MONTESQUIEU'S PHILOSOPHY

O F

LIBERALISM

D0896974

MONTESQUIEU'S PHILOSOPHY

OF

LIBERALISM

A Commentary on
The Spirit of the Laws

Thomas L. Pangle

The University of Chicago Press

CHICAGO AND LONDON

THE UNIVERSITY OF CHICAGO PRESS, CHICAGO 60637
THE UNIVERSITY OF CHICAGO PRESS, LTD., LONDON

International Standard Book Number: 0-226-64543-6 (cloth);
0-226-64545-2 (pbk.)
Library of Congress Catalog Card Number: 73-77139

To My Father
JAMES L. PANGLE

CONTENTS

Contents

8. Religion
249

9. Natural Law and the Prudence of the Legislator
260

Notes
307

Index
327

PREFACE

This book grew out of my doctoral dissertation; it therefore represents a kind of testimonial to the efforts of my teachers. Joseph Cropsey served as the chairman of the dissertation committee. The help he gave in this capacity is but a very small part of the aid and encouragement given by him to me throughout my graduate career. To a degree to which he cannot be aware, the gentle power of his heart and mind illumines all my studies. Richard Flathman and Herbert J. Storing also served on the dissertation committee. From the latter I have learned much of what I know about the American tradition of political life and thought; and since "I do not know how it is, but somehow our own things please me more," I owe to him a debt of a special kind. Ralph Lerner read the manuscript and made characteristically careful and thoughtful suggestions for improvement. During much of the time I spent writing this book I lived away from the United States, but in the same city as Allan Bloom. Only those who know what it means to live in the atmosphere of taste and thought created by that benevolent being will understand how much I owe to him. And finally, whatever grace this work possesses is due to the painstaking and most perceptive criticism of my wife, Diane.

Unless otherwise noted, all references to the works

ix

of Montesquieu are to the Pléiade edition edited by Roger Caillois: *Oeuvres complètes*, 2 vols. (Paris: Librairie Gallimard, 1949–51). This edition will be cited as *Works*, followed by the volume and page reference (for example, *Works*, II, 100). Clarity and ease of reference have suggested that we refer to books of *The Spirit of the Laws* by capital roman numerals and to chapters by arabic numerals (for example, X 5 for Book X, chapter 5). Occasionally a more exact reference within a chapter and book cited will include the page number of the second volume of the Pléiade edition (for example, X 5, p. 381).

All translations appearing in the text from this and any other work not printed in English are the author's own except where otherwise indicated.

THOMAS L. PANGLE

1

INTRODUCTION

The necessity and importance of the study of Montesquieu is more evident today than it has been for many generations. Serious reflection on books like *The Spirit of the Laws* should be a central part of our response to the growing crisis in the theoretical foundations of our political principles. Liberal democracy, or the regime devoted to the principle that the purpose of government is the securing of the equal right of every individual to pursue happiness as he understands it, has for about two centuries dominated the life and thought of the West. But as we enter the final quarter of the twentieth century we find that the regime and the tradition of thought which have for so long reigned supreme are exposed to ever more widespread and searching questions and to increasingly serious doubts. A heterogeneous combination of thinkers frequently referred to as the New Left appear as the spokesmen or inspirers of a radical ferment that has been developing for a number of years and now pervades much of thinking society in America as well as Europe. This ferment, which threatens to provoke some degree of serious political transformation in the coming years, has brought about an end to the "end of ideology" and has aroused in almost all thoughtful observers a renewed awareness of the need to understand our liberal principles and to be able to give a coherent defense of them. We find today an increasing consciousness of the fact that there exist in the tradition of political philosophy powerful and legitimate alternatives to liberal republicanism. As Hanna Pitkin has expressed it:

> We have begun to rediscover that other tradition of political thought which does not regard political life as a means for achieving pragmatic, nonpolitical goals, but takes political participation as a positive value in itself, necessary to the good life and to the completion of a human being's full development.[1]

More and more we are forced to see liberalism as something problematical; we are hence impelled to think through again its foundations.

What we require and what we do not meet with in contemporary attempts to defend the liberal, open society is a sympathetic inquiry that goes to the roots, that does not take this society's existence or its desirability for granted. We seek an analysis that does not attempt to see in liberal society the rational means to every attractive political aspiration or way of life, an analysis which takes seriously the fact that the choice for liberal democracy is a decision for one way of life and a decision against other ways of life, and which tries to demonstrate the extent to which this way of life more nearly fulfills the needs of human nature than the alternative ways. What must be shown is not only the superiority of liberal democracy to totalitarianism or tyranny, but its merit as compared with other forms of republicanism and limited monarchic rule.

This situation in which deep and long-standing

political commitments are being shaken makes only more evident the always-present need to understand the kind of human being our modern democratic regime was intended to foster. Only by becoming much more aware than we now are of what distinguishes the, political and social goals of liberalism from the alternatives will we come to understand what is compatible and what is incompatible with the basic principles of our modern liberal world. Only thus will we understand the bounds within which we must act—what things we can hope and build for and what things we must, in public life at any rate, do without. And the latter half of this double lesson may not be a merely negative part of the reward for undertaking such an investigation. For it may be that it is only when our commitment to public action is qualified that our commitment to private thought and the truth can be unqualified.

It is clear that to engage in such an inquiry it is necessary that we move beyond the familiar horizon of the modern world. We must try to place ourselves vicariously in a situation where there exist viable and attractive alternatives, in thought and action, to our modern republican order. We must try to assume a perspective which sees the proposal for liberalism as a truly debatable proposal. Given our own lack of direct experience of such a world, the only trustworthy procedure is to turn to the thought of the founders of liberalism to find the analysis we seek. It is there that one finds reflections by intellects of the first rank who did not live in a climate of opinion where any of the modern principles were taken for granted. Those thinkers were compelled to justify a new form of political society and a new way of thinking about politics in the presence of a well-established and skeptical world with its own solidly based theoretical tradition.

Of the handful of thinkers who truly stand at the origins of the liberal tradition—Hobbes, Spinoza, Locke, and Montesquieu—Montesquieu emerges as the most helpful and relevant for us. Montesquieu adopted the principles of his great predecessors. But he subjected those principles to a new analysis based on a comprehensive investigation into political experience as revealed by the history of the European nations and the accounts available to him of non-European peoples. The result was a considerable modification of his predecessors' teaching. An important part of that modification was a new and much broader presentation of the liberal principles, a presentation which included careful study of a variety of possible objections to liberal republicanism and of the kinds of regimes implied in such objections.

In particular, Montesquieu examined at length the kind of republicanism he considered the greatest challenge to his principles, that characterized by extensive direct political participation, de-emphasis of material prosperity, and a deep sense of community. He drew his empirical information from numerous republics ancient and modern. He focused on the passion of public spirit or "virtue" which animates such a community. In this examination of political virtue Montesquieu became the unknowing founder of the moral-political tradition to which the new, as well as the old, Left's attack on liberalism is the heir. For the classical or traditional understanding of virtue was inegalitarian: virtue set demands on men which not all were equally capable of meeting, and by the standard of virtue the most just form of government appeared to be aristocracy. Montesquieu claimed to reveal the truth about what virtue actually was in the republics that practiced it, as opposed to virtue as the philosophers interpreted it. Following a trail blazed by Machiavelli, Montesquieu gave a theoretical account of virtue as egalitarian and of participatory democracy as the only truly virtuous regime. In this he prepared the way for Rousseau and Kant. However, one must immediately add that *The Spirit of the Laws* is a massive demonstration of the irreconcilable tension between virtue and freedom. Beginning to some extent with Rousseau, but unambiguously in Kant, Hegel, and Marx, this tension was denied or thought to be superable. In studying Montesquieu we come to see the fascinating gulf between the origins of the modern moralism and its eventual development. While giving credit to the virtuous republic's claim to greatness, Montesquieu tries to show in a dispassionate way its contradictions and its incompatibility with human nature.

Montesquieu was also much concerned with the establishment of what is now often referred to as a "humanized" or "humane" society. Indeed, it was with Montesquieu that "humanity," as a substitute for Christian charity, came to occupy a central place in political discourse. He wanted to uncover the root of this passion and to discover the political conditions that promote it. He claimed to have shown that, in what Rousseau and his successors were to call the "bourgeois" world, humanity would be less threatened than in any other political order.

At the same time, Montesquieu recognized a certain lack of romance and of poetry and art in this new bourgeois way of life. According to him, such things find their home in monarchical political orders like that of France. On this account he held certain reservations against liberal republicanism; but for reasons we will examine he believed that these reservations were not ultimately compelling.

Finally, Montesquieu opposes to our modern critics' vague pronouncements about man's need for creative self-expression an exhaustive empirical examination of human nature—its needs and its potential. In the course of this examination he shows himself to be aware of a considerable malleability in man. But at the same time he claims to show the necessary limits to this malleability, the limits formed by the needs of human nature. Exactly what "human freedom" is, and what political system most truly provides this freedom, is the chief theme of *The Spirit of the Laws*.

In reading Montesquieu we confront a thinker who in the course of laying down the principles of liberal republicanism comes to grips with the most important of the persistent theoretical objections to that political doctrine. But the value of *The Spirit of the Laws* goes beyond what is involved in the peculiar breadth of Montesquieu's presentation of these principles. For in studying *The Spirit of the Laws* we will also come to understand better that profound transformation of thought which is the deepest source of the dilemmas of modern liberal thought: the replacement of Nature by History as the final standard for normative judgment.

As every reader of the Declaration of Independence knows, liberalism originally understood itself to be based on the idea of natural right. All of the great founders of the new republicanism conceived their project to be grounded in deductions made from a nonarbitrary insight into the permanent hierarchy of needs of human nature. This conception persisted in most quarters until the late years of the nineteenth century. At that time there began to spread, from Germany to England and eventually to America, a new, unprecedented "historical consciousness" which claimed to have discovered that man, unlike all the other beings, lacked a permanent nature or natural hierarchy of needs. This new way of thinking asserted that not only peripheral or secondary characteristics, but the very core of man's being—his heart, his soul, and above all his mind—changed throughout history. As a direct consequence, it came to be asserted that all comprehensive understandings, and in particular the liberal understanding, were in fact only the limited and erroneous "world views," the "ideologies" or self-deceptive myths, of a particular "culture" in a particular time.

For a long time it was believed by some of the greatest of the philosophers of history that this historicist insight did not necessarily imply the fatal undermining or chaotic destruction of man's evaluative reasoning faculty. It was claimed that all past historical change must be understood as a growth toward a final

7

or culminating epoch, the end of history, in which the human situation would fully reveal the permanent potential toward which all earlier epochs had been aiming and in the light of which every earlier period was to be seen as a stage in a meaningful and rational historical process. A serious attempt was made to integrate the liberal principles into this framework: the liberal state and society was to be understood as the goal of the historical process. But more and more the modern consciousness, including that of the most thoughtful Marxist,[2] has come to doubt the notion of a term or completion to the "growth" of the knowing mind in history; as a result the modern mind has become increasingly doubtful of its own capacity to discover solid and lasting moral or political standards of judgment.

This new, radical skepticism about reason represents *the* intellectual dogma of our time: no established school of thought dares seriously to question the fundamental presupposition of the new historical consciousness. Liberal intellectuals have lost the ability to satisfy the dissatisfied, to refute the critics, because they have lost faith in the validity of evaluative reason. The crisis of liberalism has its roots in the modern crisis of reason itself.

The philosophy of history emerged as a response to what were seen as decisive weaknesses in the liberal tradition of natural right. This modern liberal tradition had itself come into being through a conscious break with the classical tradition of natural right. If we are ever to understand our situation, as the first step toward overcoming it, we will have to rediscover what it was about the modern tradition of natural right which compelled political philosophy to take the eventually self-destructive step of transforming itself into the philosophy of history, or what it was about the new conception of nature which led the greatest thinkers to think it through to the point of abandoning it. Only when we have ourselves rethought the reasons for this transformation will we be able to judge whether the transformation was necessary, and whether other alternatives, including a return to the classical tradition, may not have been prematurely and unwisely rejected.

When one attempts to trace the historical approach to its roots one is led, by the authority of observers so competent as Kant and Hegel, to Rousseau. But the precise bearing and significance of Rousseau's truly seminal reflections on nature and history will not be fully understood until one sees these reflections as the attempt to provide answers to problems that Rousseau had been taught to recognize through long meditation on the philosophy of Montesquieu. It is in the thought of Montesquieu that the need to derive some moral and political standards from history, history understood as opposed to or as the replacement for nature, comes into the foreground of the tradition of political philosophy. Yet although *The Spirit of the Laws* opens the door to the historical consciousness, it denies the necessity for a complete surrender to that perspective. In Montesquieu we see more clearly perhaps than in any subsequent thinker the reasons why the historical approach became in some sense a necessity, and at the same time what are some of the grave objections to the full development of that approach.

The elaboration of these themes is the purpose of the commentary on *The Spirit of the Laws* which follows. Such a commentary is, however, exposed to a massive difficulty: the peculiar style and manner of Montesquieu's writing.

2

MONTESQUIEU'S STYLE AND
MANNER OF WRITING

Any commentary on *The Spirit of the Laws* must confront the almost universal scholarly opinion of two centuries that the work lacks order and a unifying plan: "Everyone is convinced that this book lacks method, that there is neither plan nor order and that after one has read it one doesn't know what he has read. . . ."[1] The disorder of Montesquieu's greatest work is held to reflect the disorder of his thought—a thought which is unconsciously enmeshed in fundamental contradictions: "The fact is that we are dealing in the *Esprit des Lois* with an eclecticism that accepts discordant viewpoints and that fits them into a system with apparently little idea of the confusion arising thereby."[2]

The only well-known commentator who persuasively opposes the general view is d'Alembert. Speaking of "the pretended lack of method of which some readers have accused Montesquieu," d'Alembert says:

> An assiduous and meditative reading can alone make the merit of this book felt. . . . One must distinguish apparent disorder from real disorder. . . . The disorder is merely apparent when the author puts in their proper places the ideas he uses and leaves to the readers to supply the connecting ideas: and it is thus that Montesquieu thought he could and should proceed in a book

destined for men who think, whose genius ought to supply the voluntary and reasoned omissions. The order which makes itself seen in the grand divisions of *The Spirit of the Laws* reigns no less in the details: we believe that the more one penetrates the work the more one will be convinced of this. . . . We will say of the obscurity that can be permitted in such a work, the same thing we said about the lack of order; what would be obscure for vulgar readers is not for those whom the author had in view. Moreover, voluntary obscurity is not obscurity: Montesquieu, having to present sometimes important truths whose absolute and direct enunciation might wound without bearing any fruit, has had the prudence to envelop them, and by this innocent artifice, has veiled them from those to whom they would be harmful, without letting them be lost for the wise.[3]

This enlightening and too often neglected statement is substantiated by the testimony of Montesquieu himself, who spoke with considerable frankness about the purposeful obscurity of his manner of writing. In the Preface to *The Spirit of the Laws* Montesquieu voices a fear that this "work of twenty years" will be attacked after only a brief reading. He speaks of the importance of the "plan of the work" and tells the reader that it is only in discovering this plan that he will find "the plan of the author":

Many truths will not make themselves felt until after one has the chain which links them to others. The more one will reflect on the details, the more one will feel the certitude of the principles. These details themselves, I have not always given: because who could say all without a mortal boredom?

These remarks are in full accord with Montesquieu's more extensive discussion of the proper way to read in his *Pensées:*

> When one reads a book, it is necessary to be in a disposition to believe that the author has seen the contradictions that one imagines, at the first glance, he is meeting. Thus it is necessary to begin by distrusting one's own prompt judgments, to look again at the passages one claims are contradictory, to compare them one with another, then to compare them again with those passages that precede and those that follow to see if they follow the same hypothesis, to see if the contradiction is in the things or only in one's own manner of conceiving. When one has done all that, one can pronounce as a master, "there is a contradiction."
>
> This is, however, not always enough. When a work is systematic, one must also be sure that one understands the whole system. You see a great machine made in order to produce an effect. You see wheels that turn in opposite directions; you would think, at first glance, that the machine was going to destroy itself, that all the turning was going to arrest itself, that the machine was going to halt. It keeps going: these pieces, which seem at first to destroy one another unite together for the proposed object. This is my reply to the [critique of *The Spirit of the Laws*] of the Abbé de la Porte.[4]

Montesquieu denied that his way of writing was peculiar or unique in the philosophical tradition. He did not read philosophical texts the way they are usually read today; he tended to think that many of the philosophers had hidden their true doctrines. For example, he claimed that Spinoza was an atheist;[5] that Descartes denied the existence of the soul;[6] that the Stoics were atheists;[7] and that "the doctrine of a superior intelligent being was founded by Plato only as a safeguard and a defensive arm against the calumnies of zealous pagans."[8] A style of writing that requires so much effort to lay bare its meaning is likely to appear somewhat perverse to the modern reader. But there are sound reasons, alluded to by d'Alembert, for such reticence.

The first and most obvious is the fear of persecution. Some scholars are aware that,

> Montesquieu wrote with the Censor and the Index always before his eyes. . . . In Montesquieu's time, it was not always safe to dot your i's. And that his nervousness was not unfounded is shown by the fact that, notwithstanding his precautions, his book found its way onto the Index, and remained for two years under the ban of the civil censor.[9]

Montesquieu himself makes the situation abundantly clear. The Preface to *The Spirit of the Laws* begins with a disclaimer of any criticism of the existing order of things. In the rest of the Preface and, indeed, throughout the whole work, Montesquieu never tires of reiterating such disclaimers.

But while this fear is sufficient to account for many more obscurities than most scholars have acknowledged, it is by no means the sole reason for Montesquieu's elusive style. A more important reason is revealed by d'Alembert's suggestion that Montesquieu wrote for two different kinds of readers. As d'Alembert explains, Montesquieu believed that men are radically unequal in their intellectual capacities, that only a few are capable of understanding the truth and benefiting by it, and that the vast majority would find the truth, if openly stated, both confusing and harmful. An additional reason for Montesquieu's "voluntary obscurity" is, then, the desire to hide the truth from the many unwise readers.

The possible harmfulness of the truth about human nature and politics will be clearer after our exposition of Montesquieu's teaching. We shall see that Montesquieu's understanding of man as a selfish or egoistic being is shocking to generally held views of morality and religion, the views which formed the legitimating principles of most regimes in his time, if not in ours. It is true that Montesquieu wished to change the basis of political life and that he was willing to go very far in weakening morality and religion. But as he emphasizes in the Preface, he feared the effects of unguided, radical change. And even in the kind of political order he envisioned as a goal, he did not feel it was possible to dispense entirely with salutary moral prejudices. Some remnant was needed to help preserve order and cooperation. He wished to lessen the restraints on human selfishness, but he still held that the selfishness must be channelled and guided.

At the same time, it is not sufficient to say that Montesquieu wished only to hide the truth from the vast majority of readers. D'Alembert fails to remark that Montesquieu wished to have a widespread popular effect. As he says at the beginning of Book

XX, he hoped that his book would have a far-reaching influence on political thought. In order to have such an influence, Montesquieu not only had to educate the few wise or philosophic readers; he also had to set in motion a large number of less intelligent and less studious men. The wise need "followers" who will be the "leaders" of the multitude. Accordingly, while veiling the first principles of politics, Montesquieu portrays with attractive clarity many key practical proposals for specific nations and situations. Montesquieu is famous for having presented with inimitable power and unforgettable clarity the case for federation, separation of powers, moderation of criminal law, the encouragement of commerce, and the necessity for prudent attention to the particular character of each nation. No one who reads *The Spirit of the Laws*, no matter how little he understands its unity or ultimate basis, can fail to be affected by these and other forceful ideas. Montesquieu's rhetoric is so successful because he bases his appeal for these proposals partly on principles acceptable to almost everyone—freedom and prosperity—while he refuses to delineate too clearly how these principles come into conflict with others—like piety or moral virtue.

In addition, Montesquieu pleases and attracts us through his stimulating and graceful prose. The beauty of this prose style is often noted, but its underlying rhetorical intention seems to have been perceived and described only by Hippolyte Taine. The first, and most lasting, impression conveyed by Montesquieu is a tone of moderation:

> No writer is more master of himself, more outwardly calm, more sure of his meaning. His voice is never boisterous; he expresses the most power-

ful thoughts with moderation. There is no ges-
ticulation; exclamations, the abandonment of
impulse, all that is irreconcilable with decorum
is repugnant to his tact, his reserve, his dignity.[10]

The intention to instill such moderation in the reader
is part of the reason for the numerous brief chapters
in *The Spirit of the Laws*. In a series of these chapters
Montesquieu can sketch quickly but incisively the
manifold particularity to which any universal political
principle must be applied: he thus succeeds in imitating the complex multiformity of political life. While
making both particular and general proposals, he at
the same time educates the reader in political prudence
and caution.

But the more fundamental rhetorical intention is
that which is divined by those who call Montesquieu's
style epigrammatic. This characterization is not
unjust, for the style often seems to be a kind of imitation of the Latin writers whom Montesquieu found
most beautiful.[11] An epigram is graceful, brief,
memorable, and clear, yet it summarizes in a paradoxical or thought-provoking manner a whole range of
reflections. In reading Montesquieu, one experiences
a similar effect, repeated many times. Not only do
the brief chapters resemble epigrams, but often the
relation of a chapter or series of chapters to what pre-
cedes and follows is perplexing. What begins as light
paradox in a single passage turns into a deeper puzzle
of obscure transitions and connections. But the
puzzles are so presented as to invite attempts at solution:

> He seems to be always addressing a select circle
> of people with acute minds, and in such a way

as to render them at every moment conscious of their acuteness. No flattery could be more delicate; we feel grateful to him for making us satisfied with our intelligence. We must possess some intelligence to be able to read him, for he deliberately curtails developments and omits transitions; we are required to supply these and to comprehend his hidden meanings. He is rigorously systematic but the system is concealed, his concise completed sentences succeeding each other separately, like so many precious coffers or caskets. . . . Open them and each contains a treasure; here is placed in narrow compass a rich store of reflections, of emotions, of discoveries, our enjoyment being the more intense because we can easily retain all this for a moment in the palm of our hand. . . . he thinks in summaries; . . . the summary itself often bears the air of an enigma, of which the charm is twofold; we have the pleasure of comprehension accompanying the satisfaction of divining.[12]

Montesquieu's is a style that can at once create widespread and deeply felt support for certain concrete proposals while making perfectly clear to all but the most vain or obstinate the need for prolonged study and reflection in order to grasp the whole teaching.

Montesquieu's rhetorical intention with regard to the readers capable of such study and reflection constitutes the third and most important reason for his manner of writing. Strange as it may initially seem, Montesquieu wishes to veil the truth not only from the careless reader but from the thoughtful reader as well. The paramount reason for this is that he wishes to truly *educate* such readers. At the end of the key

book of *The Spirit of the Laws,* Montesquieu remarks
on the book's incompleteness, saying, "One should
not always exhaust a subject, and leave the reader
nothing to do. The aim is not to make people read
but to make them think" (XI 20). Education is not
indoctrination; it is the stimulation of thought. Montesquieu intended his greatest work to be an education
in the true sense: a philosophic education. His work
shares with all philosophic teaching the characteristic
of making the fundamental questions, the great
alternatives, at least as evident as the correct answers.
The greatest contradiction in *The Spirit of the Laws*
is that between Montesquieu's apparent espousal of
the virtuous republics of antiquity and his espousal
of commercial England. Eventually his preference for
England is made clear enough. But his apparently contradictory presentation forces the reader to grapple
with the issue for himself. This kind of writing, with
its coyness and unmalicious falsehood, partakes to a
special degree of the playfulness associated with the
most serious teaching. Voltaire makes a character in
his dialogue say of Montesquieu, "It seems that the
author wished always to play with his reader in the
gravest matters."[13] In reading Montesquieu we must
be prepared for this ever-present irony.

The foregoing remarks must, of course, be merely
preliminary to our discussion of Montesquieu's plan
and teaching in *The Spirit of the Laws.* Their purpose
has been to combat the conventional prejudices which
might close the reader's mind to the exposition which
follows.

3

HUMAN NATURE AND
NATURAL LAW

Montesquieu introduces *The Spirit of the Laws* with a brief Preface in which he discusses the nature and intention of the work. The Preface opens, as we have noted, with a defensive denial of any intention to offend anyone, especially the rulers of Montesquieu's own country. He then warns the reader against the temptation to give an unfavorable misinterpretation to what is contained in *The Spirit of the Laws*. It appears that Montesquieu's concern with the possibility of dangerous misinterpretation is what leads him to write a Preface describing the contents and intended effect of his book. This description in the Preface of the contents of *The Spirit of the Laws* appears, then, to be made primarily with a view to self-defense or reputation.

Montesquieu begins by implicitly admitting that the book, because of its obscurity and the great effort required to uncover its meaning, lends itself to misinterpretation. An obscure style, while it protects against attack, can invite attack if it is not brought to the reader's attention and justified. In this case, the obscurity is said to be required by the complexity of the subject matter. Prudence allows and requires Montesquieu to emphasize to the reader at the very outset the theoretical character, the profundity and breadth, of the book he is about to read. *The Spirit of the Laws* will present the comprehensive truth about political life, "the principles . . . from which the histories of all the nations are but the consequences" (Preface, p. 229).

Montesquieu can dare to defend the purity and harmlessness of an obscurely written book by speaking of its theoretical character. This boldness reflects to some extent the changed political situation in Montesquieu's time; in mid-eighteenth-century France, despite the continued fear of persecution, science and enlightenment are already more at home and less suspect than they were in most previous times and places. But Montesquieu's boldness goes beyond what is justified by the increased tolerance shown to science. After all, tolerance of natural science is one thing; tolerance of political science is something else.[1] A book which teaches the true political principles would seem at the very least to challenge and thereby "offend" *some* of the various conflicting principles on which existing political regimes are based. Montesquieu's decision to be perfectly frank about the theoretical character of his book requires him to give a justification of the harmlessness of the practical effects of political science.

Anticipating or drawing attention to the threat to established regimes which is implicit in his characterization of the book as theoretical, Montesquieu immediately restates, with even greater emphasis, his claim that he does not write "to censure what is established in any country whatever it may be" (Preface, p. 230). Yet having said this, Montesquieu seems in almost the same breath to contradict himself. For in the next sentence he begins to speak of the propriety of proposing changes if one is "happily enough born to be able to penetrate with a stroke of genius all the constitution of a State." And he goes on to say later that his purpose in writing is to *improve* the lot of man through teaching him the truth about his "nature." In short, Montesquieu says that the theoretical truth he will reveal both does and does not imply a need for change.

The contradiction would be resolved if we could understand Montesquieu to mean that while the principles of all existing governments, the principles which determine who rules, will be shown to be correct or legitimate, the application and administration of the principles of some governments will be shown to require improvement. This seems implied in Montesquieu's statement that he wishes

> to make it so that everyone will have new reasons for loving his duties, his prince, his fatherland, his laws; that one can better feel his happiness in each country, in each government, in each state where he finds himself. . . . (Preface, p. 230).

But there are three reasons which make the reader reluctant to rest satisfied with this understanding of Montesquieu's practical intention. First, Montesquieu's repeated remarks about his fear of offending and his fear of misguided change remind us of the considerations outlined in chapter 2 above. In the very act of denying any wish to criticize existing orders, Montesquieu points to the reasons why he would have to hide any criticism, especially in the Preface, the most accessible and exposed part of the book. Second, we wonder how any theoretical understanding could justify all the conflicting principles based on conflicting interpretations of man and reality, of all the governments that exist. Third, the modesty and conservatism of this posture seem inconsistent with Montesquieu's emphasis on both the originality of his teaching and on the predominance in the world of "prejudice." According to Montesquieu, the world is in need of enlightenment: "It is not indifferent that the people be enlightened. The prejudices of the magistrates began by being the prejudices of the nation."

Will not Montesquieu's "new reasons" for loving one's government include new, more rational principles of government?[2] Our sense of the necessity of this implication is strengthened when we compare what Montesquieu indicates about his intention in the Preface with the other statement of his intention. At the beginning of the twenty-ninth book, he says that in this work he intends to show what should be the "spirit of the legislator." The legislator Montesquieu wishes to form or educate is the lawgiver par excellence—not the follower of established political orders but the creator of new ones. Montesquieu is silent about "the legislator" in the Preface, but he speaks constantly of him throughout *The Spirit of the Laws*.

For these reasons we may doubt the sincerity of Montesquieu's protestations of conservatism in the Preface. Nevertheless, we cannot simply dismiss these prefatory remarks as a mask. For the ambiguity with regard to the practical consequences of Montesquieu's teaching, the tension between implications about reform on the basis of new universal principles and advocacy of conservatism on the basis of sound present-day institutions will be present throughout *The Spirit of the Laws*. The Preface, although it prudently over-emphasizes the aspect of conservatism, introduces us to the deep ambiguity of practical intention which characterizes the work as a whole. This practical ambiguity is a consequence of Montesquieu's theoretical principles. Let us then turn immediately to the body of the work where Montesquieu promises to reveal these principles.

In the Preface, Montesquieu has indicated that *The Spirit of the Laws* is a treatise on law which goes to the roots, revealing the "principles" of politics and the "nature" of man (Preface, pp. 229, 230). Human nature is a part of the "nature of things"; to give a description of man, one must have some view of man's place in the "universe" (Chap. 1, p. 232). Montesquieu therefore opens his work with a brief account of the principles which govern the whole. He obviously does not intend here a complete exposition of "physics"; he rather means to sketch the way things must be if his political teaching is to be true. Montesquieu no doubt relies on previous modern science.[3] But the best justification for the doctrines of this first chapter is to be found in the persuasiveness of the political teaching which requires such a view of nature.

He begins by asserting the lawfulness, that is, the permanence, orderliness, and knowability of the whole. The things that are, the "beings," fall into a scheme of five classes or kinds: "the Divinity," "the material world," "the intelligences superior to man," "the beasts," and "man."[4] Each kind of being has its own kinds of "laws" or "necessary relationships."

Montesquieu proceeds to discuss each kind of being in the order stated, except that instead of discussing the "intelligences superior to man," or the angels, in the central place after "the material world," he begins to discuss "individual intelligent beings" in that place and never again mentions intelligences superior to man. Soon afterwards it is made explicit that "individual intelligent beings" refers to "men"; at the outset of *The Spirit of the Laws*, angels are replaced by men at the center of the scheme of being.[5]

By this device Montesquieu conveys more than the lesson that angels and angelic ways do not exist, or are irrelevant to reflections on man and politics. By first mentioning prominently, and then dropping, "intelligences superior to man," he intimates that there is no intelligence superior to man's and that therefore nothing is inherently mysterious or incomprehensible to perfected human reason. God is never referred to in chapter 1 as an "intelligence superior to man"—in fact, in the central section, man's relation to God, as creation to creator, is described as a "relation of equity" between "an intelligent being" and "an intelligent being."[6] The implied adequacy and completeness of the knowledge potentially available to unassisted human reason emerges even more clearly when one considers Montesquieu's discussion of the first kind of being, "the Divinity."

Montesquieu begins his discussion of "the Divinity" by saying that it is subject to law like all other beings, and he supports this assertion with a reference to Plutarch. This is the closest thing to a reference to authority in Montesquieu's thematic treatment of the subject "Divinity." The reference is not to the Bible or to any theological or even Christian source; it is to a pagan philosopher. Montesquieu does not refer to any theological authority because no theological authority could support the view which implies that God is wholly lawful or rational in all his doings and is incapable of performing miracles.[7] *The Spirit of the Laws* begins by asserting the sameness of reason, human and divine, and by denying the God of revelation.

In what follows Montesquieu immediately shows, however, that the denial of a God transcending human reason does not imply strict materialism or atheism. The phenomenon of the mind, with a reason which is in principle free and limitless in its capacity to know, cannot be said to have originated from the blind movement of matter. Montesquieu therefore says that "an original reason" is at the source of things. In the fourth paragraph he drops the term "original reason" and begins, for the first time, to use the term "God." "Original reason" is given the name "God."

When Montesquieu turns to the discussion of the nature and origin of the material world, he seems at first to assume that his argument for the existence of a God as "original reason" is sufficient to prove the existence of a God who "created" the world and "made" the laws by which it moves. The complete lack of demonstration of God's power to create ex nihilo goes with an ambiguity in Montesquieu's discussion of the creating. On the one hand he says "God" is "creator"; on the other hand, that "the world . . . subsists always." On reflection, it can be seen that God's "creating" must probably be understood as a purposely, or prudentially, misleading metaphor.

For "the laws according to which God created are the same as those according to which he conserves"; these are the "invariable laws" of a world which "subsists always"; and "thus creation, which *seems* to be an arbitrary act, supposes rules as invariable as the fatality of the atheists" (my italics). In other words, there is no fundamental difference between the way the atheists describe the origin and nature of the material world and the way Montesquieu describes it. It is only "intelligence" which is not explained on grounds acceptable to atheistic materialists. (As for animals, Montesquieu says: "However it may be, they have no closer relationship to God than the rest of the material world" [Chap. 1, p. 234].) It thus becomes clear that the invariable laws by which the material world is governed are the laws of mechanistic physics. There is no teleological element in Montesquieu's understanding of the nature of the physical world. And, as we shall soon see, neither is there any in his understanding of the nature of "intelligent beings."

Montesquieu gives no thematic account here or later in *The Spirit of the Laws* of the relationship between "the intelligent world" and "the physical world." The last topic of five which Montesquieu will discuss in chapter 1 is "man" as a whole—that is, man both as "physical being" and as "intelligent being." As physical being, man is like other bodies—wholly lawful; as intelligent being, he is free to violate his natural laws ceaselessly. As the oscillating order of the list of beings at the beginning implies, man is somehow in between, a partaker of two worlds.[8] The problem of this dualism, the problem of the manner in which these two worlds coexist, will recur.

Chapter Three

After discussing God and the material world, Montesquieu turns to man as "intelligent being." Montesquieu's discussion of the "laws" peculiar to man's nature as intelligent being has created considerable confusion among the commentators. The difficulty arises because Montesquieu asserts in the same sentence that there are "invariable laws" of intelligent beings and yet that these laws do not always obtain (Chap. 1, p. 233). He adds that the "legislator" must therefore strive to extablish them (Chap. 1, pp. 233, 234).[9] The difficulty is overcome by taking account of the fact that man's nature differs from all other natures in that man is extraordinarily "flexible" (Preface, p. 230). This peculiarity follows from man's potential reasonableness and the freedom implicit in this potential. Man can be rational but is not always rational. He is capable of guiding his own activity, of deliberating and choosing; but it is possible for him to deliberate badly, to choose a course contrary to the needs of his nature. One can say that it is a necessary part of human nature to be capable of acting contrary to nature. Wherever man lives together with his fellow man there are certain rules deducible analytically from the nature of social life, which, if followed (that is, if "positive law establishes them" [Chap. 1, p. 233]), preserve social life or, if not followed, destroy social life. These are the rules of natural justice as described in chapter 1, of which Montesquieu gives a partial enumeration.

Montesquieu's examples of principles of natural justice therefore include nothing more than the rules of conduct which are the bare minimum necessary to preserve the existence of almost any society or league.

There is no indication of any *natural* purpose of society which transcends the preservation of the society and its members. This impression is strengthened by Montesquieu's remarks at the end of chapter 1 where he indicates that "laws of religion" and "laws of morality" are not within the province of the "legislator" (Chap. 1, p. 234).[10] For the explanation of the bearing of these indications and for a fuller elaboration of the principles of natural law, we turn to the second chapter.

The title of the second chapter, "On the Laws of Nature," brings to our attention the fact that Montesquieu never called "the relationships of justice prior to positive law," "laws of nature." And the reason immediately becomes clear: while it is true that there are necessary rules of justice deducible from the nature of society, society itself is not strictly natural; its laws are therefore at best only quasi-natural.

In order to understand what man's nature truly is, in order to see what, if any, are the permanent needs of man, we must think of him in that "state . . . prior to the establishment of societies." "Natural law" describes man's needs and the behavior resulting from the reasonable attempt to satisfy those needs in the "state of nature." In contrast, the rules of reciprocity or the "relationships of justice prior to positive law" mentioned in chapter 1 are the product of "the natural light" of reason, which deduces from the original and permanent needs, from the natural law proper, principles of action applicable in the new circumstances of society (cf. X 3). While there is then no justice in the state of nature, nevertheless the *reasons* for justice and therefore the standards for justice are derived from the state of nature. There is a natural source of justice: justice is not simply created by human making.

Man in the state of nature is a being who lacks almost all recognizable human traits. Man is an animal of "feelings" (*sentiments*) without "understanding" (*connoisances*). He "would feel only his weakness." His "timidity" is "extreme": "Everything makes them tremble, everything makes them flee." Montesquieu's understanding of the state of nature and therefore of the elemental in man is, if not in every respect, in the most fundamental respect identical to that of Hobbes. *The* human situation is that of a being characterized by "extreme fear," the fear of painful death: a being whose "first ideas" are of "the conservation of his being." The fear of death, the longing for security, are prior to and stronger than the desire for food and sex.

Montesquieu explicitly criticizes Hobbes by drawing attention to the difficulty in the identification of the state of nature with a state of war. If men were really fearful, solitary, and dispersed, they would avoid rather than fight with one another. In their nomadic solitude and poverty they would have nothing for which to compete or fight. Vanity and the desire to dominate other men are passions that arise only after men are in society and have lost some of their fear of one another. The first "law of nature" would be peace, a peace brought about by man's desire for security and fear of his fellow man. Montesquieu agrees with Hobbes that men are independent and equal by nature because all are more or less equally able to threaten one another; but this fact implies a state of peace, not of war.

In these circumstances, repeated accidental encounters would bring recognition of reciprocal fear and therefore a reduction of that fear. Moreover, men would feel that "pleasure which an animal feels at the approach of another of his species." The weak natural sociability which all animals have is possessed also by man, and would give a certain pleasure to the first human meetings. The pleasure would be "augmented" in the case of sexual attraction. The first of these pleasures is the natural basis for compassion or "humanity"; from the second develops gradually an attachment to the family. This attachment to the family is a much stronger bond; from it seems to develop the first "society." Montesquieu leaves unexplained the extent to which family attachment is derivative from the selfish desire for security. But the family love which comes into being through sexual lust, while not as natural or as strong as the desire for self-preservation, can be said to have some independent and natural status. On every later occasion when Montesquieu speaks of natural right or law among men, he refers either to a right deducible from man's desire for self-preservation or to a right deducible from what is needed to preserve the family (mother, father, and children).[11] However, the latter is clearly second in status and power; in addition, the principles of right based on the family are more subject to change because the family is not necessarily monogamous.[12]

Montesquieu thus interprets human nature as endowed with a weak sociality, a weak positive attraction to other men, which is an addition to, or a qualifying transformation of, the purely selfish desire for security. Man is by nature led toward a familial society, and this society gives to his prepolitical, natural existence an element of sweetness, a slight but important counterweight to the primeval terror. It is in this familial situation that "in addition to the feeling which men had at first, they come to have understanding [*connoisances*]." Montesquieu does not describe this process of development of intelligence: nothing is said about the emergence of speech.[13] Nor is he expansive about the character of this understanding. He leaves it at saying,

> man, in the state of nature, would have rather the faculty of knowing than knowledge itself. It is clear that his first ideas would not be speculative: he would think of the conservation of his being.

Perhaps it is at this point, then, that man's "feeling" of insecurity is transformed into the "knowledge of death" which all animals lack (Chap. 1, p. 234). At any rate, man's knowledge makes him aware of the advantages of cooperative effort, for with the coming into being of understanding, the "desire to live in society" is strengthened. The fourth "law of nature" is this desire to live in society.

Whatever sweetness and sociability this familial society may contain is overshadowed, however, by the ugliness and antisocial behavior to which such society necessarily leads. The opening sentence of chapter 3 dispels any illusions about the degree of man's natural sociability: "As soon as men are in society . . . the state of war begins." As soon as men lose their fear of one another, the competition for scarce resources and the desire to attack and subjugate one another plunge them into bloody conflict. While man's first contact with his fellows is pacific and even somewhat pleasant, his first permanent contacts lead directly to war, a war of families and even of individuals. Following Hobbes, Montesquieu teaches that the state of war is the *permanent* state of man's relation to man insofar as *civil* society or the "State" does not intervene to impose peace: "The individuals in each society . . . try to turn in their favor the principal advantages of that society, which creates among them a state of war" (Chap. 3, p. 236; compare X 2, entitled "Of War": "Among *citizens* the right of natural defense does not at all carry with it the necessity of attack" [italics mine]; cf. also XXVI 20 and XI 3–4).

Montesquieu all but agrees with Hobbes that the state of nature is a state of war, for although the state of nature is first a state of peace, this state of peace develops, almost inevitably, into a state of war. In the only other explicit discussion of the state of nature in *The Spirit of the Laws*, Montesquieu identifies the state of nature with a state of war, a state of "enemy" families with no common superior (XXX 19). Montesquieu not only agrees with Hobbes as to the most powerful natural motivation of man, he agrees as to the necessary consequence of that motivation. Man's situation of fearfulness and anxiety gives him as his deepest desire the desire for self-preservation or security, and the dynamic of that desire leads eventually to a state of war.

Civil society is not natural to man, but man's natural situation is such that he is forced toward civil society.

Nature is not friendly or good to man; it is inimical and stingy. Man's nature is not directed by any *telos* which solicits, through its fulfillment, human happiness. Nature gives no satisfying pleasure or goal to man. It provides only a negative guide, a "greatest evil" as Hobbes might have put it. The terror of death shows man the direction in which he must flee. Civil society is man's attempt to undertake this flight, to transform and overcome his natural situation, but on the basis of, guided by, the negative passion which is produced by this situation. The principal reason for civil society is the same as the principal reason for most human actions in the state of nature: the fear of death, the desire for security. But civil society is man's way of attempting to go beyond the bare self-preservation, the constant insecurity, of the natural state. Through civil society man tries to gain a *secure* self-preservation, a lasting peace and a protection for material goods that will insure lasting satisfaction of the body's needs.

In order to see the full implications of Montesquieu's doctrine of the state of nature, it is necessary to contrast it with the classical tradition of political philosophy which Montesquieu joins Hobbes in opposing. While classical political philosophy reflected upon the possible prepolitical state of man, it saw in that savagery not a "natural state" but an unnatural and mutilated human condition. By nature, or in his natural state, man was understood to be political; that is to say, the truly human needs are expressed, and the truly human faculties of the soul come into play, only when man is in civil society. Man is a being who needs to participate in joint

endeavors with other men—to give and receive love
and honor, to create and contemplate noble men and
beautiful things, to engage through speech in the dis-
covery of truth. These activities were understood not
as reducible to or as derivative from the needs for
security and reproduction which are shared with the
animals, but as ends in themselves, the *telē* which
define and shape human nature.[14]

We must be careful not to let Montesquieu's polemi-
cal remarks against Hobbes blind us to this larger
issue. Montesquieu, like Locke, whom he to some
extent follows, wanted to differentiate himself from
Hobbes partly for the sake of personal prudence and
partly because he felt that Hobbes, like Spinoza and
Bayle, had been recklessly bold in revealing the low
and unsightly first principles of human nature. This
is why Montesquieu overemphasizes his difference
with Hobbes and presents his radical teaching about
natural law *after* his more acceptable teaching about
"principles of justice prior to positive law."

Only when this community of thought at the deepest level is fully recognized, can we understand the
precise meaning of the secondary but not unimportant
differences between Montesquieu's and Hobbes's state
of nature teachings.[15] These differences reduce to
the contention by Montesquieu that what Hobbes
describes as the state of nature must have been a situation which developed later—be it understood, almost
inevitably—from the original state.

To some extent it can be said that Montesquieu
simply completes what Hobbes left incomplete. For
in Hobbes the exact history of the state of nature is
ambiguous. The actual historical existence of the state

of nature is essential to his thought. But he was more interested in giving a typical historical account, or an account of the essential moments in that historical development, than he was in showing the actual development. He left open the question whether the original situation was one of warring individuals or warring families, or sometimes one and sometimes the other at different times and places.[16]

In the course of clarifying Hobbes's state of nature Montesquieu was led, however, to go beyond Hobbes's teaching. For he believed that one's understanding of the essential elements of human nature depends, more than Hobbes had thought, on how one understands the exact historical chronology of the state of nature. As we have seen, Montesquieu contended that the state of war depends on the previous development of some kind of association among men; he was therefore led to elevate the natural status of compassion or humanity on the one hand and of the family bond on the other.

In this modification Montesquieu was no doubt motivated by more than what was needed to complete the historical description of the state of nature: he was also concerned with giving a broader and more convincing explanation of the human phenomena as they appear in civilized society. Indeed, it may be that Montesquieu was originally led to rethink the Hobbesian description of the state of nature because he was dissatisfied with Hobbes's attempt to derive all sociability from purely selfish motives. Montesquieu does not challenge the notion that the selfish desire for security is the predominant and crucial human desire; but he argues that it is tempered by weak social desires, and that these latter must be taken into consideration in any reflections about the natural standards for political life. Since Montesquieu holds that aggressiveness is less deeply rooted in human nature, and that affection is more deeply rooted, than Hobbes had thought, the political order which Montesquieu eventually indicates to be the solution to the human problem is much less strict or tough and much more soft and gentle than Hobbes's solution.

Montesquieu's modification of Hobbes may provide a broader basis for, and in this sense a more convincing explanation of, man's sociability. But the description of the state of nature which results is unsatisfactory. Montesquieu raises an objection to Hobbes for which he himself fails to provide a sufficient answer. Montesquieu criticizes Hobbes for assuming the existence, in presocial man, of aggressive motives that can only arise in society. In other words, Montesquieu exposes what one may call the crypto-teleology of Hobbes's state of nature: if man is to be understood as naturally apolitical, individualistic, and independent, then man's natural condition cannot be one which points toward, or leads necessarily, in the direction of civil society. The state of nature cannot be a state containing passions and motives which can be explained only by reference to social conditions. The emergence of society must be explained in terms of unnecessary and unforeseeable accidents.

But having exposed Hobbes's crypto-teleology, Montesquieu is unable to replace it with a nonteleological account. In fact, after having removed the hidden social mechanism which Hobbes had illegitimately placed in the state of nature, Montesquieu is compelled

to assert more emphatically the teleological character of what is left in the state of nature. He is compelled
to contend that "the desire to live in society is
a fourth natural law." It is true that Montesquieu stops
short of saying that the desire to live in *civil* society
is a natural law; but whereas Hobbes is able to present
the creation of civil society as a sharp break with the
state of nature, in Montesquieu the sharpness of the
break is blurred because the establishment of civil society comes at the end of a natural and necessary
development from asocial to social man. Montesquieu
denies the naturalness of human aggressiveness, but
is forced to retain the notion that aggressiveness is the
cause of the establishment of civil society. He is therefore led to understand aggressiveness as the necessary
outcome, or end, of the development of human nature.

And this is not the end of the difficulty. Not only
does Montesquieu fail in his attempt to escape the
need for a hidden teleology. His unsuccessful attempt
leads him to make that teleology, or the explanation
of the natural basis for man's leaving the state of
nature, less convincing. Montesquieu expunges from
the original state of nature any desire to dominate or
attack other men, leaving as the principal motive only
a cowardly fear. This fear is the crucial cause of the
unsatisfactoriness of the solitary state and of man's
openness to the attraction of permanent familial society. But in eliminating human aggressiveness, Montesquieu undermines the reason for the fear. In Montesquieu the difficulty of the notion of an asocial "state
of nature" as the source of man's sociality, the difficulty of trying to understand political man as a being
motivated principally by the selfish fear of death,
becomes acute.

Human Nature and Natural Law

The inadequacy of Montesquieu's attempt to provide a coherent historical account of the state of nature opens the way to Rousseau's critique. In reading this passage in *The Spirit of the Laws,* Rousseau raised a simple but decisive objection: if men do not attack one another, why should they fear one another?[17] And if that greatest of all dangers, the threat of attack by man, is removed, how can one say that the lesser dangers left in the natural state make it full of terror? If the natural state is not a state of terror, why should it have been unsatisfactory? The attempt to claim that it was hideously terrifying rests in every case on the unjustified introduction of a natural impetus toward society. In Montesquieu, this lack of justification becomes palpable.

In Rousseau's thought, the above objection is the opening wedge for the elaboration of a picture of the original, natural human situation as sweet, as not dominated by fear of death. According to this natural standard, Rousseau criticizes in the first place the Hobbesian bourgeois state, and eventually all political regimes, as incomplete solutions to the natural human needs.

It is quite possible that Montesquieu was unaware of the question and difficulty raised later by Rousseau. On the other hand, the question inevitably arises from reflection on Montesquieu's discussion of the state of nature. Insofar as there is an answer implicit in Montesquieu's thought, it takes the following form. In the first place, does not the fact that the state of nature did not last imply that it was deficient or bad? But whatever the state of nature was, it is agreed that it was a state of animality. The problems of civil society cannot be solved by a return to the state of nature, for civilized man cannot become an animal again. The only part of the nature of the animal-man which can serve as a sure guide or standard for social man is that part which led or forced man to become civilized, that element which was and remains the first cause and reason for full sociality. Only that part of nature which led to civil society can be of relevance to civil society. Civil society which is in its essence a reaction against the state of nature or its outcome must be guided principally by nature insofar as nature is the negative pole, the insecurity, it seeks to avoid. This negative pole is not by itself the sole or sufficient guide; it must be supplemented on the one hand by the sentiments of compassion and attachment which arose in the seminatural familial society and on the other hand by the characteristics man acquires in the historical development of each nation. But the desire for security remains fundamental.

The path chosen by Rousseau, the attempt to take one's bearings by an understanding of the natural state prior to the coming into being of any impetus to society, would have seemed to Montesquieu to run the risk of so weakening the connection between natural and social man as to cast doubt on the applicability of any natural standards to political life. Such a line of thought would seem to lead either to the abandonment of nature as a standard or to the questioning of all political life in the name of some ideal reconstruction of or return to the state of natural individuality. This, it appears, is indeed the problem we have inherited from Rousseau.

Let us return to our discussion of chapter 3. According to Montesquieu, the "state of war" is the reason for the coming into being of the "state" with its "law" or "right" (*droit*). For Montesquieu just as for Hobbes the state is the "union" of the "particular forces" and the "particular wills" of its members into one force and one will. For Montesquieu as for Hobbes the state is essentially force and will, not thought, because the aim of the state is simple and clear: the establishment of security and peace. Because this aim can be achieved by a variety of different forms of government, no one form of government is simply best, although in given circumstances one form may be preferable to others (Chap. 3, p. 237; cf. Hobbes, *Leviathan*, chap. xix, p. 122; Locke, *Second Treatise*, chap. x).

But while showing in chapter 3 his agreement with Hobbes and Locke as to the nature and end of the state, Montesquieu also shows his disagreement with the consequences which they draw from that understanding. In Hobbes and Locke the discussion of the origin of civil society is put in terms of a "social contract," a notion which is clearly a kind of legalistic reconstruction of a process which must have been considerably less rational. This reconstruction is made with a view to the immediate application of the discoveries about natural right to present-day political life. The discussion of the state of nature is followed by an enumeration of natural laws and a description of the rights of man and the rights of the sovereign, all of which are to guide civil society. These rights are intended to be universally valid and to give general guidance to political life everywhere. This theoretical doctrine, which came to be called "universal public law," is meant to supply universal standards of legitimacy for laws and governments: "The science of natural justice is the only science necessary for sovereigns and their principal ministers" (Hobbes, *Leviathan*, chap. xxxi).

After reading the first few pages of *The Spirit of the Laws*, we might well expect Montesquieu to take a similar course: having outlined the natural principles which are the source of right or law, what would seem to follow is a discussion of the juridical norms which represent the application of those principles.[18] In other words, we would expect that after having described the laws of nature as they appear in the state of nature—the laws which describe man's essential needs and the behavior resulting from those needs—Montesquieu would proceed to show how those natural laws lead to natural laws or rights useful as guides in civil society. But in fact, except for his earlier brief discussion of the "relations of equity prior to positive law," Montesquieu here refrains from any such elaboration. Later, as we shall see, such natural rights or laws are mentioned and discussed. But here Montesquieu refuses to discuss any normative *rules* deducible from the natural laws of the state of nature. Instead, he turns to a classification and examination of the "nature and principles" of the various "forms of govenment" which have emerged in human history. We are thus presented with the first great difficulty in the plan of *The Spirit of the Laws*, a difficulty which has led some commentators to see in the transition from Book I to Books II through VIII an unresolved tension between an adherence to modern natural right teachings and a return to something like Aristotle's

de-emphasis of universal standards of justice in favor
of a concentration on the variety of legitimate political
regimes.[19]

Actually, however, Montesquieu's procedure follows from the fact that he laid much greater emphasis
than Hobbes and Locke on the enormous distance
between the original, natural situation of man and the
situation in which man finds himself in developed,
civilized society. The original nature and purpose of
civil society has been overlaid by centuries of convention, an "infinite diversity of laws and manners"
(Preface, p. 229) caused by the manifold ways societies
responded to the variety of geographical and historical
accidents which confronted them: "Although all states
have in general the same object, which is to preserve
themselves, each state has nevertheless one object
which is peculiar to it" (XI 5). The legislator or statesman cannot cut through this variety and particularity;
the principles of justice deducible from the natural
law describing man's fundamental needs must be
adjusted or diluted, often drastically, before they can
be applied to civilized political life. This thought in
all its profound ramifications is the key to Montesquieu's political philosophy. Montesquieu agrees with
Hobbes and Locke that "law, in general, is human
reason . . . and the laws . . . of each nation ought
to be only the particular cases where that human
reason is applied" (I 3, p. 237); but at the same time,
the laws "should be so appropriate to the people for
which they are made, that it is a great piece of luck
if those of one nation can suit another" (I 3, p. 237).
This appropriateness, this *relation* between the universal principles of human nature understood by reason

and the particular sociopolitical environment to which this reason is to be applied in the form of laws, is the "spirit of the laws" (I 3, pp. 237–38). Having outlined the principles of human nature, Montesquieu turns to a study of the particular environments.

Montesquieu's investigation focuses first on that factor which he considers most important in the sociopolitical environment: the "nature" of the government and its "principle." The most influential sphere of social life is the political sphere, the sphere in which men deliberately, intentionally, and authoritatively choose and shape a collective way of life. Because Montesquieu's opinion about the fundamental factor is so different from the opinion prevalent today, he is frequently misunderstood: he is sometimes even called the founder of sociology.[20] But for Montesquieu, the nature of a *society* is derivative primarily from the nature and principle of the government, not vice versa. "The principle of each government has a *supreme* influence on the laws. . . . One will see the laws flow from it as from their source" (I 3, p. 238; italics mine). This is why the notion of "the legislator" plays so great a role throughout *The Spirit of the Laws*. Those who interpret Montesquieu as aiming at something like sociology criticize his emphasis on the legislator as inconsistent.[21] But according to Montesquieu's explicit statement, *the* purpose of *The Spirit of the Laws* is the formation of the legislator (XXIX 1). Montesquieu will later make it clear that the legislator's decision for a given form of government is influenced and limited by geographical, historical, and other accidental factors; and it is true that Montesquieu lays considerably more emphasis on nonpolitical factors than previous thinkers did. But the political decision is by no means determined by such other influences and, generally speaking, its role is not even equalled by the role of the other influences. Notions of "the social" and "society" play at best a secondary role in Montesquieu's study. In this fundamental respect Montesquieu is in accord with the tradition of political philosophy as opposed to modern sociology.

Montesquieu's turn to something like Aristotle's study of regimes is not inconsistent with his natural right theory because it is part of his conscious modification of modern natural right theory; it is not inconsistent with his sociology because he has no sociology.

The chief purpose of Montesquieu's study of the forms of government is to discover how and to what extent each serves man's freedom or security. In order to achieve this aim, Montesquieu must try to arrive at an understanding of these governments as they really are, with the least possible imposition of abstract doctrine or alien principles: "When I have been recalled to antiquity, I have tried to take on its spirit, in order not to regard as similar, cases which are really different" (Preface). This is why the principles discussed in Book I fade so far into the background in Books II through VIII. Of course, the principles do not entirely disappear: they are the source of Montesquieu's unhesitating condemnation of tyranny and his initial preference for republicanism. And they are part of the reason for his suggestions for the improvement of each kind of government: his suggestions are directed at making each form of government more stable and consistent and, at the same time, making each more moderate and free. But generally speaking, Montesquieu lets the regimes appear as they are on their own terms. Eventually, in Book XI, he introduces a new form of government, represented by England, which is superior to the traditional forms of govenment in that it is based directly on the satisfaction of the fundamental natural need for security. But he forces us to see England in the context of the insuperable heterogeneity of political regimes.

In addition to his intention of showing the character of the variety of conventional political arrangements and how each serves human security, Montesquieu has a second purpose in the seven books that follow. The understanding of human nature which he reveals in Book I seems at this point somewhat a priori or, at any rate, to lack conclusive evidence. This political theory, partly borrowed from "so many great men in France, in England, and in Germany" (Preface, p. 231), is controversial; it has opponents. The opponents are of two kinds. In the first place, there is the classical tradition of political philosophy, whose opposition has been sketched earlier in this chapter. In the second place, when Montesquieu asserts that the true end of government is security and later that the only regime dedicated to the true end is that of England, he opposes himself to the practice of politics down through the ages, for almost none of the other regimes we know of have had liberty, or security, for their end (XI 5).[22] The various regimes are devoted to various ways of life; each implicitly raises a claim on behalf of its way of life. Montesquieu was aware that there are in civilized history two great kinds of regime not based on some form of barbarism, superstition, or despotism—the virtuous republicanism characteristic of antiquity and the more or less limited monarchy characteristic of Europe since the Middle Ages. We will find that the investigation of these regimes in Books II through VIII will be at the same time the demonstration of the inadequacy, and even the contradictoriness, of their principles. The refutation of the principles of these regimes is the substantiation of the truth of Montesquieu's own principles.

Montesquieu saw as the greatest challenge to his principles the republic devoted to virtue. Political men have always been attracted by the freedom, the power, and the glory that seemed possible in the city-states of antiquity and above all in Rome (cf. XI 13, XXII 12, XXIII 20). This attraction had been given new impetus by the writings of that "great man," Machiavelli (cf. VI 5). In addition, the general notion of a regime devoted to virtue was seen by Montesquieu to be the core of the classical political philosophy of Plato and Aristotle. The books which deal with republican virtue will therefore also deal with Machiavelli, Plato, and Aristotle.

In the seven books that follow, then, Montesquieu intends to show: (1) the essential character of each of the traditional forms of government and which laws are in harmony with each character, (2) the advantages and disadvantages of these forms of government from the point of view of man's natural desire for security or freedom from fear, (3) the contradiction or inadequacy of the particular aims pursued by each of these forms of government and the consequent validity of the analysis of human nature in Book I. Our commentary will focus primarily on his analysis of republicanism.

4

PARTICIPATORY REPUBLICANISM

Montesquieu begins his discussion of the various forms of government by giving an enumeration of the possible "species" of government, each of which is characterized by a specific "nature." Every actual government belongs to one of the species or is a mixture of more than one of the species.[1] What differentiates the species, what determines the "nature" of each government, is its "particular structure," or the persons to whom it gives the "sovereign power" of the state (III 1, II 1). This particular nature of each government requires and calls forth a particular way of life, a "modification of the soul," a particular set of "human passions" ("Advertisement of the Author"; III 1). Montesquieu calls this modification of the soul the "principle" of each form of government. The principle dominates the lives of all the citizens and is the motivating force, the "soul," of the government: it has "a supreme influence on the laws" (III 4; I 3).

Montesquieu's understanding of government, or "the constitution" (III 4), is reminiscent of Aristotle's. But the profound similarities are accompanied by no less profound differences. For Aristotle, government in general is understood to have as its nature or purpose the creation of a certain way of life or human type; the nature of each kind of constitution is therefore defined above all by the particular way of life which it has as its purpose or end (*Politics* 1280^a 25–81^a 4, 1295^b 1–2). Montesquieu retains something of this understanding insofar as he emphasizes the importance of the principle, or particular "modification of the soul" of the citizens, of each constitution. But whereas for Aristotle the principle defines the nature of a government, for Montesquieu the principle is *derived* from the nature or structure of each government; it does not itself define the nature. As one might say, the "soul" of a government is derived from its body. Aristotle adopts the viewpoint of the citizen, who believes that the fundamental thing, the thing that defines his regime and differentiates it from others, is the particular, praiseworthy way of life which appears to be the regime's purpose and the reason for everything else. Montesquieu breaks with this viewpoint.

For Montesquieu, the purpose or nature of government in general is the creation of security, or freedom, for its citizens—freedom from domination and from threat of death or attack by other men. The purpose of government is to use the power of the state to suppress the natural war among individuals. To a far greater degree than Aristotle supposed, the "end of government" is the same in all regimes (III 6; I 3).[2] What defines and differentiates the types of government, therefore, is the way each arranges or structures the "sovereign power" or "general force" (II 1, 2; I 3). Despite the tremendous practical importance of the differing principles or motivating passions, they are ultimately derivative from, and means to, the different ways of structuring sovereign power in order to

49

enforce peace. As will gradually be made clear, this change in the understanding of the nature of a "constitution" is at the root of Montesquieu's new understanding of each particular type of constitution.

Montesquieu divides government into three, or four, kinds: republic (aristocratic and democratic), monarchy, and despotism. As the editor Caillois notes, Montesquieu "breaks with the tradition since Aristotle" in making such a classification.[3] His innovation does not, like that of Hobbes,[4] follow from an obfuscation of the distinction between good and bad; the fundamental distinction between monarchy and despotism is retained. The "break" appears more clearly in his treatment of republics (by which he means small city-republics). Aristotle and the tradition arrived at a fourfold classification of republics by understanding them not only in terms of their "particular structures," that is, whether the few or the many rule, but also in terms of justice, or the degree to which the rulers pursue the public good of the whole as opposed to the private interest of the ruling part (*Politics* 1279[a]26ff.). Aristotle denied that the common good was simply identifiable with either the interest of the few or the interest of the many. Montesquieu recognizes only two forms of republic because he considers that the degree of pursuit of the common good is directly implied by the "particular structure": the common good is identifiable with the good of the many. Rule of the many, democracy, is in principle more just than rule of the few.

The striking sign of Montesquieu's new approach is the fact that whereas Aristotle's classification of gov-

ernments arises from the viewpoint of a mediator ("one
who studies philosophically" the claims and characters
of the partisans of the various regimes), Montesquieu's
classification is based on "the idea which the least
instructed men have": Montesquieu adopts the viewpoint of the uninstructed many, the partisans of
democracy (cf. *Politics* 1279^b 13 with II 1). This becomes clearer from the remarks made on the merits of
the two kinds of republic; Montesquieu practically
adopts the arguments of the partisans of democracy as
presented in Aristotle's *Politics*. The democratic argument emerges as follows.

Government should pursue the common good—and
the common good is the good of all the people. But
any government which is aristocratic is the rule "of
a *part* of the people" (II 1; italics mine) and this part
will not care for the whole, the common good, except
as a means to its own interest. From the democratic
point of view, once you know the "structure" of a
government, once you know who rules, you know
whose good is served: "the nobles in an aristocracy
form a body which . . . for its particular interest, re-
presses the people" (III 4). Lacking the undisputed
power and hence security of a monarchy, individual
nobles will be more ambitious and oppressive than
a monarch (XII 13). These powerful individuals will
even have a tendency to disagree over their particular
interest: they "require terrible magistrates who vio-
lently lead the state back to liberty" (II 3; V 8). The
nobility will not share their power with meritorious
non-nobility. They "establish the most distressing distinctions" (II 3). As for the particular virtue of aristocratic government, it consists only in the "lesser vir-

tue" of "moderation"—that is, moderation of the nobles' selfishness (III 4). Aristocracy is not adequately described as the rule of "part of the people"; it is the rule of "certain families" (III 2; II 3; V 8; VIII 5) over "the rest who are no more than . . . tne subjects are in a monarchy" (II 3). Aristocracy is "a monarchy with several monarchs" (VIII 5; III 4). In general, "the closer aristocracy approaches to democracy, the more perfect it will be" (II 3).

Democracy, in contrast, is the government of "the people" simply (II 2). Because power rests with the whole, democracy does not "repress for a particular interest" but concerns itself with "the public interest" (IV 6; VI 8).

The democracy Montesquieu has in mind is a limited or moderated democracy. Each citizen has a direct and equal voice in the important decisions of the community made in open assembly. There is considerable access to posts of leadership; election is by lot wherever possible (II 2). Yet Montesquieu recognizes that certain rather weighty concessions to inequality must be made if the magistrates and officials are to be men of sufficient capacity and leisure to perform their functions well. The people in assembly cannot perform all public business; they need an executive council or "senate" to advise them and to conduct foreign and other affairs requiring secrecy, dispatch, or prolonged deliberation. They need generals and other specially talented functionaries. Montesquieu is flexible about precise institutional details. He recommends following the arrangements of Solon, who restricted the access to office of the poor because the poor lack leisure to serve and to familiarize them-

selves with details (II 2; V 5). Nevertheless, these
inegalitarian qualifications are all made solely with a
view to strengthening and approaching as near as possible to a regime devoted to egalitarian self-rule.[5]

Aristotle recognizes a certain power and justice in
this democratic argument. The city seems to aim at
democracy, for it wants to be a society of friends,
a partnership in the good life of free and equal brothers
(cf. *Politics* 1295^b 20ff.). But the proper understanding
of "the good life" reveals that it is misleading to identify the common good with a good which all can share
in the same way. For the good life is the life in which
man fully exercises his natural capacities, and this is
the life according to virtue. Only a minority of men
is endowed with the natural capacity for such a life,
and, in addition, only a few can have the equipment
or wealth which provides the leisure for such a life.
The city must therefore in the best case have as its
end the life of the few gentlemen who have the chance
to be fully virtuous. The virtue of this gentlemanly
class must be counted on to take care of the lower
classes, giving them a fair share of the things they
need. But the rest of the citizens can only partake
of the truly good life in a very diluted form, through
the tone the gentlemanly class gives to the life of the
whole city (*Politics* 1277^{b}34–78^{b}5, 1329^{a}17–39). In
most cases such an aristocracy is impossible; in many
circumstances democracy is the best possible alternative. But democracy can be good only insofar as it
is a "mixed regime" with some ingredient of rule by
the few.[6]

Now while Montesquieu agrees that virtue is essential to a republic, he objects to Aristotle's interpreta-

tion of the good life which is the goal of the republic. He thereby rejects Aristotle's understanding of virtue and substitutes a new understanding of his own. The core of Montesquieu's objection and of his new interpretation of the good life can be stated as follows. Aristotle had held that the goal of a republic was not so much freedom as the virtuous or educated use of freedom. Liberty is inseparable from a liberal education; freedom is subordinated to virtue. Montesquieu reverses this priority. The goal of a republic is not so much virtue as freedom. What "freedom" means when no longer subordinated to virtue becomes clear when we reflect on the source of the human desire or need for freedom. The natural source would seem to be the desire for self-preservation. It seems to be this desire which leads men to wish to be always in control of the means to their own preservation, or to be never under the control and hence under the potential threat of another human will. Freedom can thus come to be understood as not living under the will of another individual man, and this seems to be achieved only when one rules oneself. The republic aims at such self-rule, or at the closest possible approximation on the level of society. The goal of the republic is the participation of all citizens in political self-rule. The good life is the life of a fully adult human being, the life of a "free man" who exercises his capacity for self-rule, who controls his own destiny (III 3; IV 6, 8; VIII 3, 12, 16). Such a man is an active participant in great projects; he "does things that astonish little souls" (IV 4, 6). The "spirit of liberty" makes a man abandon as "slavish" all "professions" and "pleasures" which prevent him from spending time with his friends and in public affairs (IV 8; III 3). Virtue, although it necessarily takes on the appearance of being an end in itself, is a means to self-rule.

A republic understood as aiming at self-rule is properly egalitarian. For almost no adult male is incapable of participating in such self-rule; and there is no individual or group whose need for freedom or self-rule requires the deprivation of the freedom of others within the community. It is true that some men are more "talented" than others, but these talents, according to Montesquieu, are revered not as ends in themselves but only as means to self-rule. They cannot justify the exploitation of or rule over others. And the talents will not be submerged in a small democracy—they will be called upon and given a chance to develop. Indeed, the man of talent owes to the democracy, that is, to the others who are not so talented, the fact that his talents are not subject to the threat of arbitrary oppression. For if the motive of all political life is freedom or independence, then where men are not in a regime which leads them to identify their freedom with the freedom of all, they will try to oppress others in order not to be oppressed. In other words, if there is no truly *common* good which transcends political rule, then all political life is directed either at tyranny over others or collective protection from such tyranny. The latter aim is fully achieved only in democracy. This is what justifies Montesquieu in saying that in a democracy,

> the citizens cannot all render to the fatherland equal services; but they owe it all equal services. At birth, one contracts toward the fatherland an immense debt which one can never repay. Thus

55

distinctions there arise from the principle of
equality itself, even when they appear to arise
from happy services, or superior talents. (V 3)

It is, however, necessary to qualify the thought of
the previous paragraph. Montesquieu is aware that
there are some men so extraordinarily talented at
ruling that they are capable of preserving their
independence, or "coming to the top," almost any-
where. These men do not require others in order to
be free; they do not owe their freedom to the democracy and they will know that they do not. Their talents, which inevitably lead them to wish to gain greater personal freedom or self-rule than is possible in
the democratic community, are dangerous and bad.
They can be beneficial and good only in bad circumstances (if tyranny is unavoidable, it is perhaps better
to be ruled by a prudent tyrant than a blundering
one). The democracy must be wary of unusually
talented men:

> The good sense and the happiness of the indi-
> viduals consists very much in the mediocrity
> of their talents. . . . A republic where the laws
> have formed many mediocre men, composed of
> prudent men, will govern itself prudently; com-
> prised of happy men, it will be very happy.
> (V 3)

> Often the people draw from the mediocrity of
> their understanding a stronger attachment to
> what is established. (V 2)

Montesquieu applauds the ancient practice of ostracism (XXVI 17; XXIX 7; cf. *Politics* 1284[a] 3ff.). One

might say that the freedom of all requires an injustice to the few. But then these few can be counted on to take care of themselves.

Montesquieu's understanding of virtue follows from this interpretation of the goal of republicanism. Virtue is the self-sacrifice necessary for the continued existence of a community where all participate in rule. Virtue is not the goal of a republic; it is the means to the freedom or self-rule which is the goal. The fatherland (the community) does not exist for the sake of virtue, but rather virtue for the sake of the fatherland.

This in no way means that virtue is de-emphasized. Virtue is the "principle," the "soul," of republican life. For if the republic is to be truly a community where all rule, where no part aims at exploiting the rest, each individual citizen must identify his own good with the good of the whole. Each citizen must then transform his wish for personal freedom or self-rule into a wish for the self-rule of all. And he must make this transformation apply to all his wishes. Every personal desire whose satisfaction might deprive another of the freedom to satisfy his desires must be suppressed. Each, through "self-renouncement," must have "a continual preference for the public interest rather than his own interest" (IV 5): that is, for an interest capable of being shared by all. The fulfillment of interests or desires is achieved through public policy formulated as law. In making and executing law, each citizen must seek his own goals only insofar as they can be generalized in law, or become the goals of all citizens (III 3). Montesquieu thus anticipates Rousseau's "general will."

This self-sacrifice cannot be a matter of calculation. Individuals can only act in this way if they are motivated by the "feeling," the "passion," of "love of the republic" (IV 2). Virtue is the passion of patriotism. Patriotism, love of the fatherland, is possible in all regimes; but it "is particularly felt in democracies" (IV 5), for only in a democracy can and must the citizen identify himself with the whole community. One cannot love and identify oneself with all the other citizens if one envies some of them, or lives with a different style of life. Full virtue is the love of an egalitarian fatherland. Virtue loves and demands equality (V 3, 4, 5; VIII 3). The love of equality requires aversion to the attempt to amass and spend private wealth; virtue is the love of personal poverty and frugality (III 3; V 4, 5, 6). Virtue is not only the love of equality, it is itself something which is equally possible for all men. The self-sacrificing love of the community is a difficult but at the same time a "very simple" (or uncomplicated) thing: "it is a feeling, not a product of the understanding; the last man in the State can have this feeling as much as the first" (V 2).

Montesquieu emphasizes the importance of grasping the innovation in his understanding of virtue. And he underlines the fact that his innovation consists in making political virtue egalitarian and in divorcing it from moral virtue:

> It is necessary to observe that what is called *virtue* in a republic is love of the fatherland, that is to say, love of equality. It is neither a moral virtue nor a Christian virtue; it is a *political* virtue . . . . I have had new ideas; it was most necessary

to find new words or to give to old words new meanings. Those who have not understood this have had me saying absurd things. ("Advertisement of the Author"; Montesquieu's italics)

In order for us to understand clearly what is involved in this transformation of the idea of virtue, it is necessary to contrast Montesquieu's discussion with a somewhat more detailed description than we have heretofore given of the traditional or Aristotelian understanding of virtue.

Aristotle and the classical thinkers recognized the persuasiveness of the identification of virtue with political virtue, or the understanding of virtue as the individual self-sacrifice necessary in order to achieve a life of self-rule through public participation in a republican community. Montesquieu's description of political virtue is somewhat reminiscent of Aristotle's description of justice, the virtue of public-spiritedness, in the *Ethics*. Just as Montesquieu says that "the love of the laws and the fatherland gives all the particular virtues" (IV 5), so Aristotle says that justice, or obedience to the laws and devotion to public service, "is perfect [or complete] virtue" (*Ethics* 1129[b] 11–26). Justice is perfect virtue because,

the one possessing it is able to practice virtue toward others and not only toward himself; for many can act virtuously in private but are unable to do so toward others. And because of this the saying of Bias seems good, that "rule will show a man," for in ruling a man acts in relation to others in a community. (*Ethics* 1129[b] 31–1130[a] 3)

Aristotle might seem to be saying that justice or participation in community rule is the aim of life because in such participation a man exercises a much broader and more complete freedom or self-determination than he ever can in private or family life. But Aristotle immediately shows that he cannot leave it at saying justice is complete virtue: "Justice is perfect virtue, *but not simply:* rather, it is virtue with regard to others" (*Ethics* 1129^b 26–27).

What Aristotle means by this is most clearly and succinctly explained in Book vii of the *Politics* (see especially 1324^a 23–1325^a 15, 1325^a 27–^{b} 15, 1333^b 29–35). He argues that justice or political virtue can only be understood as a means to higher virtues, to the private moral and intellectual virtues. For the exercise of rule, or public service, cannot be understood simply as an end in itself. If the exercise of rule is itself the end, then the virtuous man is compelled to long for and work for permanence of his rule at home and extension of his rule abroad. He is led to seek ever greater tests of his capacities and ever greater opportunities to exercise his faculties. The desire for fascinating challenges makes him tend to enjoy war more than peace, and in peace the same desire may make it difficult for him to avoid secret longings for ever larger territory to administer abroad and ever larger responsibilities at home. The difficulties into which we are led when we try to understand political virtue as the end of life compel us to look beyond political virtue. And this accords with our common sense. After all, laws are not made for the sake of law-making; policy is not made for the sake of policy-making (cf. *Ethics* 1177^b 12–18). The political activity and virtue of each citizen is directed at the good of himself and the whole. But what is this good? Either it is something higher, beyond the political activity of the community, or it is simply the self-perpetuation of the community life, the mere continued existence of the community. In the latter case, virtue and self-rule must be understood as ultimately in the service of collective self-preservation and possession of necessary bodily goods. Political rule or freedom would then be at its core merely a means to, or identified with, safety and comfort.

But, according to Aristotle, such an understanding would distort the phenomena of virtue and the fatherland, which are seen as noble things for the sake of which we are willing to sacrifice our property and our lives.

The higher goal which immediately comes to sight is national military glory, or the proof of the excellence of the community through its victory over and conquest of all its neighbors. But this apparent solution to the problem is unsatisfactory. For the excellence aimed at is really only the excellence of force or brute strength, the capacity to secure safety and bodily goods. Besides, the community goal of glorious victory and conquest is in the final analysis contradictory. It would mean that the self-rule of a community of free men has as its purpose the tyrannical rule over subjects or slaves; and the tyranny over one's neighbors which is the end of the community might just as reasonably be the purpose of each individual with regard to his neighbors within the community.

Aristotle therefore argues that political life and political virtue have as their end some self-sufficient but cooperative and peaceful activity which develops and employs the full capacities of the souls of the citizens. This activity he understood to be the use of man's highest and distinctive faculty, the faculty of reason. The aim of the city is the life of thought and contemplation of the truth (*Politics* 1325^b 17–33). Unfortunately, this goal is all but impossible for a number of reasons. The most massive is the fact that men capable of devoting themselves to the contemplative or philosophic life are exceedingly rare—rarer than the rarest gem. The republic must therefore settle for the goal of fostering the development of a type of human being who is halfway between the good citizen and the philosopher: the gentleman. The virtue of the gentleman—moral virtue—is halfway between political virtue and intellectual, or philosophic, virtue. This moral virtue which dominates and defines the life of the gentleman includes political virtue—that is, justice or "perfect virtue with regard to others"—but it does not consider justice to be the highest peak of virtue. Public service is good not because the self-rule it implies is itself the greatest good, but because rule gives one an opportunity to exercise the higher capacities of one's soul. Virtue has another, higher, peak, that is, "virtue toward oneself." The gentleman considers the excellence or nobility of his own soul to be more important than, and in some sense independent of, public service or participation in rule. The culmination of virtue toward oneself is what Aristotle calls "greatness of soul." Greatness of soul is the habitual posture of the perfect gentleman toward public honor and office—the greatest political goods. The man with greatness of soul deserves the highest honors given by the worthiest men, and considers these honors to be the greatest external goods. But he looks down on even these greatest goods because he is aware that nothing is as great as his own soul, that the excellence of his soul is somehow the purpose or end of all political activity (cf. *Ethics* 1129^b 27 with 1124^a, 1122^b 33–1125^a 17).

In this pride, in this looking down, the perfect gentleman is similar to the philosopher, the truly perfect human being. Insofar as greatness of soul understands the nobility of political life and the political virtues to be subordinate to the beauty of the life of the individual soul, it is a reflection of the negative side of the philosophic life. The perfect gentleman divines or recognizes that the exercise of the soul in public service points beyond itself to a private exercise of the soul which would be an end in itself. The gentleman is aware of the legitimacy, and even to some extent the desirability, of withdrawing from political life for the sake of a superior private life. This awareness is a key part of the justification of his claim to greatness.

Contra Montesquieu

The perfect gentleman will be led toward a life of private leisure. He will not pursue a truly philosophic leisure. But in the best case he will, together with friends, occupy himself with the cultivation of the arts and literature (see *Politics* viii).

Such gentlemen are not as rare or as difficult to produce as philosophers, but they are still rare. In addition, they must be very wealthy in order to lead semileisured lives. Even in the best circumstances they will probably be in a minority. The best republic, the republic which is the wished-for goal of political life, is, then, an aristocracy. Perfected political virtue or justice is consequently not merely love of the laws and the community or fatherland; it is love of the laws and community of an aristocracy which fosters leisured gentlemen (the good man is rarely a simply good citizen: *Politics* 1276^b 16–1277^b 33). Justice or political virtue is not simply a "passion," but rather passion "guided by right reason." Virtue is more than political virtue, and it is inegalitarian.

Now we are in a better position to see clearly what it is that has been abandoned in Montesquieu's separation of political virtue from moral virtue. Montesquieu does not *explicitly* deny the existence of private moral virtue. Indeed, in language reminiscent of Aristotle, he alludes once to "laws of morality" which remind each man of what he owes to himself. But these laws of morality are said to be the province of "the philosophers" and not of "the legislator" (I 1; see chap. 3, note 10, above). Moral virtue has the same status as Christian or religious virtue. Insofar as it is not reduced to political virtue (compare III 5, note a and IV 5 with XXIV 8), it is silently forgotten. Montesquieu never discusses moral virtue thematically or shows any basis for it in human nature. He speaks of no political order which fosters or depends on moral virtue.

This does not mean, of course, that he denies the existence of a way of life preoccupied with a sense of personal honor and concerned with taste, art, and intellectual pursuits. What he does hold is that such a life has no intrinsic connection with the free self-government of a republic. Montesquieu implicitly refutes the contrary claim of Aristotle and Plato by having recourse to the historical facts and to the reality of republican political life. In a republic, virtue always means patriotism and public spirit: devotion to the freedom of the community. No citizen in any actual republic could seriously associate virtue or praiseworthiness with intellectual pursuits.

This line of argument emerges most clearly in Montesquieu's very curious discussion of the "laws of Plato" in the book devoted to education (IV 6–8). He treats Plato's utopian arrangements as serious practical proposals; but in order to do so he must disregard the most important aspects of both the *Republic* and the *Laws*. By ignoring all the differences between the *Laws* and the *Republic*, and by forgetting the philosopher-kings and the nocturnal council, the community of women and children, and most of the education, he can call the "laws of Plato" a "correction of the laws of Sparta" (IV 6). This is the light in which he persists in seeing Plato: if Plato's suggestions are to be taken seriously, they must be reduced to a "correction" or "perfection" of Sparta (VII 16). From this point of view, the education in music which Plato and Aristotle propose cannot be considered as the peak of the citizen's education. Montesquieu recognizes that "all the ancients thought" that "music was necessary." But, in bold contradiction to the very passages in Plato he quotes, Montesquieu explains this "paradox" by claiming that music is necessary only as a palliative to correct the excesses of the education in citizen virtue. Increased community emphasis on education in virtue turns into concentration on the defense and glory of the community through military virtue. Music was only needed to ameliorate the harsh tendencies of this warlike spirit. According to Montesquieu, "It is impossible to imagine that music inspires virtue; that would be inconceivable; but it mitigates the ferocity of the institution [of gymnastics and training for war]." But according to the remark of Socrates in the *Republic*, which Montesquieu quotes in a footnote as follows, "Damon will tell you which sounds are capable of giving birth to baseness of the soul, insolence, and the virtues opposite to these [namely, greatness of soul and moderation]" (IV 8; cf. *Republic* 400^b). As for "speculative sciences," Montesquieu mentions that they are of no use because they make men "savage [unsociable]" (cf. XIV 7).[7]

The human type concerned with honor, and tending toward an interest in artistic and literary taste, is found above all in monarchy, according to Montesquieu. In monarchic as opposed to despotic one-man rule, the power of the prince is limited and balanced by the power of an hereditary, landed aristocracy whose members are preeminently concerned with their personal and class prerogatives. Montesquieu's critical discussion of the nature and effects of honor is implicitly a critique of the pride which Aristotle saw as the core of "greatness of soul" and which he claimed reflected human perfection. It is true that Montesquieu thinks primarily of noblemen in modern Europe and Aristotle thinks primarily of Greek noblemen. And there are important differences: Christianity, the point of honor, and chivalry are all new developments. Nonetheless the core remains the same, as can be seen immediately from the similarities between Aristotle's description of the proud man and of the *kalon*, or "the noble," which is the aim of the gentleman, and Montesquieu's description of honor.

Honor is "ambition," personal ambition, for "preference and distinctions" (III 7). Honor understands
"virtue" to consist of "a certain nobility"; the man
of honor "does not judge the actions of men as good,
but as beautiful, not as just, but as grand"; "as soon
as honor finds something noble in actions, it is either
the judge who makes them legitimate or the sophist
who justifies them." In that world of honor, "one hears
always three things said: that one must have in one's
virtue a certain nobility, in one's ways a certain frankness, in one's manners a certain politeness." Honor
is the sphere of the virtues which look to oneself rather
than to others: "The virtues which it shows us are
always less what one owes to others than what one
owes to oneself " (IV 2).

Montesquieu shows the difficulty with pride or
honor in two ways. In the first place he indicates that
the pride and honor one finds in aristocracy is alien
to political virtue. The "ambition" of honor "is pernicious in a republic" (III 7). Its virtues are "not so
much those that call us to our fellow-citizens, as those
that distinguish us from them" (IV 2). Moreover,
"honor has its own laws . . . and doesn't know how
to bend" (III 8; cf. IV 2, final paragraph).

More important, the self-esteem which is the end
of honor is hollow. Both the "laws of morality" of
the traditional philosophers and the "virtues" of honor
are concerned with "what one owes to oneself " (cf.
I 1 with IV 2). But as it turns out, the honor which
Montesquieu describes in the passages quoted above
is, "philosophically speaking, a false honor."[8] It is
preoccupied chiefly with the opinions of other men—it
seeks as "recompense the noise of its actions" (III 7).
It is hence closely tied to arbitrary convention: "Honor

is a prejudice" (IV 2, p. 265, note a). It prides itself on pointless self-restraint, and is full of "caprice" (III 8); its dictates are "bizarre" (III 10; IV 2; V 19). In the *Considerations on the Greatness of the Romans and Their Decline*, Montesquieu remarks that:

> Self-love [*amour-propre*], love of our conservation, transforms itself in so many ways and acts by such contrary principles, that it makes us sacrifice our being for the sake of love of our being. . . . (chap. xii, p. 136)

The peaceful activities which are the source of the nobility's self-esteem are not based on true, permanent, or natural things. The only solid basis for the nobility's sense of superiority is its prowess in war, its capacity to conquer others by brute force and cunning. Not refined leisure or philosophy but war "in fact . . . is the distinguished profession because its hazards, its successes and misfortunes, both lead to greatness" (IV 2).[9]

Montesquieu seems to argue that, while it may be immensely attractive to find that a man "glorifies contempt for his life" (III 8) and looks down on many other things most men pursue, such contempt is not truly glorious unless it has a clear, positive goal. Politically speaking, "true glory" goes with "love of the fatherland . . . self-renouncement . . . and all the heroic virtues that we find in the ancients" (III 5). Personal honor may seem remarkable and charming, but it is seen ultimately as having no coherent aim beyond the satisfaction of exaggerated vanity.

This whole antiaristocratic line of argument is vitiated, however, by what Montesquieu is compelled to admit later in *The Spirit of the Laws*. As we shall see, he is forced to concede that in circumstances of peaceful leisure and commercial enterprise—such as existed in Athens and exist now in France—selfish preoccupation with honor and vanity can produce a society possessing a certain love of taste, wit, and intellectual pleasure for its own sake (see XIX 5–8, XXI 7, and chapter vii below). In other words, Montesquieu seems compelled to recognize the potential in the love of honor which Aristotle advances as the justification of aristocracy. It is not certain that Montesquieu ever adequately disposes of this difficulty in his defense of democracy. Our detailed investigation of how he interprets the aristocratic concern for what one might call the pleasure of contemplation of the beautiful must be postponed until chapter 7 below. Here Montesquieu draws our attention to the fact that this concern is principally only a vehicle of vanity; later he will show that insofar as it transcends vanity, it is ultimately not a serious concern of the aristocrat. The aristocrat himself does not consider it to be serious, and this posture on the part of the political class most in touch with "the life of the mind" reveals, according to Montesquieu, the human truth about that life. Philosophy or contemplation for its own sake is not by nature a serious concern of man. Therefore it cannot ultimately justify any regime.

as Aristotle would have it.

Having arrived at an understanding of what is implied in Montesquieu's new democratic teaching on the nature and principle of the participatory republic, we are ready to examine in more detail the way of life in such a regime. But before doing so, it is appropriate to pause briefly in order to complete our analysis of Montesquieu's classification of the forms of government.

Montesquieu's rejection of the possibility of unselfish virtue outside the context of the democratic community is reflected in his understanding and evaluation of the forms of one-man rule. For although he agrees with Aristotle in separating monarchy from despotism, his reasons for this division are quite new.

> Aristotle's difficulty appears clearly when he treats of monarchy. . . . He doesn't distinguish the species by the form of the constitution but by accidental things, like the virtues and vices of the prince; or by irrelevant things like the usurpation of the tyranny, or the succession to the tyranny. (XI 9)

Montesquieu uses Aristotle's opposite terms, monarchy and tyranny, interchangeably. What counts is not whether the prince gained the throne legitimately, or whether he will use his power virtuously; what counts is the "form of the constitution," its "nature" or "particular structure." One cannot rely on virtue to keep the holder of power from abusing it; "it is an eternal experience that every man who has power is led to abuse it" (XI 4). Accordingly, whenever all power is in the hands of one man, the government is almost always a despotism where all citizens are slaves to the pleasures of the prince. All are motivated by fear and insecurity. Despotism is an assault on "human nature" (II 4; VIII 8, 21). Compared with the insecurity and even atrocity of this government, all other governments can be said to be good, or "moderate" (III 9, 10; V 15; VI 1, 2, 9,

16, 19; VIII 9). Only in a political system where the power of the prince is checked and balanced by independent powers are the citizens not subject to despotic slavery. Montesquieu thinks that such a system has been most nearly achieved in the monarchies of medieval and modern Europe, where the power of the king has been balanced by the independent power of the aristocracy. This structural balance of powers is strengthened and enforced by the "principle" which the structure calls into being and which pervades and animates it: honor, pride, or the sense of personal glory. Despite the unjust usurpation on which monarchy is based (VII 4) and the many irrationalities to which its honor or exaggerated vanity leads, it has the advantage of requiring that individual persons be respected—in a degree varying with social class.

Montesquieu must be somewhat cautious in evaluating monarchy as opposed to republicanism, for, as he often notes, "we" are subjects of a monarchy. He begins *The Spirit of the Laws* by expressing his gratitude for being born in monarchic France (Preface). Nevertheless, in Books II through V he *seems* to indicate the superiority of the participatory republic: "They did things [in the ancient republics] which we do not see any more today, and which astonish our little souls" (IV 4; cf. IV 6: "the corruption of our modern times"). "In monarchies . . . the state subsists independently of . . . all those heroic virtues which we find in the ancients, and of which we have only heard in speech" (III 5). The far-reaching qualifications which must be added to this praise emerge only gradually, as Montesquieu unfolds his examination of the consequences of the republican principles.

The first step in that examination is the discussion of education in republics (Book IV). Every regime must imbue its citizens with the motivating passion which is the principle of the government. The laws of education are therefore the most important after the "fundamental laws" themselves, and especially in a republic: "it is in republican government that one has need of all the force of education" (IV 5). The necessary devotion of each citizen to the rest has a link to man's natural inclinations insofar as the love of the small community can be understood as an enlargement on the one hand of man's capacity to love his family and on the other hand of his sense of "humanity" or attraction to members of his own species (cf. I 2 with IV 1, 7; V 2; VI 15; and *Persian Letters*, nos. 11–14). But these inclinations are so much weaker than man's natural egoism that a transformation of that egoism is required in addition. Democracy stands or falls by the strict subordination of each to the whole; yet men are selfish enough that they will always be tempted to neglect their political duties in the assembly, in public office, or in war, in order to pursue private pleasure and gain. The community must therefore guide and restrict the private lives of its citizens. The citizens must be enthusiastic about such restriction and control. Enthusiasm about subordinating the private to the public requires education.

Montesquieu begins his description of republican education by underlining the distance which separates its spirit from the spirit of education in modern times. Ancient republican education produced men capable of far more noble and self-sacrificing deeds than does modern education. The chief cause of this difference is not that the ancient education was more strict or more detailed, but that it was simple and uncontradictory. In modern times we receive three different and contradictory educations. Montesquieu alludes here to the pernicious effect of Christianity on political morality. Our first education is from our father. This is that simple moral training and humanizing process common to all civilized peoples; the moral training would seem to include the quasi-natural principles of equity existing prior to positive law. In all except the public-spirited republican regimes, this teaching is at a certain tension with what is required "in the world" in order to protect oneself from other selfish men. Nevertheless, the simple morality is commonsensical; it is based on the rational requirements of social life. It therefore retains a certain force. But in modern times the moral education given by our fathers is distorted by our "masters," the Christian moral authorities, in the light of an impractical ideal of perfection. This transformation makes the tension between public-spiritedness, or morality, and the world seem much greater. It has the tendency to make men believe that the requirements of success "in the world" rule out any adherence to unselfish virtue. In modern times then, especially in Catholic monarchies, Christianity contributes to the contempt for virtue, the extreme self-regarding tone of public life, and makes more difficult the establishment of a regime based on political virtue. Political virtue is not only "not a Christian virtue"; it is endangered by Christian virtue (cf. II 4: in a republic there can be no independent clergy).

The primary aim of educational policy in a republic

is the removal of any influences which might contradict the education given by the father to his children. Contrary to what Plato and Aristotle taught,
even in the best republic the laws of education are
not "laws given by the legislator." This is first
indicated by the title of Book IV in contrast to the
title of Book V. And in the chapter on "education
in a republican government" Montesquieu says that,

> it is to inspire [love of the laws and fatherland]
> that education ought to be attentive. But, in order
> that the children have it, there is a sure means;
> this is that the fathers themselves have it. One
> is usually the master of giving to one's children
> one's knowledge; one is even more so the master
> of giving them one's passions. If that doesn't turn
> out so, it is because what was done in the paternal
> home is destroyed by impressions outside. (IV
> 5)

Montesquieu does not seem to think it necessary to
go into the details of this family education; it would
not seem to be difficult as long as the institutions of
the society do not corrupt the education "by impressions outside." After all, virtue is "a very simple
thing."

After thus describing republican education, Montesquieu turns somewhat unaccountably to an examination of "some institutions of the Greeks," to which
he devotes the remaining three chapters of Book IV.[10]
The institutions discussed are the institutions actually
in Sparta and some other Greek cities like Sparta,
and the institutions suggested as improvements or
"corrections" of Sparta by Plato. These institutions,
which Montesquieu calls "singular," create a society

radically devoted to political virtue and opposed to private life. Lycurgus "shocked all accepted usages": while promoting justice among the citizens (making them fully political and thus self-determining, and moderate about private indulgence), he encouraged larceny to promote valor, enforced a harsh rule over a slave population in order to give citizens leisure for fully public lives, and permitted "atrocious sentiments" of homosexuality while weakening private family love (cf. XXIII 7). He deprived the citizens of all access to private wealth by banishing the arts, commerce, and money. Plato is said to have improved on this nearly total communization by abolishing all private property, emphasizing polytheistic piety in order to support self-renunciation, and keeping all strangers away (IV 6).

Such institutions require that the city become like a large family. Privacy is all but eliminated. These laws "suppose a singular attention of all the citizens one to another" (IV 7); education ceases to be a concern of the fathers and becomes a concern of the magistrates.

Montesquieu does not at first reveal the extent to which these extreme republican communities should or should not serve as guides for political life. He speaks of the "wisdom" and "genius" of the legislators and of the "grandeur and the glory" Sparta reached as a result of such laws, but he does not endorse the institutions. He says that "these sorts of institutions can go well in republics . . . , but for inducing honor in monarchies, or for inspiring fear in despotic states, so much care isn't needed" (IV 7); he does not say whether "so much care" is *needed* in republics.

Montesquieu's repetition of the pejorative term "singular" in describing the institutions points to his recognition of the fanaticism, or extremeness, of such communities (cf. IV 6, 7 with XII 30; XXIII 7, 17; and XIV 14; XVIII 19; cf. also *Persian Letters*, no. 116). The core of the difficulty appears in the last chapter (IV 8), where Montesquieu shows what such communities have as their aim or goal. The Greek "popular governments" (including Plato's as interpreted by Montesquieu) were preoccupied with the preparation for war; the total devotion of the citizens to this as well as other public business required a large number of slaves (cf. XXIII 17). Montesquieu gives two examples of such communities which are not warlike; but these are communities of Christian priests or zealous Christian pacifists living, isolated, in America and possessing firearms (which the natives lack). Montesquieu seems to imply that the uncompromising participatory community, if not aimed at religious fanaticism, becomes dedicated to war and slavery. He cannot endorse these institutions because of their ugly consequences, as well as the tremendous sacrifices they require. Yet he cannot simply dismiss, or criticize, or even remain silent about these warlike communities because he recognizes that they express a natural and inevitable tendency of the full dedication to political virtue. That they reveal the tendency of virtue appears, if we reflect on the implications of Montesquieu's description of the way of life of a virtuous republic. As we shall see, he in great part concedes the difficulties which Aristotle found in the goals of political virtue.

Participatory Republicanism

After his discussion of education, Montesquieu describes in Book V what he considers to be the appropriate institutions of a democracy. The greatest danger to public-spiritedness is concern with private property and gain. The *best* practical solution is strict equality of property (V 5). But equality of property is usually impractical. The practical substitute is "a census which reduces or fixes the differences at a certain point," that is, an establishment of classes of property-holders and a confiscation of property in excess of a certain "mediocre amount" (V 5). The classification will make it possible to establish "particular laws to equalize, so to speak, the inequalities by charges imposed on the rich and help given to the poor" (V 5). And "it is not sufficient, in a good democracy, that the portions of land be equal; they should also be small" (V 6). Private property "beyond what is necessary for the family" brings a taste for private pleasures and greater wealth (V 3, 6). Community of property is introduced as much as possible by heavy taxation on all superfluity, maintenance of a large public treasury, and great expenditures on public monuments and projects (III 3; V 3; VII 3). All gifts, inheritances, doweries, every transference of property ("in short, all the ways of contracting") must be strictly supervised with a view to preventing inequality (V 5).

These property regulations are accompanied by restrictions on private business. Private commerce must be forbidden. The spirit of commerce is the spirit of private gain; it leads to inequality and the forgetting of virtuous self-renunciation. A city cannot

moderate the spirit of commerce: "In order to maintain
the spirit of commerce, it is necessary . . . that this
spirit reign alone, and not be hindered by another"
(V 6). Solon's Athens, though admirable in some
institutions, leads to Periclean Athens where "a rich
man would despair to think some believed him dependent on a magistrate" (V 7). At the same time, Montesquieu prefers Solon's Athens over Sparta insofar as
the citizens are not "idle" in Athens. Idleness leads.
if not to luxury, to militarism (cf. IV 6–8 with XXIII
17). In addition, idleness requires many slaves, and
Montesquieu wishes to avoid a slave population: "In
a good democracy where one doesn't spend except
on what is necessary, each ought to render account
of how he gains his living; because from whom else
will he receive it?" (V 6). It is best, therefore, that
the citizens be yeomen farmers (IV 8, note g).

Insofar as these economic arrangements cannot
achieve perfect equality, they must be reinforced by
careful public supervision of manners and morals. We
note in passing that Montesquieu understands moral
supervision to be necessary for the sake of equality,
not for the development of individual excellence.
Virtue exists for the sake of equality, or for the preservation of each man's self-governing freedom. A powerful body of censors, preferably holding office for life,
should supervise public life and life within the family
to make sure the traditional simplicity and austerity
are everywhere preserved. The wide-ranging authority of this body will leave punishment of "crimes"
to the law; it will "note laxity, judge negligences, and
correct faults." Its punishments will include even the
death penalty. The "subordination" of young to old

and of all citizens to magistrates must be "extreme," as it was in Sparta. Most extreme of all is the subordination of children to fathers, which should be as it was in Rome where fathers controlled the property of their children throughout their lives and had the power to punish them even with death (V 7, 19). The harsh inhumanity and arbitrariness of such regulations are sacrifices necessary for the sake of preserving equality and virtue.[11]

Montesquieu does not emphasize the fact, but this rigid control of manners and morals is supported by popular belief in divine sanction: the members of "the fixed body which is by itself the rule over morals" will be "exposed to the view of the people as the similitudes of the gods" (V 7). Citizens will be encouraged to give up their superfluous wealth as offerings to the gods (V 3). The most virtuous republics were the most religious:

> There was no people, says Livy, where dissolution introduced itself later than among the Romans. . . . The holy oath had so much force among that people that nothing attached more to the laws. . . . Rome was a ship held by two anchors in a storm: religion and custom. (VIII 13: cf. XIX 22)

> Religion is always the best guarantee one can have of the morals of men. (*Considerations, Works,* II, 120–21)

The republic requires a civil religion which places no reservations on whole-hearted devotion to political life, a religion whose tenets are no more and no less than a support for the laws and customs. For this reason there is no need for Montesquieu to discuss religion at length; and, for obvious reasons, he does not want to underline the fact that virtue is incompatible with Christianity and, indeed, goes hand in hand with paganism (IV 4; cf. *Considerations, Works*, II, 176–77, 196, 199, 203; *Persian Letters*, nos. 2, 11–14; "Dissertation on the Policy of the Romans in Religion," *Works*, I, 81–92).

The democracy Montesquieu pictures for us is one where the commitment of private individuals to public life is great but not total: where there is a modicum of private land, where the citizens farm their own plots and thus escape the idleness and some of the reliance on slaves characteristic of Sparta (although there must still be a few slaves to perform the functions of artisans, IV 8). The citizens must be poor, without the comforts commerce brings. They must sacrifice much privacy and security to the watchful scrutiny of the public censors. They do not give up as much as Lycurgus and Plato demanded, but the degree of self-renunciation and lack of liberty is severe. It appears justified by the freedom of participation in self-government.

Yet even as he does homage to this freedom, Montesquieu casts doubt on its status and true worth. Two considerations lie at the root of his reservations. First, although freedom originally meant personal freedom, the citizens of the democracy are forced to sacrifice almost everything personal. Second, and more fundamental, freedom as self-determination is in principle not an end in itself, but a means to personal safety and comfort; but in a democracy, self-rule becomes an end in itself. These theoretical difficulties are manifested in the actual content, or lack of content, of the lives of the citizens.

For what, after all, is this participatory freedom, this free community life, for the sake of which so much is given up? On the one hand, the republic does guarantee to each individual a certain degree of safety and comfort. But this is considered by all to be of secondary importance; the self-renunciation which is virtue exists for the community as a whole and for its common good, not for individuals and their private goods. But what is the common good, the common life, beyond the practice of self-restraint? Virtue or self-restraint tends to become not only in appearance but in reality an end in itself. To a degree, the activity of virtue can be an end in itself. Beyond the maintenance of defense, the securing of food and other necessities, political activity will be occupied with regulating and supervising the behavior of all. Still, once the "great things," the fascinating work of revolution and founding (V 7) is finished, once no one is too poor or too rich, once public and private education is under way, can this kind of domestic political supervision be understood as a sufficient content for human life? Can it justify the tremendous sacrifices made in its name? Can men be expected to be satisfied with it?

We have learned in Book I that man is attracted to his fellow man by two natural social bonds. There is a sense of kinship, compassion, or humanity for other members of the human species in general; and there is family love, which sharpens and focuses the sense of humanity and adds to it yet another tie. If these passions were man's primary and deepest passions; if in addition they could be extended to embrace all the members of a small democracy; and finally, if the democracy could become like a large family in its institutions and customs—if, in short, the picture Usbek gives in the story of the stateless Troglodytes (*Persian Letters*, nos. 11–13) represented the truth about man—then the virtuous democracy would approach a natural and satisfying solution to the political problem. But in fact none of these conditions is possible: above all, man's egoistic desire for security and comfort is far stronger and more deeply rooted in his nature than any social passion. Republican self-devotion is therefore always a restraint, a distortion of human nature. Unless it leads to some reward or satisfaction beyond itself, it is profoundly unsatisfying.

Montesquieu indicates the questionableness, even the emptiness, of the life of virtue that animates a republic most clearly and succinctly in the chapter entitled, "What Virtue Is in the Political State." He compares the republican community to a monastery, saying:

> Why do monks love so much their order? Precisely because of what makes it insupportable. Their rule deprives them of all the things the ordinary passions aim at—there is left only one passion, the passion for the rule itself. The more austere it is, the more it restrains their passions, the more power it gives to the only passion it leaves unrestrained. (V 2)

Political virtue, as we have seen, does not point beyond itself; but political virtue is only restraint. The passion which fills most of the life of a republican citizen resembles therefore a kind of blind devotion.

a "self-renunciation" for the sake of self-renunciation. Like a monastery, a republic represents a way of life which is to a great extent a pointless, or fanatical, asceticism.

The kind of democracy Montesquieu presents as best—poor, public-spirited, peace-loving, unambitious—may be able to exist in some times and places. But Montesquieu indicates that there are tremendous forces which draw it in the direction of war or at least to constant preparation for war. Let us picture for a moment the virtuous republic: almost all private aims have been sharply choked off; great human energies have been harnessed, high-spirited selflessness and devotion to the community or fatherland are pervasive. Lacking any satisfying or rewarding goal within the community, the citizens tend to find their happiness in the contemplation and fostering of the glory of their country, its greatness as revealed in its superiority to its neighbors. The citizens' love of the fatherland becomes identical with their devotion to the glory of the fatherland. Personal ambition has been transformed into "the desire for true glory" (III 5). "Heroic virtues" look to the performance of "great things."

> To people for whom nothing is wanted except *which leads to war.* the necessities, there is left only the desire for the glory of the fatherland and themselves. (VII 2)

The desire for glory and national preeminence leads naturally to the desire for superiority and victory in war. Military prowess appears as the test of virtue: it is the criterion Montesquieu himself suggests (III

3; cf. VIII 11, IV 6–8). And it is not necessary to invent enemies. Practically every republic has neighbors; it is eventually in competition with or threatened by them, especially if it is small: "Little societies have more often the right to make war than great societies, because they are more often in the situation of fearing destruction" (X 2). The threat is lessened, but the desire for glory remains, even if the republic enters into a federated defensive alliance (IX 1–3). And citizens of a republic, because all their love for fellow men is turned inward upon their fellow citizens, are not restrained from the full brutalities of war by a sense of humanity (IX 1; X 2, 4–6).

Montesquieu's unambitious republic is a possible regime, but it will not possess those "heroic virtues which we find in the ancients"; its virtue will not be exercised, or reveal itself, in "great things." It must count on a kind of "mediocrity" and barrenness in its own virtue (V 3). Montesquieu shows most clearly the difficulty in the persistence of such a situation by his use of examples. He does not give a single example of a republic that even approximates the conditions he sees as best. His proposals remind one of his description elsewhere of Rome under Numa (*Considerations, Works*, II, 70–71), but a regime like Numa's Rome is and remains a monarchy. As soon as Rome became a republic, it was set on the road to empire (*Considerations, Works*, II, 71). Most of Montesquieu's examples are drawn from Greece. Yet he tells us that "it is necessary to regard the Greeks as a society of athletes and warriors" (IV 8; XXIII 17; cf. *Considerations, Works*, II, 99: "the spirit of liberty, honor, and glory . . . animated the Greeks"). The only alternative in Greece to regimes which somehow imitate Sparta were commercial regimes: "There were in Greece two kinds of republic: one kind was military, like Sparta; the others were commercial, like Athens" (V 6). Montesquieu seems by his examples to teach that republics must either take the path of war and glory or surrender to private aims:

> It is necessary . . . that a republic fear something.
> . . . Justin attributes the extinction of virtue at Athens to the death of Epaminondas. Having no more emulation, they spent their revenues on holidays. . . . (VIII 5)

Montesquieu begins by rejecting Crete and Sparta, but the nature of virtue and the history of republicanism force him to accept Crete and Sparta as the outstanding examples of republicanism.

But one cannot even leave it at saying that republicanism points in the direction of the warlike Greek republics. To gain a comprehensive understanding of Montesquieu's interpretation of republicanism, it is necessary to compare what he says about virtue and republicanism in *The Spirit of the Laws* with what he says about the same subjects in the *Considerations*. For our purposes, it is sufficient to mention some of the salient points.

It would at first seem unfair to take Rome as the model for the small, public-spirited republic, for Rome had a unique history which appears to be a distortion of republicanism. Yet Rome represents the outcome, or the full development, of the same profound tendencies which lead in the direction of Sparta. The Romans, like the Spartans, were "a people who loved glory" (*Considerations, Works,* II, 113, note a; 85; cf. XXIII 21, 23 with VIII 16). The predominant cause of Rome's wars was the patriotic ambition of its most talented citizens:

> Princes have . . . periods of ambition . . . , but in a republic that has chiefs who change every year, and who seek to make signal their magistracy in order to get another, there is not a moment lost for ambition; they get the Senate to propose a war to the people. . . . (*Considerations, Works,* II, 72; cf. 70, 85, 140)

The incentive to war given by public ambition is enforced by the factional strife between rich and poor, or nobles and freemen, which leads the city to seek unity and greater wealth in war. This factionalism may have been partly due to faulty arrangements and chance occurrences at Rome, but these cannot explain it fully, for "at Rome the fortunes were nearly equal" (*Considerations, Works,* II, 84; cf. 81 and V 5). Faction seems a rather natural consequence of a free-spirited, self-governing people (XXIX 3). The mass of citizens, passionately devoted to public life, seem likely to magnify minor class differences into serious quarrels. Montesquieu disagrees with the traditional censure of faction in republican Rome; faction is a sign of republican health:

> One hears, in the authors, only that the divisions destroyed Rome; but it isn't seen that these divisions were necessary, that they have always been and always will be. It was only the expansion of the republic which was bad. . . . It was very necessary that there were divisions in Rome: and

these warriors, so fierce, so bold, so terrible in external affairs, could not have been very moderate in domestic affairs. To ask, in a free state, for men hardy in war and timid in peace is to wish for impossible things, and as a general rule, every time you see everyone tranquil in a state that gives itself the name of republic, you can be sure that there is no liberty there. (*Considerations, Works*, II, 119; cf. 116, 187, and Machiavelli, *Discourses*, I, iv)

For these reasons, the Roman engagement in "eternal war" subsisted "by the principle of its government" (*Considerations*, II, 73). The "good laws" and "virtue" of the republic led to empire, and empire is the destruction of virtue and good laws. For democracy is most endangered by the spirit of extreme equality, or the loss of the habit of obedience (VIII 2). Great national successes give the people an overweening pride which destroys the spirit of obedience; the citizen army loses not (at first) its military prowess and discipline, but its sense of subjection to the city (VIII 3; *Considerations, Works*, II, 117). Empire brings corrupting luxury and swells the population with foreigners who destroy the homogeneity and intimacy necessary for a self-governing community (*Considerations, Works*, II, 117–18):

This is a thing that one has seen always, that good laws, which made a little republic become great, become a burden when it has grown large; because they were such that their natural effect was to make a great people, and not to govern it. (*Considerations, Works*, II, 119–120; cf. 173)

Not only is the republic corrupted internally, but

its conquests naturally require it to exercise "a kind of tyranny" (cf. *Considerations, Works*, II, 71–72, 153, 178, with X 13, 14, esp. p. 390). Since tyranny exercised by a city is no more justifiable than tyranny exercised by a man, Rome's principles fostered the internal tyranny of the emperors: "That terrible tyranny of the emperors came from the general spirit of the Romans. . . . the Romans, accustomed to playing with human nature . . ." (*Considerations, Works*, II, 147–48). Well may Montesquieu say:

> It is here that one must see the spectacle of human things. That one should see in the history of Rome so many wars undertaken, so much blood spilt, so many peoples destroyed, so many great deeds, so many triumphs, so much of political skill, of wisdom, of prudence, of constancy, of courage; this project of invading everywhere, so well formed, so well sustained, so well completed, to what end is it, except to serve the happiness of five or six monsters? What! This senate did not destroy so many kings except to fall itself into the basest slavery under some of its most unworthy citizens, and to exterminate itself by its own decrees! (*Considerations, Works*, II, 150)

As David Lowenthal has remarked, the *Considerations* is a "melancholy" book.[12] Contemplation of the outcome of virtue is deeply disquieting.

The free, participatory life of a republic, the political role for which the individual sacrifices so much, thus emerges as profoundly dubious. It has an emptiness and a powerful tendency to fill that emptiness with war, conquest, slavery, and despotic empire.

Democracy at first appeared to be the only form of government not devoted to the domination of some men over others for the sake of low and selfish ends. But the virtue, the political freedom, of democracy, is revealed to be a means which is aimed at no stable or consistent end. And for the sake of this political freedom the individual is forced to make tremendous sacrifices of his freedom to pursue his selfish wants, his security, his physical comfort and preservation.

But this pursuit of selfish wants can be the basis for another, more limited, but more consistent understanding of freedom, and even for another kind of regime founded on freedom in this other sense. Prior to the notion that "liberty" means freedom for positive political participation in self-rule, is the notion that "liberty" means freedom *from* domination, pain, and fear. Prior to any positive goal, project, or activity which can be thought to be the end of government, government is intended to protect the citizenry. Montesquieu can claim to have shown how the supposed great positive goals of government—virtuous public-spiritedness and private honor—are unsatisfactory as ends in themselves. This is in a way the substantiation of his teaching about human nature in Book I. The demonstration of the inadequacy of the various historical proposals leaves as the only solid end of government the negative aim of merely providing security. Political experience supports the view that human nature is directed *at* nothing and is guided only by the impulsion to avoid discomfort and the threat of death. This understanding of liberty, implicit in the presentation of the nature of man and of government in Books I and II, is brought to the foreground again in Book VI, when Montesquieu turns from an elaboration of the principles and the "political" laws of the various regimes to a discussion of the effect of the political laws on the "civil" laws, the laws which protect the individual.[13]

It has been noted that Book VI seems out of order and should be put with Book XII, or vice versa, for both treat the same theme.[14] It might seem more reasonable to postpone the material in Book VI until Book XII, for it naturally follows the introduction of the theme of "liberty of the individual," to be introduced in Book XI.

But there is a good reason for adumbrating the theme of individual liberty here in the present context. For, in addition to showing which political and civil laws are most conducive to individual liberty (Books XI-XIII), Montesquieu wishes to study and compare the status of personal liberty in the traditional forms of government. Having revealed the dubiousness of the positive goals of those regimes, he now displays their merits and demerits from the point of view of the true, negative goal. On the one hand he will show to what extent and by what means each of the regimes is conducive to security; on the other hand, he will reveal the extent to which they fail to protect the individual from his fellow citizens. Especially insofar as the latter fact becomes clear, Book VI serves to recall the reader from the perspective of participatory freedom to the perspective of Book I, that of freedom as security. Book VI forces him to reflect on the difficulties of republicanism, and prepares him for the great issue of *The Spirit of the Laws*, the issue between ancient republicanism and modern England, which becomes explicit in Book XI. We see here, as we will see again and again, the characteristic style of Montesquieu's presentation: much of the apparent contradiction or disorder in *The Spirit of the Laws* is caused by the way in which its teaching *unfolds*, revealing at each stage the incompleteness or inadequacy of a previous perspective.

Montesquieu begins Book VI with a chapter on the simplicity of noncriminal "civil law." The simplicity or complexity of "civil law" is directly related to the security of life and property because complexity of law helps guarantee against arbitrary fiat in judging and administering. Complexity of law forces the judge to take account of the variety of individual circumstances, and requires that precedent be investigated and followed. Simplicity permits a thoughtless universalism in the one institution where the individual seeks to compensate for the crudeness of law's universality. Complexity is characteristic of law in monarchies, where the hierarchy of independent powers requires differentiation in law and the pervasive sense of honor requires meticulous treatment of each individual. Simplicity is characteristic of despotism, where all men have the status of slaves. In a chapter which by its title claims to deal with all three kinds of government, Montesquieu is silent about republics. He indicates that this is not caused by a slip in memory by the remarkable fact that here, and only here in the whole of *The Spirit of the Laws*, he says that he "was forgetting to say" something. Montesquieu remembered all that he wanted to say in this chapter. His silence about the simplicity or complexity of civil law in a republic forces us to think about the topic and why he should not mention it. The reason would seem to be that since in a republic private property is severely restricted and each citizen has very little private business with other citizens, noncriminal civil law would be unimportant and simple (cf. XVIII 13: "It is the divisions of lands which principally extends the civil code"). Montesquieu does not spell this out because it implies the unseemly fact that in a republic civil law will be closer to the simplicity of despotism than to the complexity of monarchy. A republic treats all citizens the same, and it does not respect private honor or property nearly as much as does monarchy. Indeed, as we have seen, a republic tries to overcome the private sphere to a very great degree. Of course, in a despotism the individual is left with nothing; in a republic he is recompensed by participation in public business and property.

After this single chapter on noncriminal civil law, Montesquieu devotes the rest of Book VI to the subject of criminal law. He immediately makes clear the great importance of this theme and the new sense of the word "liberty" which is emerging. Criminal law is "the thing in the world that it is most important for men to know," since it is directly connected with "the liberty and safety of the citizens." At first Montesquieu uses the two terms—liberty and safety—as if they were not identical. But at the end of the same paragaph, and twice in the rest of the chapter, he uses only the one term—liberty. Liberty no longer refers to participation in government; it is identified with "safety," and especially protection from arbitrary injury *by* government.

Participatory Republicanism

While Montesquieu seemed to indicate that the civil law of a republic is simple, he says that the criminal law in a republic "should have at least as many formalities as in monarchies." He continues: "In each government, the formalities are augmented to the extent to which one is concerned with the honor, fortune, life and liberty of the citizens" (VI 2). There is clearly a difficulty here; for, as we have seen, a republic lacks the differentiation of classes and groups, and the pervasive respect for individual "honor and fortune," that bring complexity to law in a monarchy. On the one hand, the criminal law in a republic is gentle because each citizen is cherished; but on the other hand, republican law is characterized by simplicity and uniformity, which would imply harshness. The republic counts on the self-restraint of magistrates instead of relying on more trustworthy institutional restraints in order to prevent abuses threatening to the individual. In addition, a republic places much greater demands on its citizens: they have more to do with public affairs, where their weaknesses or vices are more likely to be seen as criminal, and they are in general under closer scrutiny. For the same reason, the civil law is far more extended. In a monarchy, and even within the ruling class of an aristocracy,

> although all crimes are public by their nature, one distinguishes, nevertheless, crimes truly public from crimes private, thus called because they offend a particular person more than the whole society. But, in republics, private crimes are more public, that is to say, shock the constitution of the state more than they shock individuals. . . . (III 5; cf. III 4, note a; XI 18)

The consequences for individual security of these conflicting tendencies of republican criminal law are illustrated in the rest of Book VI.

In republics, criminal judgments follow the strict letter of the law. This prevents arbitrary bias: "There is no citizen against whom one can interpret a law" (VI 3). The prohibition on interpretation goes with the fact that in a republic the people as a whole act as the judge. But this means at the same time that the judgment is strict, without any possibility of moderation or adjustment. There is in fact no real "judging" in the criminal courts of a republic:

> In monarchies, the judges act in the manner of arbiters; they deliberate . . . they take council . . . . At Rome and in the Greek cities the judges do not communicate with one another. . . . This is because the people judge . . . but the people is not a jurisconsult; all those modifications and temperaments of arbiters are not for it. . . . (VI 4)

The fact that the people judge means that in a republic the sovereign is judge, as well as prosecutor: something which is characteristic of despotism, but not of monarchies (VI 5, 6, 7; XI 6, p. 404). This situation is of course particularly dangerous in republican trials for treason where, unless the institution is modified, "the political interest forces, so to speak, the civil interest, for it is always an inconvenience that the people itself judge offenses committed against it" (VI 5). To protect "the safety of the individuals" in trials for treason, the law must, like Solon's, introduce some form of independent appellate judiciary or make some other ad hoc provisions, such as allowing voluntary exile before trial.

Just as there is no independent and permanent judiciary in a republic, so there is no independent prosecutor:

> At Rome, it was permitted to a citizen to accuse another. That was according to the spirit of a republic, where each citizen ought to have a zeal without limits for the public good; where each citizen is understood to have all the rights of the fatherland in his hands. (VI 8)

Everyone is continually subject to the scrutiny of his fellow citizens for any indication of crime. Indeed, Montesquieu points out, there may be a penalty for failing to inform on others. The abuses to which such "zeal without limits" may lead are obvious ("even virtue has need of limits" [XI 4]). In contrast, "today," in the modern monarchies, the public prosecutor performs this function, leaving the citizen "tranquil."

Having thus discussed some of the salient topics of criminal procedure, Montesquieu devotes the rest, or the greatest part, of Book VI to a discussion of the penalties of criminal law. The penalty—the infliction of death and suffering—is that part of law which most directly endangers the security of the individual. Nothing reveals Montesquieu's own interest, in contrast to that of a good republican, more clearly than this emphasis on the penalties. Montesquieu is almost completely uninterested in the moral effect of criminal law. In fact, he seems more interested in the danger to the individual from criminal penalties than he is in moral education altogether: he devotes twelve chapters and fourteen pages to his discussion of penalties, whereas he devotes only eight chapters and twelve pages to the book on education.

In the context of the discussion of penalties, Montesquieu begins to refer with some frequency to "human nature." While human nature faded into the background in the earlier discussions of republicanism and virtue, it comes to the foreground again in the remarks about the proper limits on the harshness of penalties. The threat of arbitrary death or suffering is against nature and "natural defense" (VI 9, 13, 17); numerous harsh physical penalties are not necessary to preserve order; therefore, "let us follow nature" in prescribing, wherever possible, penalties which do not lead to physical harm (VI 12).

Both republics and monarchies, in contrast to despotisms, are characterized by gentle penalties. Both can rely on the sense of shame which accompanies virtue and honor instead of on the fear of physical punishment. In both, but especially in republics, there are neither extremely happy nor extremely unhappy men, and it is men in such conditions who are "carried to harshness"; "it is only the mediocrity and mixture of good and bad fortune which gives softness and pity" (VI 9). Nevertheless, here again the gentle tendencies of the republic are mixed with harsh tendencies.

Montesquieu agrees with Livy that one can praise the "humanity" of the Romans, and say that "no people ever more loved moderation in punishments" (VI 15). Yet he indicates that at least on one occasion "the people were strongly carried toward terrible punishments" and had to be restrained by the Senate. Montesquieu explicitly criticizes Livy for overlooking the cruelties Rome permitted under the Decemvirs. At the end of the previous book he pointed

out that "one is astonished" at the harsh penalties of
the Aereopagus in Athens. He remarks that "savages"
and "monks" are harsh because of their poverty and
hardness; but the republic was earlier compared to
a monastery, and the warlike education in the Greek
republics tended to incite "anger and cruelty" (VI 9;
V 2; IV 8).[15] Montesquieu finds himself literally
incapable of speaking about the harshness of the treatment of "slaves among the Greeks and Romans": "I
hear the voice of nature which cries against me" (VI
17). Finally, in the very chapter where he follows Livy
in praising the Romans, he refers us to the *Considerations*, where he says:

> The Romans, accustomed to playing with human
> nature in the person of their children and slaves,
> could scarcely comprehend that virtue we call
> humanity. . . . When one is cruel in the civil
> state, what can one expect of mildness and
> natural justice? (II, 148; cf. V 7; II 283; IX 1,
> note b; X 3)

Montesquieu continues the general theme of the
effect of the various regimes on the liberty of the
individual in Book VII, dealing with laws regulating
pleasure, luxury, and the condition of women. Here
he explicitly returns to some extent to the discussion
in Books IV and V of the impact of the principle
of government on private life, private property, and
the family (VII 2, note a).

Luxury is constituted by "commodities which one
gives oneself by the work of others." Luxury therefore
goes hand in hand with an inegalitarian order in which
some work for the sake of others. It follows that "in
order that the riches remain equally divided, the law

must give to each only the physically necessary" (VII 1). Where men have more private property than the minimal necessities, some will attend to private pleasures, and spend; others will attend to amassing private wealth, and acquire; and inequality will be established. Republics therefore require strict sumptuary laws (VII 2).

In a monarchy, on the contrary, there should be a promotion of luxury and the commerce based on luxury in order to promote a greater flow and distribution of the wealth possessed by the nobles. In monarchies, luxury is "a usage one makes of the liberty one possesses." Citizens of a monarchy can say that "the examples of the harshness of the ancients have been changed into a way of life more agreeable." Monarchies are not interested in "self-renunciation" for the sake of public service; the nobles, through luxury and commerce, render to the poorer citizens "the physical necessity" they once took from them and gain an "agreeable way of living" for themselves (VII 4).

Intimately connected with the question of how much luxury political society allows or encourages is the question of the status of women. Montesquieu, perhaps more than any other political philosopher, calls attention to the importance of the place of women in a political order. He does not believe that the nature of women is the same as the nature of men; and every form of government must somehow come to terms with this natural division in the human species. The source of woman's unique nature is her role in sexual love and motherhood. These roles are very different in the different forms of government; under most, it is not possible for women to fulfill both roles equally.

In particular, in a republic requiring self-renunciation and strict education, the sexual freedom of women must be sharply restricted.

Chastity, continence, simplicity, and fidelity of women are of supreme importance in a republic, for "public incontinence . . . is joined with luxury, which always follows it and which it always follows" (VII 14). Luxury arises because erotic love weakens or replaces the passionate love of the fatherland which makes self-renunciation and endurance possible: "If you leave in liberty the movements of the heart, how can you restrain the weaknesses of the spirit?" (VII 14). Men refuse to do their public work: "The commerce of gallantry . . . produces laziness" (VII 8). Instead of being preoccupied with public affairs, men become concerned with obtaining things which please or adorn their women: "Gallantry . . . gives a price to all the little nothings, and lowers everything important" (VII 8). Men forget the dictates of glory and "one conducts himself only according to the maxims of ridicule which the women know so well how to establish" (VII 8). Where women have "liberty," "their weakness does not permit them pride, but only vanity," and therefore they will not occupy themselves and their men with great things but only with the adornments of luxury, "their quarrels, their jealousies, their indiscretions, their dislikes, their inclinations, their piques, that art which little souls have of interesting great souls" (VII 9). They will corrupt the men and ignore or corrupt the children. In these remarks Montesquieu presents only the worst side of a regime where women are free; we saw in his discussion of the warlike sense of honor in Book IV, and we will see in his later descriptions of France and England, that the evil effects of woman's freedom are counterbalanced in nondemocratic regimes by other good effects. But in a republic based on renunciation of private interests,

> there are so many imperfections attached to the loss of virtue in women. . . . When this principal point is lost, so many others fall that one can regard, in a popular state, public lack of continence as the last of misfortunes and the certitude of a change in the constitution. (VII 8)

In a republic, therefore, in contrast to a monarchy, women lack "liberty." They are not slaves, as they are in despotisms, but neither are they free: "In republics, women are free by the laws, and held captive by the customs" (VII 9); "the institutions of the Romans put women in a perpetual tutelage . . . and it appears . . . that they were very much confined" (VII 12). This of course means that women cannot have within their own control any property to speak of (VII 15). But the restrictions go much beyond that. Lightness must be banished from woman's life: "the good legislators have in republics required of the women a certain gravity in their manners" (XVI 9; VII 8). The republic enforces this code of manners through special censors or inspectors and "domestic tribunals" which "watch over the general conduct of women" (VII 10). These tribunals are closely allied to the more general censors who supervise and correct the conduct of all the inhabitants (cf. VII 14 with V 7, V 19, VIII 14). Of course, any artistic presentation must conform to these manners (VII 10, note d). In the administration of this "correction," the individual is not protected by the strict letter of any law:

> The punishments of this tribunal must be arbitrary, and were in fact; because all that which regards customs, all that regards rules of modesty, can scarcely be comprised in a code of laws. (VII 10)

In a participatory republic women cannot be free, and the love of men and women, "the movements of the heart," cannot be free. A republic will strive to follow that "beautiful custom of the Samnites" which made "love and beauty . . . so to speak, the reward of virtue" (VII 16). According to Montesquieu this tends to lead, however, to unseemly consequences. If the love of male for female is prevented, the love of male for male, which does not run all the risks caused by the "weakness" of women, may well have to be tolerated or even encouraged to some extent:

> In the Greek cities where one didn't live under that religion which, among the men too, established purity as a part of virtue . . . , a blind vice reigned in an unbridled manner, where love had only a form which one does not dare to name, while in marriage only friendship was found. . . . (VII 9, cf. note a ad. loc.; IV 8; VIII 11; XII 6)

The risk of such distorted passion is part of the price one pays for participatory republicanism. In attempting to substitute love of the community for love of the family, the republic undermines the love of the family.

The democratic republic, by establishing legal

equality, imitates the equality of the state of nature (VIII 3); no man is ruled by the arbitrary will of another. But for the sake of this equality in government, the democracy makes a considerable sacrifice of the security, comfort, and freedom from constraint or imprisonment, of the individual. By the end of his presentation of participatory republicanism, Montesquieu has made perfectly clear the inadequacy of the republic's protection of the individual, his life, his comfort, his property, his family, and his natural inclinations.

Insofar as the status of republican government and its participatory freedom is called into doubt, the status of monarchy rises, and it becomes more a question which of these two regimes is preferable. For in a monarchy there is no need to restrain man's selfish natural passions: "In monarchies, politics does great things with the least virtue it can" (III 5). The principle of monarchy, unlike that of a republic, "is favored by the passions" (VI 5); "in a monarchy one doesn't need so much constraint" (V 7; cf. IV 7). The competition of selfish independent powers and selfish individuals seeking honor prevents anyone from having despotic power, and promotes respect for the individual throughout the society:

> Ambition is dangerous in a republic. It has good effects in a monarchy; it gives the life to this government. . . . Each aims at the common good believing that he aims at his particular interests. (III 7; cf. V 14)

As we have seen, monarchic civil and criminal law give greater procedural protection to the individual, and there are fewer acts which are considered crimes. In a monarchy, more than in a republic, men and women are left alone in comfort, unthreatened and unconstrained. For these reasons Montesquieu begins in Book VI to use frequently his twofold categorization of regimes as "moderate" or "despotic." A regime is "moderate" insofar as it pursues a course opposite to despotism. Despotism is characterized by *fear;* moderate regimes are characterized by *security.* Monarchy seems at least as secure, or "moderate," as a republic (V 14; VI 1, 2, 9, 16, 19; cf. III 9, 10; V 15; VII 17). Thus Montesquieu can say at the end of the presentation of the traditional forms of government:

> The inconvenience is not when the state passes from moderate government to moderate government, as from a republic to a monarchy, or from a monarchy to a republic; but when it falls and throws itself from a moderate government to despotism. (VIII 8)

Montesquieu also points out in his book on the corruption of the principles of the various regimes that monarchy is less threatened by corruption than is republicanism. The selfishness of the monarchical principle goes less against the grain than the self-renunciation of the republican principle. In addition, monarchy is less dependent on the maintenance of its "principle" than is republicanism. Montesquieu seems at first to say that all forms of government are equally endangered by corruption of their principles; but most of his examples and much of his discussion of the downfall of the constitution and the laws caused by the contamination of the principle deals with republics (VIII 11, 12, 14; note especially the silence about monarchy in VIII 12 and 14). The maintenance of the nature or structure of monarchy, the balance of competing powers, is at least as important as the maintenance of the principle, and is somewhat independent of the principle (VIII 6–7).[16] A monarchy depends more on institutional restraint than on human restraint. Monarchy may be more stable than republicanism as well as being more moderate.

In addition to the second, monarchical kind of "moderate government," there is a third, to which Montesquieu makes a number of rather Delphic allusions in the first eight books: the commercial republic. He has told us that "there were in Greece two sorts of republics; some were military, like Sparta, others were commercial, like Athens" (V 6). In commercial republics public spirit is attenuated; the citizens are concerned primarily with private aggrandizement. If the citizens are prudent enough to enforce limits on the evil effects of commerce—inequality, selfishness, growth in size—a kind of stable compromise between republicanism and anarchy is possible. Of course, from the point of view of participatory republican freedom and military power, such a republic is inferior. Nevertheless, it has some advantages. It is truly peaceful, for the citizens are occupied with commerce, and its riches can to some extent help it to defend itself. It is therefore possible for it to avoid the consequences of great success in war. It is much easier for a commercial city to enter into defensive federations, for it need fear less that the purity of its morals will be corrupted by close associations with

neighbors, and its way of life is less threatened by
the dilution of patriotism that association with other
cities must imply.[17] The spirit of commerce, prudently understood, brings with it certain virtues—
"frugality, economy, moderation, work, prudence,
tranquility, order, and rule" (V 6; cf. VII 2,
6)—which give the city stability and some strength.
The citizens are not subject to as much constraint as
in a pure republic. And these advantages appear even
greater once one has seen the difficulties in pure
republicanism.

The commercial republic has the difficulties
inherent in its compromise. It is too committed to
republicanism to give its citizens as much individual
freedom as monarchy gives; and its commitment to
republicanism also keeps it small and hence poorer
and more vulnerable. On the other hand, it is too
committed to private wealth to enforce vigorous public
spirit: Athens and Syracuse are the great examples
of republics corrupted from within (VIII 2); the growing power of the commercial class helped destroy
Rome (XI 18). Commercial republics tend to grow
in wealth and power even without war, and when
they do grow they are even more vulnerable than
growing noncommercial republics (*Considerations,
Works*, II, 83; VIII 4). Nevertheless, Montesquieu
draws our attention to the example of classical Marseilles, a city one hears little about in the writings
of the ancients. The history of Marseilles, a city which
remained moderate, shows that the internal balance
of opposites in a commercial republic *can* sometimes
endure in times and places where small republics are
possible (VII 15, note b; VIII 4; XI 5; XX 4–5;

although consider XXI 11). The alternative represented by this uneasy combination of natural selfishness and virtue is never entirely dismissed by Montesquieu, insofar as he never entirely dismisses the attractiveness of participatory freedom. Yet because he finds the justification for virtuous republics so weak, Montesquieu is more attracted by the commercial aspect than by the public-spirited aspect of those republics. Dedication to commerce is a dedication to individual security, comfort, and gain which brings with it certain "virtues" beneficial to others in the community. It therefore has many of the advantages of the concern with honor and none of the inconveniences or "bizarreness" of exaggerated vanity. What commerce does not bring per se, and a key part of what the small commercial republic lacks, is the balance of competing selfish powers which at once restrains and gives energy to monarchy. The commercial republic is therefore required to continue to count on political virtue and all it entails, while at the same time undermining that virtue. Only a regime which somehow combined the monarchical balance of powers with commerce could successfully devote itself wholeheartedly to individual liberty or security. Such a regime Montesquieu finds in England.

5

LIBERAL REPUBLICANISM

In the Second Part of *The Spirit of the Laws* Montesquieu turns to a study of the relation between the
laws and the liberty of citizens. From the progression
of the argument in the first eight books the reader
might at first expect Montesquieu simply to draw out
the consequences for liberty of the three constitutions
and their principles (see especially the plan as stated
in I 3). But instead, as is indicated by the title of
Book XI, Montesquieu ceases to give a central place
to the consideration of the three forms of government
to which we were introduced in Books II through
VIII, and confronts us with a new kind of constitution
devoted exclusively to liberty. On the other hand, the
reader has been prepared for this development.

In his presentation of the traditional forms of government, Montesquieu has revealed the inadequacies
of their particular principles and the aims which derive
from those principles. He has thereby pointed to the
desirability of a government having no other purpose
than the security and comfort of its citizens. He finds
the principles of this desired government in the modern
constitution of England, properly understood and
interpreted. Book XI is the presentation of this constitution, and the books which follow all deal in one
way or another with its consequence for political life
in all times and places.

Chapter Five

The books immediately preceding Book XI form
an appropriate conclusion to the study of the traditional forms of government and a fitting transition to
the new English form. These books deal with the preservation of the lives of the citizens through the prevention or moderation of war. In them Montesquieu
moves from a discussion of the principle of each
regime, of what is unique to each, to a discussion
of what all the regimes and all men have in common—the need for defense (compare the titles of
Books II through VIII with the titles of Books IX
and X).[1] In the discussion of defense, Montesquieu
returns emphatically to the themes of "human nature"
and "natural law." He does this in chapters entitled
"On War" and "On the Right of Conquest" (X 2,
3). Montesquieu thus reminds us of the natural condition of man—the state of nature which becomes a state
of war—and of the principles of politics deduced from
that natural condition as presented in Book I. While
the needs generated by the particular principles of the
various regimes Montesquieu has presented may not
be solidly grounded in man's nature, the need for preservation most certainly is. As we have seen, the
ancient virtuous republic is not very successful at fostering peace or encouraging humanity in warfare.
Indeed, it seems to foster war and encourage brutality.
It is therefore not surprising that in this context, when
speaking about concern for the preservation of life in
warfare, Montesquieu for the first time praises the
superiority of modernity over antiquity: "It is necessary here to render homage to our modern times, to
contemporary reason, to today's religion, to our
philosophy, to our morals" (X 3). Montesquieu thus

prepares us for his presentation of a new regime devoted to security.

Montesquieu begins Book XI with a rather difficult and compressed résumé of the understanding of liberty we have seen emerging in the earlier books. He starts from the mixture of truth and error in the most generally held opinions about liberty; his intention is to show the error in the common opinion which holds that republics, especially democracies, are free while monarchies are not.

Liberty means many things to many men because men's inclinations and tastes vary, but in general it means doing as one wishes. Therefore "each has called liberty the government which conforms to his customs or his inclinations." Almost every kind of government has been called free at one time or another. Yet liberty has most often been associated with republics, for there the laws, rather than men, seem to rule or, in other words, men seem to be less enslaved to other men's wishes. Moreover, since doing as one wishes seems to require not only not being ruled by others but also ruling, or "having power," oneself, liberty has been understood to be most at home in democracy. It is there that "the people seem almost to do what they want" (XI 2).

But in placing liberty in democracy, men have "confused the power of the people with the liberty of the people" (XI 2). It is a mistake to understand liberty as the "power" to do "as one wishes"—that is to say, it is a mistake to identify liberty with independence (XI 3). Montesquieu identifies liberty with a life lived under the rule of law. A man is free only when he limits his doing as he wishes to activities not forbidden by law. In order to understand this somewhat paradoxical definition of liberty, a definition which separates liberty from independence, we must remind ourselves of the implications of human independence.

We remember that if men living together in society were all independent, or free to do as they wished, the result would be a state of war (I 3). All men are naturally in competition for the scarce material goods necessary to live and live comfortably; men free to do as they wish will steal, will kill or dominate one another in order to get goods for themselves and to prevent others from depriving them of these goods. Doing as one wishes in society is self-destructive or self-contradictory: men in a position to do as they wish in society are not free because they are threatened with force, violence, and death (XXVI 15, 20). The only free men are those who are secure and safe from these threats; this security is achieved through the creation of a "state" which regulates the behavior of men so as to put an end to war and the acts which bring war. The essence of the state is the "union" of the individual "wills" with the "power" to enforce those wills (I 3; II 2). The state "unites" the wills by making each individual limit his selfish desire for security and other things so as not to endanger the similar desire of others. The state does this through laws which can thus be called expressions of a "general will" (XI 6, p. 399). Life under law is the only life which is secure and therefore free (XI 3).

The essence of law is therefore will and formal universality. Human will and its object, security, predates law; what law contributes to man is the means for universalizing and thereby making truly enforceable the selfish human will. Law does not, as was traditionally thought, embody dictates of gods or of reason which show to man better and higher objects of aspiration. Law gives to man only a rationality in *form*. Hence Montesquieu's definition of liberty in terms of the restraint imposed by law is not a return to the *traditional* understanding of liberty in terms of restraints imposed by reason and law. That restraint was understood to be imposed for the sake of the cultivation of certain higher human faculties. For Montesquieu, the necessary legal restriction is limited to what is required in order to achieve universally what each man originally desires. What initially appears to be a definition of liberty in terms of law is in fact a definition of both liberty and law in terms of security of the individual. This is made perfectly clear two chapters later: "Political liberty in a citizen is that tranquility of spirit which comes from the opinion which each has of his security" (XI 6; cf. XII 1, 2). The liberty of government is rule of law; but liberty of government exists for the sake of liberty of the citizen (cf. XI 1 with XII 1).

Montesquieu understands law as, above all, form. The form of law, its universal applicability, becomes more important than its content; more precisely, the form guarantees the goodness of the content. Since no man in his senses wills insecurity for himself, no matter how much men's tastes and desires vary, the rulers of a state will always promote liberty, their intentions will always be good, as long as they express their authoritative volitions in the legal form—universal applicability to themselves as well as others. In order to achieve security or liberty it is therefore sufficient to construct a system that insures the rule of law. One must hasten to add that the rule of law is not quite enough. Rule of law insures the goodness of the government's intention; but the rulers may be victims of factual error, mistaken judgment, or even blinding superstition. There must therefore be provision for enlightenment and prudence. <u>Still, the key to liberty is law as formal universality</u>.

Now it is evident that not every authoritative civil pronouncement constitutes a law (cf. XXVI 20). Montesquieu does not emphasize this because he wishes to avoid as much as possible undermining obedience to law. For in almost any civil society which makes some attempt at rule of law most men are better protected than in the state of war—that total absence of law resulting from revolution. Initially, then, Montesquieu keeps in the background the standard by which law can be judged and termed false law. Nevertheless, when identifying liberty with obedience to law, Montesquieu makes it clear enough that he does not mean that obedient subjects of despotic "laws" are free: "Political liberty is found only in moderate governments" (XI 4).

Moreover, even in nondespotic governments there exists true rule of law only in the degree to which the government promulgates and enforces laws which make all citizens secure. Republics, including democracies, do not necessarily possess liberty or rule of law: "Democracy and aristocracy are not free states by their nature" (XI 4). They may provide their citizens with some security but they are willing to dilute that security in the name of another goal—virtue. One can say that democracies make the mistake of supposing that true political liberty requires autonomy or self-legislation. But we have learned from the analysis of human nature in Book I and of autonomous virtue in Books II through VIII that this exercise of the will in self-government has no justification independent of its contribution to security. Completely free exercise of the will is a desirable thing in thought or philosophy but not in action or politics:

> Philosophical liberty consists in the exercise of one's will or at least (if it is necessary to speak in all the systems) in the opinion one has that one exercises one's will. Political liberty consists in security or at least in the opinion one has of one's security. (XII 2)

Political autonomy, while it may produce security, is not necessary for it and can in fact be dangerous to it. Virtue is an insufficient restraint on those who hold power; more important, virtue itself tends to threaten the security of individuals—"virtue itself has need of limits" (XI 4).

Montesquieu carefully refrains from saying that monarchy is "not free by its nature." By this silence he implies that monarchy is free by its nature.[2] Monarchy does not require the self-sacrifice of virtue. And by its system of checks and balances monarchy prevents any group or individual from gaining the power to make nonuniversal rules which oppress some other group or individual. In monarchies, we remember, "the laws take the place of all those virtues of which there is no need" (III 5). The difficulty with traditional monarchy, of course, is that it excludes the non-noble classes from many of the benefits of the

regime, and the security it does provide is based on
the irrationality or insecurity of the "code of honor."
A truly free regime would require at the least some
combination of republican egalitarianism with a more
rational balance of power.

In perfectly characteristic fashion, Montesquieu's
presentation of the government which represents the
rational solution of the problem of human nature does
not take the form of an imagined model. Instead, he
draws a picture of the living regime of England. This
picture is not intended as an exact or complete replica
of English political life (XI 6, p. 407); but it
extrapolates or modifies only in the direction of making more reasonable the principles and possibilities
Montesquieu sees in England's laws.

The English government is characterized by almost
complete abandonment of reliance on virtue. Montesquieu never mentions virtue or education when discussing England in Books XI and XIX; it was ridiculous,
a "spectacle," to see England try to establish a democracy founded on virtue because "those who took part
in affairs had no virtue at all" (III 3). Nor does "honor"
play any more than a secondary role. England is a
"republic" and even a "democracy" (V 19; XII 19;
XIV 13), but it does not rely on the principle which
seemed essential to a republic. England is a new kind
of republic which "hides under the form of a
monarchy" in order to achieve the end of freedom
(V 19; XI 5; XIX 27, p. 580).

Here in his discussion of political liberty and the
English constitution devoted to liberty, Montesquieu
surely does not emphasize the fact that free govern-

ment neither requires nor encourages virtue, not to speak of the fact that it requires and encourages lack of virtue. Several hundred pages later, when he returns to a discussion of England, with a description of its way of life—its "customs, manners, and morals"—he makes explicit that

> all the passions being free there, hate, envy, jealousy, the ardor for enriching and distinguishing oneself, will appear in their full extent. . . . Each individual . . . will very much follow his caprices and his fantasies. . . . Often, in that nation, one can forget the laws of friendship. . . . (XIX 27)

By the silence here, and by his refusal to state clearly how England is related to the enumeration of regimes in Book II, Montesquieu is willing to allow the careless reader to become confused about the sharp distinction between English republicanism and the virtuous form of republicanism, and about the distinction between English monarchy and the form of monarchy based on the principle of honor.

[margin note: England stands alone]

There would seem to be two reasons for Montesquieu's reticence. First, although the English constitution is based on the collective selfishness of its citizens, it still requires a minimal devotion to the whole on the part of each citizen. We have seen in Book XI the importance of law-abidingness for freedom; we remember from Book I that every society requires adherence to certain principles of equity or reciprocity; and national defense will require a certain capacity for self-sacrifice. While Montesquieu thinks that enlightened selfishness can go far in supplying

the motive for these restraints, he still thinks it necessary that the principle of self-interest be somewhat
muted.

Second, the advocacy of free government is much
more effective rhetorically if it does not underline the
distinction between freedom and virtue, or freedom
and honor. And as long as one succeeds in getting
men to support freedom and to emulate English
institutions, one need not be too worried by the effects
of their talk about virtue. In this rhetorical enterprise
Montesquieu was amazingly successful. Probably the
greatest failing of most commentators on *The Spirit
of the Laws* has been their blindness to, or confusion
about, Montesquieu's radical opposition between
ancient republicanism and modern English republicanism, and between traditional monarchy and English monarchy.[3]

England is free because it provides security for every
individual. It is republican or even democratic because
it gives sovereignty to the people (XI 6, p. 399). It
achieves this without the "inconveniences" of the virtuous government of all by all, but by making government the product of an institutionalized competition
of selfish individuals and private factions whose
struggle checks the possibility of oppression without
destroying the force necessary to government.

Of "the principle" of the English form of government Montesquieu does not speak. The English constitution does not have "a principle" in the same way
that the other forms of government do. For in the
other forms of government the animating principle
was "a particular passion," a "modification of the
soul," while England is animated by the conflicting

struggle of "all the passions," which are left "free" (XIX 27). Where all the passions are free, or where there is the least "modification" of man's soul, it is the course of nature for the selfish passions for security to become dominant. England achieves the natural and legitimate end of government—the provision of selfish security for each citizen—without distorting, threatening, or modifying man's natural selfishness in the process.

This understanding of the true nature of the English system emerges clearly enough in Montesquieu's description of the principles of the English constitution. The idea of preventing oppression in a republic by balancing selfish competitive factions was of course not invented in Montesquieu's England. Nor is the scheme of institutionalizing this balance through a division of governmental power an innovation. But in the English system as described by Montesquieu these ideas take on a radically new form. In addition, Montesquieu's new principle of the "separation of powers" goes beyond the classical aim of stabilizing the balance of competing factions and tries to create out of the competition of selfish interests a new guarantee for personal security and the rule of law.

Since we now live in a world where all republican government has a form derived from the principles Montesquieu first described here, we have difficulty in grasping the unique and peculiar character of these principles. We can best gain a clear perspective by comparing the modern, Montesquieuian balance of power and separation of powers with the older forms of republican balance of power. Montesquieu himself invites us to do so in the chapters of Book XI which follow chapter 6. Let us begin by examining Montesquieu's new plan for balancing power.

It was well understood in classical thought and practice that for many, or even most, republics the population was not homogeneous enough, or patriotism strong enough, to prevent the formation of factions, especially of rich and poor, or nobles and commoners, one of which might usurp all governmental power and oppress the other. In such situations the classical authors endeavored to balance the power of the competing factions by giving each a share in the rule. Such a regime, part democracy and part oligarchy, was known as a "mixed regime" or what Aristotle calls a "polity." Now classical political science also recognized that there are three naturally distinguishable functions or powers of government—what Aristotle called the deliberative, the magisterial, and the judicial functions. This distinction of function is the source of our modern distinction of government into legislative, executive, and judicial "powers," although the two distinctions are by no means identical. The difference appears most clearly in Aristotle's understanding of the deliberative and magisterial functions. By the "deliberative function" of government, Aristotle refers to all the general policy-making, whether expressed in the form of law, in administrative guidelines, or in the judicial trials of the most important political crimes. Aristotle attributes to the deliberative function or "power" a considerable part of what we would call the "executive power" and some of what we would understand as the "judicial power." The "magisterial function" Aristotle tends to see as more purely administrative, more the tool, so to speak, of the deliberative function.[4] In this understanding of the articulation of government, Aristotle keeps in the foreground the fact that ruling means above all deliberation, or taking comprehensive thought about the good of the community. What Aristotle means is perhaps best understood by us when we speak of the need for political "leadership."

While the classical authors were aware that this threefold distinction of governmental functions tended to influence the actual formation of the institutions of government—the magistracies often being separate from the deliberative body and so forth—a strict threefold institutional arrangement along the lines of the threefold distinction of governmental *functions* was by no means necessarily implied. Aristotle indicates that the same institution or office may exercise two or all three of the functions. And even where the functions are exercised by separate institutions, it is obvious from the great preponderance of the deliberative function that Aristotle does not envision a *balance* of these functions. The balance takes place not between but within the institutions and powers of government; the balance is a balance of *factions*, achieved by "mixing" the factions in each institution and in the exercise of each function of government.

It is clear from a little reflection on the scheme itself and from the historical data presented in the *Politics* that such a balance of factions does not in itself possess great stability. Insofar as rich and poor become more selfish and more unequal the common government threatens to dissolve into a war between the two factions which directly control it. The institutions of the

Aristotelian or classical mixed regime are inadequate to control factions; the regime must rely not on its institutions but on its citizens. It must cultivate certain human virtues and certain kinds of men. In brief, it requires a large, stable, and public-spirited middle class, with a predominantly agricultural economic basis (*Politics* 1295ª ff.; cf. XI 18, pp. 426–27).

The instability to which the mixed regime was exposed suggested the need for a modification of or supplement to the Aristotelian discussion. The theoretical formulation of this modification appears most clearly in Polybius's somewhat idealized account of the Roman republican constitution.[5] The "judicious Polybius," as Montesquieu calls him, suggested that the balance of factions could be made more stable if it were institutionalized. In Polybius's Rome, each faction, the rich patricians and the poor plebeians, is given a role in government through an institution of its own—the senate for the nobles and the assembly for the commoners. Where the governmental powers of each institution are well defined by law and custom, each faction is more permanently maintained and a shift in their respective strengths is less likely. In addition, Polybius praises the Roman revival of monarchy in the form of a third institution, the office of consul. The independent interests of the consuls lead them to enter the factional struggle, transforming the two-way struggle for power into a shifting three-way struggle where the likelihood of any one institutionalized faction permanently gaining the upper hand is much diminished.[6]

Polybius's suggestion takes the first step in the direction of replacing reliance on the public spirit or virtue of men with a reliance on institutions which preserve the free republic by channeling and manipulating man's naturally selfish passions. This is for Montesquieu the great value of Polybius's suggestion. And Polybius himself argues that the superiority of the Roman constitution is revealed especially in times of corruption (*Histories* VI xviii 5–8). Yet Polybius does not mean that the Roman constitution allows for the rule of men who lack virtue. He rather means that this constitution, by requiring less virtue in most citizens, can withstand more corruption and can thereby better preserve the power of the few virtuous citizens. The Roman constitution continues to require patriotism in all citizens, prudence and moderation in the senators, and respect for virtue in general in the mass of the people (*Histories* VI xiii, xiv 5, li).

Montesquieu's understanding of the constitution of the Roman republic seems to be at least partly inspired by Polybius (XI 17, note a, p. 421). But he challenges Polybius's analysis in two ways. In the first place, Montesquieu presents a more realistic and strictly historical account which demonstrates the failure of the Roman constitution to balance the powers of the factions. The actual Roman regime is seen as not having lived up to Polybius's theoretical account of it. Instead of a stable, institutionalized balance of powers, Montesquieu finds in the Roman constitution a slow but steady evolution toward mob rule—the same as Aristotle found evolving in many or most mixed regimes. The Roman regime required virtue; and as virtue ebbed, it became necessary for the nobles to reinvigorate the sense of attachment to the common good by means of the common enterprise of war (XI 13,

17) or by means of "terrible" officers—dictators and censors—who forced the people back to obedience or deprived them of their role as citizens (XI 16; cf. II 3). But such institutions were unable to restore virtue or to prevent the eventual accumulation of power in the hands of the poor and their demagogues.

In the second place, Montesquieu reveals a new understanding of the principles underlying a "balance of power." The Polybian system had attempted to create a stable balance by the *division* of governmental power among institutionalized factions—consul, senate, and assembly. But Polybius had not connected this with the Aristotelian analytical distinction among the functions or powers of government. It is Montesquieu's suggestion that the balance will be further stabilized if the separation of the competing institutions, each of which has been given over to a single faction, be coordinated to some extent with the distinction between the two nonjudicial functions. Montesquieu tries, not altogether unsuccessfully, to show that the stability of the Roman balance was due in some measure to this kind of coordination. Rome's constitution was neither a "mixed regime" as understood by Aristotle, nor a balance of power as understood by Polybius.

Now in order to make such a suggestion it is clear that Montesquieu had to have a rather different understanding of the two nonjudicial functions or powers of government than the understanding of Aristotle and Polybius.[7] By understanding government as essentially "rule of law," or the limitation of private wills by the union of those wills in a "general will," Montesquieu is led to understand the key function of government to be a "legislative" rather than a "deliberative" function. The legislative function remains the supreme function, just as the deliberative function was. But since this legislative function is limited to the formulation of *general* rules, and political life is actually constituted by constantly changing individual circumstances, the function of carrying out those general rules must be given greater independence than was given to the "magisterial" function. The "executive" function can claim a more legitimate right to mold the commands of the "legislators" than the magistrates could claim with regard to the commands of the "deliberators." If the two functions—legislative and executive—are assigned to separate institutions, those institutions will be more nearly equal than would have been the case according to the Aristotelian understanding.

This implication is strengthened by reflection on the needs of foreign policy: since foreign policy can hardly be regulated by laws, it cannot be said to be necessarily a part of the legislative function. And since the kind of deliberation foreign policy requires is more akin to the prudent attention to constantly changing circumstances—the energy, secrecy, and dispatch —possessed by the executor of laws, the "executive power" seems properly to incorporate most of the control over foreign affairs.

By separating and equalizing the two nonjudicial functions of government, Montesquieu's scheme gives a new and additional basis for an institutionalized balance of factional power, a basis drawn from the principles, the nature, of government itself. In particular, Montesquieu's analysis lends greater legitimacy to the independent power of the Roman senate (interpreted as possessing the executive power) even when the people possessed most of the lawmaking power (XI 17).

Unfortunately, the Romans themselves were not fully conscious of the nature of government as it appears in Montesquieu's analysis. And if they had been, Montesquieu's presentation of Roman history shows that even a balance of power thus understood is inadequate to remedy the weakness of institutions and the need for virtue in a republic. For even where the legislative and executive powers are separated from one another, as long as the legislative power is itself united, especially in the hands of the people, there will be an inevitable tendency toward legislative usurpation of all other power (XI 16–18). The legislative function or power should be divided between nobles and people. Such a division into two antagonistic or competing branches seems more reasonable if one considers this part of government to be essentially lawmaking or expression of will rather than deliberation: expression of *will* does not require as much common agreement as does deliberation. Yet if one divides the legislative power between nobles and people, the nobles will possess both legislative and executive power; this leads either to oligarchic oppression or to popular resentment or to both. The eventual outcome is again democratic decay.[8]

The difficulty would be solved if one could reestablish monarchy, giving to the king the executive power. Then the legislative power would be divided and balanced, without sacrificing the separation and balance between executive and legislative. In addition, one would reap the benefits outlined by Polybius in his praise of the Roman office of consul. Yet unlike Polybius, Montesquieu doubts whether this solution is usually available to the republic. The restless popular desire for participation and self-rule will not tolerate monarchy; kings were possible only in the early and primitive days of republics (XI 8, 11, 12; VIII 16). Rome as interpreted by Montesquieu exhausts the institutional arrangements available to a republic. Republics lack a secure institutional balance of power. A republic has no substitute for reliance on and cultivation of virtue.

The reason why a republic cannot forgo reliance on virtue is that, in order to replace virtue with a more stable and permissive institutional balance of powers, the republic would have to be combined with monarchy. And this is prevented by the power and spirit of popular self-rule. Direct popular participation—precisely that which seemed to be a necessary condition for freedom—now appears as the obstacle to freedom. Monarchy is possible only in large countries. Large monarchies can have a kind of balance of power between nobles and king; large countries are more prosperous and secure than small countries. But large monarchies tend to oppress or exploit the people. What is needed is some institution which allows the people to have a share of the political power in a monarchy but which dilutes that share of power.[9] Unknown to the ancients (XI 8), this institution, the "great advantage" of modern liberal republicanism (XIX 27, p. 576), is representative government. The representative republic Montesquieu finds in England makes possible the desired combination of republicanism and monarchy, and thereby the institutional balance of powers. Having abandoned the goal of pure popular government (III 3), England can allow and even encourage the selfishness of individuals and factions because through its largely nonpopular institutions it can channel the factions and force them to restrain one another. Even while the factions are being restrained by the institutions, they are left with enough power to check and moderate the power of those institutions.

The way in which the new balance of power actually works can be better understood if we examine in more detail the particular institutions of the model English system. Most important is the representative legislature which replaces the general assembly of all the citizens. It is through this institution that the moderation of the advocacy of popular interests is achieved. Not only will direct control be removed from the people, but the selection of representatives will tend to produce spokesmen more sober and thoughtful than the mass of the people (XI 6, p. 400; XIX 27, p..576). In addition, the representatives as a body will be encouraged to be more deliberate, more far-seeing, and less narrow than the people as a whole since their number will be small and they will be sufficiently independent of popular will (XI 6, p. 400). And finally, there will be a less monolithic, more divided popular will, since because of the large size of the republic, the constituencies of the representatives will have a variety of competing interests (XI 6, pp. 399–400; XIX 27, p. 583).

The popular interest will not, however, become

simply fragmented. Montesquieu speaks of the growth of "parties" by which the variety of interests will coalesce into rival factions on opposite sides of one issue, usually the issue of whether the king should have more or less power and money. Involved in this two-party struggle will be struggles between richer and poorer, landed and commercial property, and so forth. Different narrow or local interests will identify themselves with one or the other of the two sides to this dispute at different times (XIX 27, p. 575). Nevertheless, it would be overinterpreting to find in Montesquieu a full anticipation of the party system. Like the American Founding Fathers, Montesquieu seems to have exaggerated the extent to which the institutional system, in transforming the factional struggle and in allowing individuals to devote themselves to private pursuits, would bring about the disappearance of politics in the sense of broad and permanent contests over principles.

The representatives of the people will be united in their subdued competition with the nobles, who will occupy a separate branch of the legislature. The nobles will have less power than the people, especially in regard to the crucial matter of finances. They will possess enough power to protect themselves and to exert some influence, but not enough to become predominant and oppressive. The relative weakness of the nobles is the feature which most clearly defines the English structure as republican in contrast to the monarchical balance of powers in other European countries (XI 6, p. 399).

As we have anticipated, and as Montesquieu emphasizes in chapters 7 through 12, the most striking characteristic of this republican system is its synthesis of republic and monarchy. The new kind of republic will depend on a powerful executive which is quite independent of direct popular will. The subsequent historical development of this idea leads directly to institutions like the independent civil service and the American presidency.

By the introduction of a monarchy, the two-way factional struggle turns into an imbalanced three-way struggle with no one power capable of gaining a decisive advantage. The moderating effects of representation and monarchy make it possible to give more power to the people than to the nobles, thus satisfying to some extent the just claims of number and weight without destroying balance. Since the executive power is effectively carried out by a single man, one can create a new power without giving it to either class. The king and the royal family will have its own interests distinct from those of either people or nobles. At the same time, without relying on the virtue of the king (cf. XI 9), one can expect that the king's most selfish interests will be more likely to approximate those of the whole country than the interests of either faction, especially in foreign policy. His honor and prosperity will rise or fall with the country of which he is in some sense, and especially in the eyes of the world, the proprietor. The king is therefore not likely to be tempted to side with the stronger of the two great competing forces. Although this means he may more often than not be opposed to the people (XI 6, p. 401; XIX 27, p. 579), his hereditary identification with the whole country and his exalted position will make him less liable to resentment than the nobles (cf. *Considerations, Works,* II, 112).

Liberal Republicanism

In thus transforming the struggle between nobles
and commoners or rich and poor, Montesquieu does
not do away with it entirely. The two great classes
will continue to compete for control of the legislative
power. The royal family belongs to neither class and
is in a way a third class. Montesquieu still believed
that the competition which keeps powers limited
requires a real class division among the citizenry (see
especially XI 6, p. 398). Otherwise, he feared, there
would sooner or later be formed a single popular faction, a coalescence of the variety of popular interests
which in a country where the people are not imbued
with virtue would override the institutional restraints
and lead the country into the "spirit of extreme
equality"—the spirit which undermines the country
by endangering the private wealth and honor that are
the incentives to the productivity of the talented (VIII
2). And a nobility must be preserved not merely in
order to maintain a countervailing force to the popular
power. The character of the nobles—their independent spirit, their education, their leisure for reflection
—enables them to contribute the prudence and moderation which the other classes tend to lack (cf. XI
18, pp. 426–27). These special qualities of the nobles
are employed not only in legislation but also in certain
judicial functions requiring true judging (cf. XI 6, p.
405). Montesquieu indicates, however, that in the
actual day-to-day working of the system, the influence
of the nobles will only rarely be exercised in direct
confrontation with the popular branch of the legislature over the issue of which great faction should have
more power. The institutions already provide for the
people to be predominant in the legislature and for
the nobles to lack the means to oppress. Instead, the

nobles will more usually play a role by becoming parts of the same factions or "parties" which are formed among the popular representatives. Added to the fact that the reduced role of the nobles will induce a number of them to turn from public office to private enterprise, this development will have the effect of making the nobles less distinct and more similar to the rest of the populace (XIX 27, p. 581). Montesquieu therefore recognizes a tendency to a more homogeneous citizenry even while continuing to call for a substantial maintenance of heterogeneity. He admits that this is a great weakness of the English constitution.[10] In the light of subsequent British history one can wonder if he appreciated enough the force of this tendency to homogeneity.

However this may be, Montesquieu's balance of power, unlike that of the American Founding Fathers, does require a noble class. Montesquieu takes the first great steps in the direction of the American system, but he does not go so far as it does in relying on institutions and dispensing with reliance on uncommon qualities in men. The American Founders created a system which dispensed with the class of nobles and the monarchical family. They tried to replace these class differences with institutions like the presidency, the Senate, and the Supreme Court which by their modes of selection first pick out from the populace educable men and then, by their definition of official functions and by the succession from one office to another, mold and shape these men, working on their selfish interests, to the point where their performance imitates or approximates the performance of monarchs and nobles.[11]

The discussion so far explains part of Montesquieu's aim, but only part. The balance of power insures each of the two great factions against oppression by the other. It is not certain, however, that it insures every individual against oppression:

> It is necessary to remark that the three powers can be well distributed with regard to the liberty of the constitution, although they are not so well distributed with regard to the liberty of the citizen. (XI 18: see the context)

The desire to remedy this deficiency, to prevent as much as possible *any* deviation from the rule of law, is the most important reason for Montesquieu's teaching about the need for separating the three powers. For by separating the three powers, the English system leads the powers to check one another and thus prevent the improper exercise of authority by any one of them. Every act of government expressed as law must pass through the control of three independent authorities, each of which can prevent or correct any inequities introduced by either or both of the other two. The legislators are compelled to reckon with the fact that an independent authority will interpret their laws and apply them equally to everyone. The executive knows that there exists a separate judicial power which reviews his application of law in particular cases. The separation of powers aids the factional balance of power, but it has a purpose—the maximum protection of each individual from oppression by government—which goes far beyond the classical concern with balanced power. Indeed, the balance of competing factions finds a great part of its value in the fact that it makes possible the separation of powers.

This intention of Montesquieu's English system is seen most clearly in the arrangement of the judicial power. The separation of the legislative and executive powers from one another is made partly for the sake of the balance of factional power; and to some extent the separation is blurred (for example, by the unrestrained executive veto) in order to contribute to the interaction which creates that balance. But the separation of the judicial power has nothing to do with its playing such a role (XI 6, p. 401). The only reason for separating the judicial power is to keep it independent; the judiciary is given only enough power to defend itself from the other two powers.

The separation of the judicial power is the most important part of the separation of powers, for it is in the actions of the "judicial power, so terrible among men" (XI 6, p. 398), that the government and its law most directly confront the individual. It is here that the barrier government maintains against the possibility of its own lawlessness must be most effective. And it is this part of government which can and should be the weakest. Even if the legislative and executive branches are not separated, the separation of the judicial power can make a government "moderate" (XI 6, p. 397).[12]

The judicial power will be made less "terrible" and its separation from the other powers will be reinforced if it is in part given directly to the people by means of the jury system. The constant rotation of judges will insure against the courts becoming the tools of any individuals. On the other hand, the need for careful attention to and knowledge of the law, as well as for training in jurisprudence, calls for a well-trained and stable corps of judges who will supervise and balance the power of the juries. Although the juries will be supreme, the judges will uphold the law itself, and must therefore adhere strictly to the letter of the law. In order to provide for cases where the particular circumstances make this system too rigid or dangerous to an individual, it will be arranged so that the noble branch of the legislature can serve as a court of final appeal, bringing to bear its qualities of education and moderation (XI 6, p. 404).

Up to this point we have concentrated on the most important aim of Montesquieu's English system—the balancing and channelling of governmental power in order to protect every citizen from oppression. But the new republican system has an additional aim: the greatest efficiency and efficacy of the governmental power thus channelled. We have already noted how the arrangement of each of the three branches is meant to promote smooth exercise of power as well as separation and balance of power. For the purpose of governmental effectiveness, even more than for the purpose of balance of powers, the key element is the new executive, the element of monarchy which has been added to republicanism. Although the range of affairs supervised by government is more restricted in the liberal republic than it was in the classical republic, Montesquieu still sees a need for vigorous government (cf. XIX 27, p. 575). A much larger nation must be defended against foreign enemies and policed against domestic dangers. Management of population growth and of the economy, administration of relief for the poor, and other such projects are included in the task

Weber thought so as well

of providing security (cf. XX 18; XXII 3, 10; XXIII 28, 29). Yet the liberal republic lacks the popular energy of the participatory republic. Even more important, the system of checks and balances might seem to require a sacrifice of governmental vigor; Hume at any rate wondered whether Montesquieu had not overlooked the danger of repeated deadlocks.[13]

The monarchic executive is meant to be the answer to these difficulties. The power and unity of the executive, combined with the fact that it alone is the power which is "always active," means that it will be responsible for much more of the real work of government than were the "magistrates" in the classical scheme. The weakness of the Dutch republic is caused by its lack of a king (XI 6, pp. 406–7; see note 9 for this chapter, below). The need to limit government does not imply a need to weaken government: the executive is the key to the achievement of both limited and forceful government.[14]

Yet one can wonder whether the Montesquieuian system entirely solves the problem of effective government. The real problem is not so much the sacrifice of vigor as the sacrifice of deliberation and thought. While it is true that the arrangement of the legislative branch tries to promote sound deliberation, the system undermines the attempt somewhat by restricting that deliberation to lawmaking. This restriction threatens to distort and suffocate the range of prudential deliberation which is concerned with political affairs not subject to regulation by law. As we have indicated, the system meets this threat by placing such deliberation in the hands of the executive. But this cannot be said to solve the problem. In the first place it seems doubtful whether this arrangement completely frees political prudence from the straitjacket of legalism. The great attachment to rule of law which animates Montesquieu's system as a whole will tend to cast doubt on the legitimacy of executive actions not done in accordance with law. As Montesquieu himself predicts, the system will be characterized in its day-to-day working by a tug of war between the extralegal prudence or prerogative of the executive and the more powerful forces seeking to limit that prerogative (XIX 27, pp. 575–76). This situation is good for the balance and separation of powers; it also tends to limit the dangerous effects of bad use of prerogative. But does it not tend to choke off the good and necessary use of prerogative?[15] Whereas Montesquieu's general reflections about politics are much more prudential and much less legalistic than Hobbes's or Locke's, Montesquieu's recommendations for the best constitutional arrangement give far less latitude to prudence than either Hobbes's doctrine of "sovereignty" or Locke's doctrine of "prerogative."

There is a second and deeper difficulty, a difficulty shared by Hobbes and Locke as well. The unified executive is well constructed for "instantaneous action"; it is obviously not well constructed for collective deliberation. Montesquieu's system places a crucial part of the deliberative function in an institution admittedly not well designed for such a function. More than that. Insofar as the system requires the chief executive to subordinate himself to another separate power even as he attempts to deliberate authoritatively himself, it seems more awkward and more restrictive of deliberation than traditional monarchy. The problem is succinctly indicated in a paradoxical phrase often heard today. Political observers, in the spirit of Montesquieu, speak of the need for "executive leadership": the Montesquieuian system requires that the executor, he who carries out what is ordained, be also a director, one who decides what is to be ordained.

Reflection on the reasons why the prudence which transcends the rule of law has come to be called "leadership" helps to reveal why Montesquieu felt enabled to go so far in sacrificing the needs of good deliberation to the requirements of a stronger system of checks and balances. "Leadership" refers more to the capacity to guide and control followers than to the capacity to deliberate. Thinking of politics in terms of "leadership" moves the emphasis away from thought toward force and initiative. In classical discussion of republican government one does not find such emphasis on "leadership." Good leadership was held to be the characteristic advantage of monarchy; republics were thought to compensate for a certain lack of leadership by possessing better deliberation as a result of their better facilities for collective consultation and discussion (cf. V 10). It appears that emphasis on good leadership ("virtù") as a necessity and even as an advantage of republics begins with Machiavelli. Machiavelli prefers republican to monarchic Rome because it produced more good leaders and generals.[16] The distinction between the excellence of monarchy and the excellence of republics becomes obscured, leadership and generalship become the key considerations, when the traditional goals of domestic policy are lowered and the goals of foreign policy—defense, aggrandizement, and glory—take precedence over the domestic goals. The classics held that the preeminent goal of a republic was the domestic task of cultivating moral virtue. The complexity of this task necessitates great thought and deliberation in government. And an important means to the cultivation of moral virtue is the encouragement of its exercise in collective political deliberation. Machiavelli, by lowering and simplifying the goals of government, makes deliberation less important and forceful initiative more important.

Montesquieu carries further this Machiavellian tendency. By focusing more on the lowered domestic goals—security and prosperity—Montesquieu is led to give less weight to the requirements of foreign policy. He thereby reduces somewhat the importance of leadership. Machiavelli's leadership can for Montesquieu be partly replaced by manipulative institutions. For Montesquieu, even more than for Machiavelli, government is not thought but "force" and "will." Political deliberation gives way to "rule of law" supplemented and stimulated by "executive leadership."

To sum up, Montesquieu's English system has three different but related aims: a balance of power which prevents oppressive rule by a faction; a separation of the powers or functions of government in order to prevent the oppression of any individual; the effective use of governmental power. At various times and at various places within the complex apparatus of government one of these aims may be predominant at the expense of one or both of the others. Generally speaking, the third has the lowest priority. Especially at the lower levels, the dynamics of three-way competition and the constant endeavor to draw legal boundaries between powers will give government a cluttered and disharmonious appearance. The difficulty of comprehending the system will be heightened by the presence in it of several different aims. This appearance of confusion is the natural and healthy appearance of a system fulfilling several purposes, the most important of which require constant discord (XIX 27, near the beginning).

After presenting the principles of free government, Montesquieu does not, as we might hope, proceed to show how these principles are embodied in or may be extended to present and future regimes. The full reason for this reticence will emerge in Books XIV through XIX; but provisionally we can say that Montesquieu is dubious about any simple or immediate application of the English principles elsewhere (XI 6, p. 407; cf. I 3). The principles of the best constitution can be shown, but their application depends on the particular character of each nation. It is fitting therefore that Montesquieu assigns this task of application to his thoughtful readers in the various particular times and places (XI 20). Eventually, Montesquieu returns to a discussion of England and the way in which it can become a more direct model; this will be treated in its proper place.

Leaving the English constitution more or less in the background, Montesquieu now turns to the completion of his treatment of liberty. It is not enough to show the constitution which most fosters liberty; liberty depends not only on how the laws are made and executed generally but also on how governmental authority is applied to and affects the individual. The constitution has a great influence on liberty. But it is not the only influence. Liberty also depends on "morals, manners, accepted examples . . . [and] certain civil laws" (XII 2).

Montesquieu does not propose in Book XII to treat all of these factors which promote liberty of the individual citizen. He will treat here the principal factor, criminal law. As we learned in Book VI, criminal law governs that sphere of life where the power of the state most directly threatens the security of the individual. The moderation and limitation of criminal law for the protection of individual security is then the most urgent task of politics. The theme of Book XII is for Montesquieu the most important theme of political philosophy:

> Political liberty consists in security. . . . That security is never more attacked than in public and private accusations. It is then on the goodness of the criminal laws that depends principally the liberty of the citizen. . . . The knowledge . . . about the surest rules that one can have in criminal judgments interests human kind more than anything in the world. It is only in the practice of this knowledge that liberty can be found. (XII 2; cf. VI 2)

The manner in which criminal law is enforced can be relatively independent of the character of the regime: "The citizen can be free, and the constitution not" (XII 1). In this important area of political life Montesquieu can be a vigorous advocate of reform without threatening the stability of regimes. Naturally, then, in this book Montesquieu manifests an increased interest in contemporary regimes. He is also drawn to modernity because the knowledge he advocates is modern knowledge. This knowledge required centuries to perfect and is susceptible of still greater perfection; it was therefore not available to the ancients:

> Criminal laws have not been perfected all at once. Even in the places where liberty has been most sought, it has not always been found. . . . (XII 2)

> The Greeks claimed that their usage had been established by the gods; but it is ours [that is so]. (XII 3)

It is not only because it took time to gain the knowledge that the Greeks and Romans lacked it. The knowledge, as appears from Montesquieu's substantive discussion, is in large part alien to the spirit of the republics which sought individual sacrifice for the sake of the fatherland.

The general tenor of Montesquieu's recommendations appears from his chapter on the correct nature and proportion of penalties. The security of the individual should be threatened by the state only when the individual violates the tranquility and security of others. This great principle of liberal criminal law of course weakens the capacity of the state to enforce laws concerning religion and morality. It depends on a point of view rather different from that of the virtuous republic; it is surely incompatible with the rigorous enforcement of morals characteristic of the censors discussed in Books V and VII.

After establishing the general orientation, Montesquieu discusses a number of specific crimes whose

which is
contra- Aristotle . *140*

Liberal Republicanism

punishment is likely to be especially dangerous to individual liberty. Here and throughout this book, Montesquieu tries to show how the efficient enforcement of criminal law, or the good of the rulers, goes hand in hand with fair and moderate prosecution of the law, or the good of the individual. The most perilous prosecutions are those connected with sacrilege, especially Christian sacrilege, and treason, as the prosecution of both may well be attended with zealous anger. Montesquieu argues for the narrowest possible interpretation of such crimes, in order to restrict the threat their investigation imposes upon all the citizens and also in order to increase the likelihood of apprehension of the real criminals.

In the context of his discussion of treason, Montesquieu advocates freedom of thought, speech, and of the press, advancing as the proper guide the now famous libertarian principle that,

> it is not words that one punishes, but an action committed in which one uses the words. The words do not become crimes except when they prepare, accompany, or follow a criminal action. One overturns everything if one makes words a capital crime, instead of regarding them as the sign of a capital crime. (XII 12)

The violation of this freedom of speech is the most arbitrary form which the law against treason can take (XII 12). Montesquieu advocates these freedoms of expression not for their own sake, or for the sake of knowledge or philosophy or culture; he advocates them for the sake of security, for the sake of protecting life (cf. XIX 27, p. 580). Nothing is more revealing of the spirit and foundation of Montesquieu's liberalism.

Montesquieu concludes the book on civil liberty with a series of chapters dealing with each of the three regimes, recommending certain practices peculiar to each which will foster individual security in criminal law. Book XII thus continues and completes the theme introduced in Book VI.

The last of the three books devoted to liberty treats of the relation between liberty and taxation. It is at first somewhat surprising that Montesquieu should consider taxation such an important part of the theme of liberty. We can best understand the train of thought which guides him here if we begin from his definition of liberty. We recall that liberty is identified with security. Security means not only life in the present, but assurance of continued life in the future; and not only mere life, mere existence, but life without anguish and suffering, comfortable life (cf. VI 9). After one has acquired the minimal conditions for safety, one is immediately concerned with the acquisition of goods which will extend that safety and provide comfort. In addition, it is to be noted that liberty is not identified with security simply, but with the subjective belief that one is secure—with what Montesquieu calls the "opinion of security." For the fact is, death cannot be done away with and therefore the fear of death cannot be entirely done away with. That fear can only be overlaid with an anxiety akin to the fear but less painful than the fear. Liberty, or the opinion of security, is not the abolition of the fear of death but the absorbing, active preoccupation with providing against pain and violent or early death, the preoccupation which assuages and obscures the fear of death. Since one is never absolutely secure, unless another aim or principle intervenes, the desire to acquire becomes infinite. Protection of the increasing acquisition of private property and of the capacity for such acquisition is therefore a key part of the protection of the opinion or state of mind which is liberty. And just as criminal law was the sphere where government most endangered the life of the individual citizen, so taxation is the sphere where government most endangers the property of the citizen.

How far the theme of liberty takes us from the spirit of virtuous republicanism is shown by the first sentence of Book XIII: "The revenues of the State are a portion which each citizen gives of his property in order to have the security of the rest, or in order to enjoy it agreeably." Public revenue is no longer seen as a means of preserving individual poverty and frugality and fostering great public monuments and endeavors (V 3, 4, 5, 6; VII 2). Montesquieu cautions against using public revenues for "imaginary needs of the State, . . . the rich desire for a vain glory" (XIII 1). The objects of state expense should be more prosaic; the citizen gives up a part of his private property in order to let the state protect the rest. So important has the preservation of property become that Montesquieu can call tax and revenue policy more important than any other domestic policy of government: "There is nothing which wisdom and prudence ought to regulate more" (XIII 1). "The most important part of legislation" is the "levy of public taxes" (XI 6, p. 405).

Chapter Five

As liberty becomes the theme of politics, economics becomes ever more important. Throughout Book XIII Montesquieu assumes that wealth and prosperity are desirable ends for the political community and that therefore "industry, arts, and manufacture" should be encouraged (XIII 2). He shows that the interest of the rulers—the wealth and increased taxes of the whole state—is identical with the interest of the individuals—retention of as much private property as possible. Encouraging private wealth is encouraging the wealth of the whole: "If the State proportions its fortune to that of the particulars, the ease of the particulars will soon make its fortune rise" (XIII 6).

The core of the practical teaching of Book XIII is found in chapter 12, whose title and theme almost reproduce the title and theme of the whole book. The relation of taxation to liberty is that "one can levy higher taxes in portion to the liberty of the subjects." There are two kinds of liberty. In most small republics "one can augment the taxes because the citizen, who thinks he is paying himself, wishes to pay, . . . in monarchy one can augment the taxes because the moderation of the government there can produce riches" (XIII 13). It is clear that from the point of view of preserving personal property, the latter, or some combination of the former with the latter, is preferable, and it is this situation which Montesquieu seeks to favor in his specific proposals. We will comment on only the most important of them.

Montesquieu recommends that taxation be primarily in the form of a merchandise tax paid directly by the retail merchant and indirectly by the customer (XIII 7). This is "the natural tax for a moderate gov-

Liberal Republicanism

ernment" (XIII 14), for it is "the one the people feel
the least" (XIII 7). Far from wanting to encourage
citizens to sacrifice their property for the sake of the
common good, Montesquieu wants a situation where
the people "are almost ignorant that they are paying"
(XIII 7). In such a situation there is the maximum
sense of security, even to the point of "illusion" (XIII
8). People will be encouraged to acquire property, to
work harder, to gain more, and to trade more. At
the same time, the state is induced to encourage and
support the merchant, who becomes the agent and
the creditor of the state (XIII 14). This kind of taxation
is characteristic not of ancient republics but of England (cf. XIII 7 with 14).

or delusion

it's a regressive tax —

Montesquieu's discussion of the relation of the laws
to property might well serve as an introduction to
his description of the English way of life, pervaded
and animated as it is by the spirit of commerce and
acquisitiveness. Montesquieu does not, however, proceed now to a discussion of the customs, manners,
and morals of England, despite his teaching that "the
customs of a free people are a part of its freedom"
(XIX 27; cf. XII 2). Instead, he interrupts his discussion of the English political and social system with
a number of books devoted to showing the obstacles
to the application throughout the world of the principles and practices of free government. After these
books Montesquieu returns to his study of England
and then proceeds to a study of the commerce which
is epitomized in England. This curious order of the
argument is perhaps the most baffling feature of the
general plan of *The Spirit of the Laws*. Indeed, some
commentators argue that beginning with the last chap-

ter of Book XIX (the chapter on the English way of
life) Montesquieu ceased to follow a discernible plan
and merely proceeded to state his reflections on a
number of more or less important topics of political
life.[17]

But in fact there is a well-ordered plan which
appears if we consider the movement of *The Spirit of
the Laws* as a whole in the following way. Having
shown the nature and superiority of the principles of
free government in Books I through XIII, Montesquieu presents the great problem for free government,
the difficulty in its application elsewhere, in Books
XIV through XIX; at the end of Book XIX Montesquieu returns to free government to describe its commercial way of life. The main reason for postponing
the discussion of the latter aspect of free government
must lie in its relation to the subject matter which
intervenes. The commercial way of life is a response
to the problem set forth in the intervening books. In
fact, as we shall see, it is the commercial spirit which
is in some measure the solution to that problem. Commerce is an important part of English liberty, but it
is also that aspect of English liberty which is most
relevant to the problem of liberty in other countries.
Our discussion of the problem of liberty in other
countries and of the reason why this theme is presented in so obscure a fashion is best postponed until
after our discussion of the problems presented in
Books XIV through XIX. But we will find it convenient to take some liberty with the order of the text
by discussing here the English commercial way of life.

Montesquieu's chapter describing the English way

of life moves from politics, or that part of life most directly shaped by the laws, to private and intellectual life, that part least directly formed by the laws. In his brief but masterful outline of the character of the new republican society, Montesquieu limns a picture which Tocqueville brought up to date and completed.

The fundamental characteristic of life in England is the ceaseless motion of competitive individual ambition and acquisitiveness. The regime which provides men security from threats of physical harm from other men does not leave its citizens in a state of tranquil repose. "All the passions being free there, hate, envy, jealousy, the ardor to enrich and distinguish oneself, will all appear in their full extent" (XIX 27, p. 575). The citizens are free to follow their natural inclination to compete with one another in the acquisition of selfish power. Political life will be characterized by constantly shifting combative factions or interests. "One abandons a party where one leaves all one's friends. . . . In that nation one can often forget the laws of friendship" (XIX 27, p. 575). Since Englishmen are not friends, they cannot really be called citizens: "Men in this nation would be rather confederates than fellow citizens" (XIX 27, p. 582). In Rousseau's terminology, this is the regime of the *bourgeois;* the ancient cities were the regimes of the *citoyen.*

The selfish competition does not lead to fragmentation because it is channelled by the institutions we have seen described in Book XI and also because men perceive the need for a certain minimum of common effort. This need is well understood with regard to war, although war must almost always be defensive and the profession of soldiery is not held in high esteem. A diluted sense of national prestige exists, but it is seen as something necessary, not as something intrinsically desirable (XIX 27, pp. 576–79). What most unites Englishmen in peacetime is anxiety about domestic tyranny, usually with regard to the monarch. Men who think constantly of themselves and the security of their lives and property will have the political virtues of independence and watchfulness but the political vice of overanxiety. Political life will frequently be swept with strange fears and mass convulsions of alarm against potential usurpation; these will require the calming influence of the more dispassionate legislative representatives. The same narrowness and restless anxiety that produce mass sentiments gives English political life a general tendency to stupidity and error in particular policies, despite the soundness of its fundamental political aims (XIX 27, pp. 577, 582).

While all Englishmen are attentive to politics, only a few are directly involved in government. Men concern themselves with politics primarily in order to foster their private pursuit of wealth. The laws created the conditions for commerce, and after those conditions were taken advantage of, politics came to be dominated by commerce (XX 7). The restless competitive motion of political life is actually the mirror of the economic life.

In England men enjoy solid bodily comfort and satisfaction in larger numbers and to a greater extent than ever before. This commercial wealth will not lead to a corruption of the independence and freedom of the country. While "opulence would be extremely great" (XIX 27, p. 578), there will be no "luxury founded on the refinements of vanity." "One will there enjoy a great superfluity, and nevertheless frivolous things will be proscribed" (XIX 27, p. 581). The spirit of commerce is not that of enjoyment but of anxious effort to increase wealth. Commercial wealth is of a different character from the older form of landed wealth gained by inheritance or conquest. In the first place, commercial property is inherently more fluid and less secure—its maintenance requires constant use and reinvestment. In addition, the wealth of the commercial man is generally more moderate than that of the traditional wealthy man; the typical merchant or tradesman recognizes a real need to achieve greater physical security. Finally, the man of commerce knows only of wealth accompanied by constant industry and watchfulness. He has none of the carelessness or even mild contempt for money of those accustomed to effortless prosperity. He is less secure in his feeling of possession and on the other hand more in love with the money he has devoted his life to making (cf. *Republic* 330 b–c). For all these reasons Montesquieu can say:

> The spirit of commerce brings in its train the spirit of frugality, economy, moderation, work, prudence, tranquility, order, and rule. Thus while it subsists, the riches it produces have no ill effect. (V 6)

Montesquieu is aware of the fact that this spirit of commerce is not automatically self-perpetuating. He advocates intervention of government to achieve redistribution of income:

> In order to maintain the spirit of commerce, it

is necessary that . . . the laws, by their disposition, divide the fortunes in the measure that commerce increases them, making each citizen poor in a great enough ease to be able to work like the others; and each citizen rich in such a mediocrity that he has need of his work for conserving or acquiring. It is a very good law in a commercial republic which gives to all the children an equal portion in the inheritance of their fathers. It happens through this law that whatever fortune the father has made, his children, always less rich than him, are led to flee luxury and work like him. (V 6)

This means that many of the very rich will "exile themselves . . . and go to seek abundance in the lands of servitude" (XIX 27, p. 578).

Thus commerce does more than spread safety and comfort and the concern with those things. Properly fostered by wise policy, it sharpens the selfish competitive energy, the independence, the watchfulness of citizens in all classes. And commerce demands a freedom of movement and a security of persons and things in order for its operations to be successful. The free laws and principles of the English regime fostered commerce; but commerce in turn fosters the laws and principles of the regime.

The most arresting part of Montesquieu's description of the way of life of commercial England is his portrayal of the noneconomic social life, especially what we would call the intellectual life. Today's reader of Montesquieu, who usually begins with a belief that we witness in the present liberal world unprecedented cultural and intellectual achievements, might well expect that Montesquieu's new republicanism with its freedom of thought, speech, and movement together with its experience of the heterogeneous influences of foreign trade, would produce an exciting and diverse intellectual life. But Montesquieu's rather gray description belies this expectation. The unmitigated commercial spirit of England fosters advances in political science, technological natural science, and some aspects of philosophy. But the pervasive selfish concern for material well-being and acquisition of wealth stifles any intense interest in taste and the arts, the beautiful and useless things which ornament and can inspire human life.

This does not mean to say that Montesquieu believed unselfish elevation or generosity is a necessary condition for preoccupation with beauty and taste: "It is not from a source so pure that graceful manners [*politesse*] customarily draw their origin. They are born from the desire to distinguish oneself " (IV 2). It is the selfish passion of vanity, the pacified and refined version of selfish honor, which gives birth to taste. Taste is therefore found chiefly in monarchies, though it is rare even there. The preconditions for a high level of sensibility throughout society are usually found in a monarchy which is leaning toward despotism, and which possesses a rather centralized but not yet despotic court—a monarchy like France, or perhaps like Imperial Rome under Augustus. There,

> one finds at court a delicacy of taste in all things, which comes from a continual usage of the superfluities of a great fortune, from the variety

and above all the lassitude of pleasure, from the
multiplicity, the confusion even, of fantasies. (IV
2)

At such a court men train themselves to look down
on the need for security and the acquisition of wealth
through labor. Assured of prosperity partly through
the benefits of forgotten robberies committed by their
fathers (VII 4; XXXI 2) and partly through the favor
of even more fortunate beneficiaries of the ancient
crimes, these men compete in displays of wit, perceptivity, and the capacity to enjoy pleasures whose
appreciation requires superior moral and intellectual
sensitivity. A character is formed which pays great
attention to form, grace, and elegance in every aspect
of life.

Devotion to such leisure requires that the most powerful men in a regime be persuaded to forsake, for
a part of the time at least, the apparently most serious
affairs of war and rule. For this reason taste seems
to be closely connected with the preeminence of
women. At any rate it was the growth of the power
of women (occurring partly, but only partly, by
accident—XXVIII 22) which released the full potential for taste in the French and other European
monarchies. The influence of women weakens the
vanity that rests on physical and material power and
strengthens the vanity of wit and beauty (VIII 8).
Women are not averse to the accumulation of wealth
and power, but their physical and intellectual disadvantages lead them to promote the power acquired
through beauty and the appreciation of beauty, refined
pleasure, and the unserious use of the mind. When

they are permitted to do so by the spirit of the regime, women use the physical empire they have over men in order to transform the objects of emulation in the direction of those things for which they have the greatest capacities or over which they can have control (VII 9).

In contrast to all this, life in England is businesslike: "Since one would be always occupied with one's interests, one would not at all have those polished manners which are founded on leisure, and really one wouldn't have the time" (XIX 27, p. 581). Luxury in England is "solid, founded not on the refinements of vanity but on that of real needs. . . . Frivolous things are proscribed." Consequently, "there one scarcely esteems men for frivolous talents or attributes, but rather for real qualities; and of this kind there are only two: riches and personal merit" (XIX 27, p. 581). Some men will become preoccupied with amusement, but when they do, they will seek it in vulgar and extravagant forms: "Some, having more wealth than occasion to spend it, will employ it in a bizarre manner; and in this nation there will be more wit than taste" (XIX 27, p. 581).[18] The English lack of taste goes together with the status of women in England:

> Where every man in his own way takes part in the administration of the State, the women scarcely live with men. They are therefore modest, that is to say timid: that timidity forms their virtue; while the men, without gallantry, throw themselves into debauchery which leaves them all their liberty and leisure. (XIX 27, p. 582)

The family is stable, and women find their place within it as mothers and virtuous wives. There is no court, society, or salon. There are only the family, the business, the club, and the brothel.

All of these tendencies will not be much stemmed by the existence of a class of nobles. For in England the nobles are imbued with the spirit created by the political principles of the regime. They too feel the need to acquire; this feeling is enforced by the taxation laws and the general fluidity of property:

> The dignities, comprising a part of the fundamental constitution, would be more fixed than elsewhere; but, on the other hand, the nobles in this country of liberty would bring themselves close to the people; the ranks would then be more separated, and the persons more confounded. (XIX 27, p. 581; cf. XX 21)

The nobles have no place, no role, except the one they find for themselves in the economic and political activities of the other citizens. Their own political power is overshadowed by the powers of the people and the king.

In England men are not brought together in a true society either by vanity, as in monarchies, or by virtue, as in ancient republics. Underlying the continual motion is a privatization or atomization of society. This privatization is the outcome of the political and economic selfishness we have seen described; men are "confederates rather than fellow citizens" (XIX 27, p. 582). In their equal little spheres of independence, men seem to themselves to be self-sufficient. They are satisfied and proud in their very equality, proud without a sense of superiority; or, in other words, they are proud without being vain (XIX 27, p. 583). Relatively inattentive to the opinions of others, they do not seek to please. Yet despite, or because of, the fact that Englishmen live apart and in a kind of isolation, they act toward one another with a certain decency and humanity. Although lacking in "politeness of manners," they manifest a certain "politeness of morals" towards one another (XIX 27, p. 582).[19] A sense of humanity arises from the fact that the independence of the Englishmen, for all its self-sufficiency and self-centeredness, is the independence of an anxious being. The Englishman's situation resembles that of original man, whose selfish neediness led him to have a certain sympathy for and attachment to his needy fellow man. The English societal situation promotes the only naturally social or unselfish human impulses.

The atomization of society has a profound effect on the thinkers and artists, and on what we might call the cultural life of England. In order for us to grasp the full portent of Montesquieu's remarks, it is necessary to read them not only in view of his later contrasting reflections about France, but also in the light of the mention of this theme in other works.[20] In the course of his discussions of this theme he frequently uses the terms "*esprit*" and "men of *esprit*." The difficulty of translating the word *esprit* reflects not only the breadth and complexity of its meaning in French but also the enrichment and deepening the word acquires through Montesquieu's use of it. We will do well to begin with a glance at Montesquieu's thematic remarks on *esprit*.

Esprit in its fullest and most general sense comprehends the soul's capacity to understand and

express knowledge of the world around it. "*Esprit* is
the genre which has under it several species: genius,
good sense, discernment, justness, talent, and
taste."[21] A man of *esprit* in this fullest sense is a man
whose soul is wholly awake and attuned to the world:

> A man has *esprit* when things make on him the
> impression they ought to make. . . . A man of
> *esprit* knows and acts immediately in the way
> which is necessary for him to know and act; he
> creates himself, so to speak, at each instant, on
> the present need; he knows and he feels the just
> relation which is between things and himself. He
> feels what other men can only learn. All that
> is mute for most men speaks and teaches him.
> There are some men who see the faces of other
> men; others who see the physiognomy; and there
> are others who see into souls. One can say that
> a fool lives only with bodies; men of *esprit* live
> with intelligences.[22]

Esprit is a synthesis of two elements whose division
reflects a division in the soul and in civilized human
life in general: "This man of *esprit* is very rare. He
must unite two qualities almost physically incompatible . . . the man of *esprit* in the world and the man
of *esprit* among the philosophers."[23] The "man of *esprit*
among the philosophers" is concerned above all with
"judging" things in order to know the truth about
them and their "intrinsic value." This man possesses
the spirit of science, the spirit of thought which does
not seek to amuse. His education comes from
"masters" or instructors. The "man of *esprit* in the
world" is the man of taste and of society. He is possessed of a perfect discernment of what pleases and
amuses the soul of man. He is above all concerned

with what men find beautiful and therefore with the "value of opinion" rather than "intrinsic value." He receives his education from "men of the world" and consequently requires a society where men "communicate with one another," a society where the art of pleasant conversation for its own sake is fully developed in all its frivolity, gaiety, rapidity, and delicacy of perception.[24]

England will be capable of producing men of science and even philosophers. Commerce promotes technology; certainly enlightened England has no reason to fear science. And since the worldly species of *esprit* tends often to prevent clear and profound meditation,[25] England may well foster the sciences better than more polished nations. But English life undermines or destroys worldly *esprit*. Montesquieu indicates that the spectrum of studies and intellectual activities often called the humane studies—those "liberal" preoccupations which range from concern for what is fitting in human society to what is beautiful in the fine arts—will manifest a certain barrenness in England: "The character of the nation would appear above all in their works of *esprit*, in which one would see men who are meditative and who would have meditated all alone" (XIX 27, p. 583). When men of natural perceptivity and intelligence do speak out about life in England they will exhibit a bitterness and moral indignation. Perhaps thinking partly of Swift, Montesquieu says,

> Society teaches us to feel the ridiculous; retreat renders us more ready to feel vices. Their satirical writings would be bloody; and one would see a number of Juvenals among them before having found one Horace. (XIX 27, p. 583)[26]

Likewise, historians will cease to aspire to embody the removed judgment, the subtlety and finesse of men who know the world. Instead, they will become the mouthpieces of narrow parties: "The historians . . . would betray the truth because of their liberty itself which always produces divisions: each would become as much the slave of the prejudices of his faction as he would be of a despot" (XIX 27, p. 583).

Above all, the level of execution and appreciation of poetry and the fine arts would reflect the general lack of taste. Montesquieu does not seem to mean that great artists will be unknown. Men of "genius," men with depth of discernment and a power of imagination and expression, will arise in every civilized nation. And given the fact that excessive delicacy together with excessive frivolity can be almost as detrimental to real taste as rudeness,[27] English poets and artists may have strengths lacking in the artists of more effeminate nations. But they will lack the discipline, refinement, and delicacy which is required for perfection:

> Their poets would have more often that original rudeness of invention than a certain delicacy which gives taste: one would find there something which would approach more the force of Michelangelo than the grace of Raphael. (XIX 27, p. 583)[28]

The absence of tasteful society in England means that great art and thought will lack the audience which it needs in order to flourish. This lack of audience will affect genius; but it will affect even more that much larger number of more ordinary men of talent. It is the gentlemen who are naturally endowed with a modest degree of intellectual merit who most need a political society which brings them into "communication" with others like themselves. Men of *esprit* require companions and a society that appreciates, evokes, and encourages their talents. This "world" does not exist in England. One cannot say of any particular artist, thinker, or man of *esprit* that he will find no pleasures and will hence be unhappy; one can speak only of a certain emptiness, a general tone of grayness which pervades society at large:

> Most men with *esprit* would be tormented by their *esprit* itself; in the disdain or distaste for all things, they would be unhappy, with so many reasons for not being so. (XIX 27, p. 582)

Montesquieu's description of the English way of life may well strike the modern reader as harsh and overly pessimistic. But we should not overlook the fact that Montesquieu by no means precludes the appearance of talent, art, and thought in England; he rather draws attention to its difficulties and its limits. As for the life of the mass of Englishmen, Montesquieu emphasizes their healthy naturalness, their sobriety, independence, and vigor—the virtue of the women, the capacity for sacrifice of the men. Perhaps, indeed, the England that Montesquieu describes does not remind one of Jane Austen's England; but we do find here the England described by Thackeray; and Thackeray's portrayal is probably the broader and more accurate. And yet something is missing; one can put one's finger on that something by thinking of what the old Tory party stood for in its noblest, if not always its wisest, moments. Throne, altar, and the landed gentlemen of England have been eclipsed in Montesquieu's picture. This appears very clearly when one compares what Montesquieu says about the place of religion in England with what Burke has to say about the same subject. According to Montesquieu, religious freedom combined with the commercial temper will divide the nation as a whole into those who possess a spirit of indifference to all religion, and therefore accept the established church, and those who possess a spirit of zeal, and therefore promote the flowering of numerous, weak little sects (XIX 27, p. 580). In contrast, Burke says that

> we know, and what is better, we feel inwardly, that religion is the basis of civil society, and the source of all good and all comfort. . . . First, I beg leave to speak of our church establishment, which is the first of our prejudices, not a prejudice destitute of reason, but involving in it a profound and extensive wisdom. I speak of it first. It is first, and last, and midst in our minds.[29]

Montesquieu did not wish simply to mirror English society. He rather looked to what he believed to be the most portentous characteristics of England, the qualities and the spirit which he hoped and believed would help shape the future of the world. The English constitution and its way of life is to be the guide, the polestar in political affairs. But there are great obstacles in the way of any attempt to use what has been learned about political liberty in England to shape the future in other lands. It is to an explanation of these obstacles that Montesquieu turns in Part Three.

6

THE OBSTACLES TO FREEDOM:
CLIMATE, GEOGRAPHY,
AND HISTORY

By the end of Book XII, or Part Two, of *The Spirit of the Laws* Montesquieu has presented the character and ranking of the fundamental political alternatives open to man; he has indicated some of the most important reasons for the superiority of the principles of liberal republicanism. He does not, however, proceed to complete his analysis of this form of government and way of life. Instead, he interrupts his discussion of England to show how the natural environment—climate, geography, terrain—and the conventional environment—history and tradition—mold and limit man. The political alternatives must be understood in light of the fact that human nature is to a great extent not uniform. The human race is divided into a multitude of diverse groups or "nations," each possessing a unique and deeply ingrained character which puts its stamp on every individual. The natural environment, especially the climate, is the primary but not the only cause of this diversity.

Many commentators have noted that in his emphasis on the limitations imposed on politics by climate, just as in his emphasis on the variety of legitimate regimes, Montesquieu returns from contemporary natural law teachings to Aristotelian political science (cf. *Politics* 1327^b 18–36). But this is true only in a very qualified way. In Montesquieu the influence of climate and geography on political life is far greater than it was for Aristotle. This is a consequence of the massive agreement between Montesquieu and those modern thinkers from Machiavelli to Locke who hold that man is much more malleable than the ancients realized. Montesquieu's emphasis on climate and history is an outcome not so much of a return to Aristotle as of a more radical thinking through of the understanding of human nature held by modern political philosophy.

Ancient political philosophy understood the moral and intellectual qualities which we find in civilized social life to be natural to man. It was considered impossible to understand the nature of man except in terms of the highest human potential discoverable in civil society. The ancients were therefore led to conceive of human nature as directed toward certain high and fixed ends. The attainment of these ends is the aim of all political activity, but chance is so powerful a counterforce to nature that attainment is extremely difficult and rare. Since these ends are natural or permanent, they cannot be lowered in order to make the satisfaction of man's needs easier. Man cannot be remade. Political life is therefore severely limited in what it can accomplish toward achievement of human happiness. The practical spirit of classical political philosophy is one of moderation or manly resignation in the face of the unchangeable nature of things. The best regime is rarely if ever possible.

Beginning with Machiavelli and Hobbes, modern political philosophy tries to understand human nature almost exclusively in the light of man's origins. It finds those origins in a precivil, subhuman "state of nature."

In the state of nature man is an animal preoccupied with the satisfaction of bodily animal passion. But while the ways of all other animals are unchangeable, man's ways are variable. Civil society, the development of reason and of all the faculties we know as human, is the product of man's capacity to mold his behavior in response to accident. Man has proven himself to be "flexible" or malleable to an almost infinite degree (see the Preface, p. 230). The proper understanding of the higher human capacities reveals that they are not the end or purpose of human life, but are rather faculties which have evolved as means to the satisfaction of the bodily passions, the only permanent and real goal of the animal man. Man's natural needs are much lower than the classics thought, their satisfaction more attainable. And, in our use of our reason and freedom we need be much less restricted by the fear of perverting these higher capacities; they are no longer to be seen as things to be cultivated for their own sake. Man's higher faculties can be molded, shaped, used in whatever way is necessary to create a civil society which will answer to the true natural needs. We can therefore be much more hopeful than was hitherto thought. We need not be dependent on chance to achieve wholly satisfactory regimes. Fortune can be mastered; the problem of human nature can be solved.[1]

As we have seen, Montesquieu agrees with this line of thought. The best regime has been realized in England. But, at the same time, Montesquieu sees the need for a modification of or addition to this modern understanding. The teaching about climate is the most striking part of this emendation. These five books deal-

ing with nonhuman nature also deal with human
nature; the section begins and ends with the most
detailed discussions of human nature in the whole of
The Spirit of the Laws. The discussions constitute an
elaboration of the theoretical principles stated in Book
I. It is perfectly fitting then that the books comprising
Part Three are literally the central books and that their
titles all refer to "nature."

Montesquieu argues that if one begins from the fact
that man's nature is as low and pliant as the moderns
have shown, one cannot conclude that the passions
of the original animal man are as permanent or remain
as universally similar as thinkers like Machiavelli and
Hobbes supposed. Man's body is affected by his
natural environment, especially his climatic environment. While it is true that "men have had in all times
the same passions" (*Considerations, Works*, II, 71), these
passions, even the most basic of them, vary in strength
and degree. All men may be dominated by the desire
for "the opinion of security," but that desire varies
according to the condition of the body which in turn
varies with the climate:

> One has more vigor in cold climates. The action
> of the heart and the reaction of the extremities
> of the fibers works better, the liquids are more
> in equilibrium, the blood stays closer to the
> heart, and reciprocally the heart has more
> strength. That greater force produces consider-
> able effects: for example, . . . more courage . . .
> more opinion of one's security. . . . Put a man
> in a hot place, . . . his present feebleness will
> put a discouragement in his soul; he will fear
> everything, because he will fear he can do
> nothing. (XIV 2; cf. XIV 10, 11; contrast
> Hobbes, chap. ii)

In trying to establish free government on the basis of man's deepest natural needs, the legislator must take into account the natural climatic variation in the capacity to satisfy these needs.

Montesquieu's emphasis on the influence of climate requires him to make more explicit the extent to which man's life is determined by the condition and behavior of his body. Book XIV begins by presenting a picture of man which is as near as one can imagine to a pure materialism without being simply so. Montesquieu refers at times to "the soul" but he leaves almost no nonmaterial thing except reason itself to constitute this "soul": the passions, the spirit, the character, imagination, taste, sensibility, sadness and happiness, all are said to be determined by the state of the body (XIV 2, 3, 4). And the human body is like all other animal bodies. In fact, Montesquieu blurs the distinction between organic and inorganic matter: he frequently refers to the human body as a "machine."[2] In a later, unpublished, essay dealing with the same theme, Montesquieu goes so far as to reduce "ideas" to "feelings" and "thought" to "action in the brain."[3] Nevertheless, we know from Book I that Montesquieu strongly doubts that "a blind fatality would have produced intelligent beings" (I 1). Men therefore have some capacity for independent exercise of reason and will. But it seems this independence is more tenuous than is usually supposed. A picture of Montesquieu's view of the relation of man's rational freedom to his physical necessity is given in the following metaphor:

> The soul is, in our body, like a spider in its web. The spider cannot move without disturbing the threads which are extended far out, and, at the same time, one cannot move one of these threads

without moving the spider. . . . The more these threads are stretched tight, the more the spider is made alert.[4]

Man is therefore determined not only by "physical causes" but also by what Montesquieu calls "moral causes" (XIV 5; VIII 21; *Considerations*, chap. 18, *Works*, II, 173).[5] Moral causes stem above all from the political actions of the "legislator" who is independent to the extent to which he uses intelligence or reason (XIV 3, 5).

We learn of the complicated way in which moral causes combine with physical causes to determine political life by following Montesquieu's argument through Book XIV. The most influential climatic factor is temperature. (While it is a mistake to say that the factor of humidity is excluded, it is relegated to a secondary role.)[6] Over generations a cooler climate tends to produce bodies which have tougher and more tense muscles and nerves, better circulation, and hence greater vigor. This makes the spirit more insensitive, independent, courageous, and free. A warmer climate, in contrast, tends to produce more relaxed and softened fibers and slower circulation—a less vigorous but more sensitive body. This leads to imagination and taste, but also to indolence and lack of courage and independence.

Modern opinion frowns on such generalization. The reason is not so much the crudity of scientific details (of which Montesquieu was probably aware) as the moral implication. We do not like to hear it suggested that climate may make peoples more or less capable of self-government. In this we share the Lockean doc-

trinairism which Montesquieu attacked so strongly.
The experimental evidence is certainly not conclusive
one way or the other, for the exhaustive studies which
would be required have yet to be made, and, given
contemporary intellectual opinion, will not be made
in the forseeable future. On the other hand, the evidence of history would seem to lend some support
to Montesquieu: liberal republicanism has yet to be
successful in hot climates. With this kind of empirical
foundation, experienced observers of international
politics today sometimes speak in Montesquieuian
terms.⁷ Whether or not this apparent empirical foundation provided by history is valid, it must be admitted
that starting from the view of human nature shared
by Hobbes, Locke, and modern reductionist biology,
it is difficult to refuse to follow the general direction
of Montesquieu's speculations.

But no defense of Montesquieu can deny that his
discussion of what has come to be called geopolitics
shares with that discipline a curious combination of
common sense and madness. *The Spirit of the Laws* is
the only work of political philosophy known to us
in which serious theoretical conclusions are drawn
from experiments performed on a frozen sheep's
tongue (XIV 2). We see here some of the aberrant
enthusiasm generated by Enlightenment scientific
research. One profits most from Montesquieu's discussion of climate if one takes seriously only those
suggestions which seem to correspond to common
sense and historical experience. Since Montesquieu
only rarely strays from this firm ground, his thoughts
seldom fail to be provocative.

Montesquieu teaches that because so much of the

Chapter Six

inhabited world lies in torrid zones, the predominant
effect of climate is to hinder man from establishing
government which provides the freedom or security
longed for by his nature. In hot climates men tend
to be timid. This is not inconsistent with the fact that
in hot climates there are "atrocious" cruelties, for those
in power imagine danger from others and those lacking
power lack the spirit to resist the outrages the powerful perpetrate (XIV 3). In addition, a hot climate tends
to make men lazy, reluctant to undertake even the
efforts necessary to cultivate the earth for sustenance
(XIV 5, 6, 7). In such climates men are consequently
much more in need of a "legislator" whose "reason"
will oppose "nature," whose "moral causes" will
oppose the "physical causes" (XIV 3, 5). Montesquieu
does not advocate the absurd climatical determinism
which Collingwood ascribes to him.[8] The goodness
of a legislator is proportional to his opposition to the
vices of the climate.

This does not mean to say that the good legislator
will usually be able to establish a free regime, for he
is severely limited by the climate. In hot climates the
legislator is limited not only by the particular vicious
tendencies inculcated by the climate, but also by the
general "immutability" of all laws and customs. The
feebleness of the human spirit there, combined with
its sensitiveness, makes the original institutions and
usages much more deeply imbedded than elsewhere
(XIV 4). The most important task of the legislator
in hot climates, and the one to which Montesquieu
devotes the most attention, is the overcoming of laziness through laws, customs, and religion: the encouragement of the agricultural industry which provides

food (XIV 5–9). The legislator must strive to create the minimal conditions for human existence. In this context Montesquieu gives high praise to the laws of the Chinese despotism. China is not free; it is unattractive from the point of view of European monarchy and republicanism; but a China is probably the best that can be hoped for in hot climates (cf. XIV 5, 8 with VIII 21).

Montesquieu wishes to show not only how climate hinders free government in hot climates but also what its relation to law is in England, where free government flourishes (XIV 12, 13). In England the climate produces "a sickness . . . a defect of the filtration of the nervous fluids" which leads to discontent, irritableness, and restlessness. This disposition destroys the patience required for political prudence. Yet it fosters the spirit of selfish independence, vigor, and courage which promotes free government. We now begin to learn that while liberal republicanism does not depend on classical virtue, it does depend on specific qualities or transformations of character which might be called virtues of a kind. These qualities are not the product of restraint or education but are rather the natural distortion of the passions brought about by climate. Nowhere do we find a climate that leaves human nature unaffected. Never can political life be based *simply* on human nature or natural right, for the core of human nature is always shaped to some degree by climate. And even if we could find a place where all influences of the climate were neutralized, it is doubtful if we should desire such a habitation. In order that it be strong enough to form the spur to free government, the passion for security at the core of human nature seems to require the supplement of a certain irrational restlessness given by a climate like England's. It is not sufficient to say that human nature supplies man with a negative standard; even in the best case this standard needs the aid of the accident of climate in order to be applied.

In the books immediately following Book XIV Montesquieu reveals in more detail first the way in which climate hinders freedom and, second, its consequences for the development of free institutions in temperate Europe. His treatment is more comprehensive than Aristotle's not only because he believes men are more shaped by climate but also because he has greater concern with the improvement of political life everywhere. Despite his return to something like Aristotle's view of the limitations on improvement, he remains more sanguine about the possibility of the beneficent widespread influence of political philosophy. This posture is to some extent the outcome of his lower view of the goals of political life and political philosophy. But it is also partly due, as we shall see in Book XX, to his confidence in the world-revolutionary power of commerce. Montesquieu wishes to educate those who will control this force.

Book XV, on civil slavery, is a continuation of Books XII and VI, whose theme was civil liberty. Although the question of slavery was only adumbrated in Book XII (chapter 21), one could reasonably assume that slavery, since it is the greatest deprivation of security next to death itself, is a fortiori always to be avoided. But now Montesquieu devotes a whole book to slavery in order to correct that impression. We learn here in the most startling fashion that no principle of civil liberty, not even the prohibition on enslavement, can be considered an "absolute." By now it should not be necessary to add that "relativism" is not the only alternative to "absolutism." Montesquieu makes it emphatically clear in the five opening chapters of Book XV that slavery is bad, and not only on his own grounds, that is, because in arbitrarily depriving a man of his security it goes "contrary to the fundamental principle of all society" (XV 2), but also on the grounds held by classical exponents of slavery—grounds of moral and political virtue (XV 1).[9] But that slavery is bad or unhealthy for human nature does not prove that it is always to be avoided. In some times and places human nature is in so miserable a state that a man has a better chance for life and minimal comfort as a slave than as a free man.

At first Montesquieu seems to justify only "a right of very mild slavery" (XV 6). But in the next chapter he provides a justification for "cruel slavery" as well. There are some countries where the heat is so severe and enervating that only the slave-holder's lash can make men do the necessary work. Montesquieu's justification of this extreme form of slavery epitomizes his understanding of the status of natural right altogether:

> Since all men are born equal, it is necessary to say that slavery is against nature, although in certain countries it may be founded on a natural reason; and it is very necessary to distinguish those countries from those where natural reasons themselves reject it. . . . (XV 7)

He then immediately adds two chapters in which he reemphasizes the lack of any justification for slavery in Europe (XV 8–9).

Montesquieu's procedure in Book XV is perfectly characteristic of his thought, and of the difference between the political philosopher and the moralist in general. After condemning and then justifying and then condemning again "cruel slavery," he gives a rare indication of his deep personal repugnance to slavery: "I do not know if it is the spirit or the heart which dictates this article." Yet instead of giving a blanket condemnation of slavery and averting his eyes from the situations which require it, Montesquieu proceeds to devote the rest of the book (chapters 10–19) to a cool and detailed discussion of the ways to mitigate the abuses and dangers of slavery wherever it exists, whether justifiably or not. Montesquieu believed that in order to benefit humanity one must never permit the sense of humanity to blur one's clarity of vision.

In the general discussion of climate in Book XIV, Montesquieu indicated that man's sexuality is radically affected by the climate (XIV 2, 14); in Book XVI he discusses the political consequences, returning to the theme of the relation between women and political life.

In hot climates the radical inequality of the two sexes tends to make polygamy and the seclusion of women necessary. There women reach puberty very early and begin to age quickly, and would be abandoned if their husbands were not permitted a plurality of wives (XVI 2). Polygamy also provides for the larger female populations of hot lands (XVI 4). Seclusion is necessary not only in order to enforce unity and fidelity in the polygamous family but also because the body is so sensitive to pleasure that lust is less controllable in both men and women (XIV 2, 14; XVI 10, 11). The seclusion of women is a prudent measure of the legislators who "force the nature of the climate" when the climate "violates the natural law" governing the relations of the sexes and the family (XVI 12). The situation of women in hot climates must then usually be one of "domestic slavery."

This climatic limitation on human freedom is at once more inescapable and more portentous in its political effects than is the tendency to civil slavery in hot climates. This is indicated by Montesquieu's de-emphasis on its intrinsic badness and by the space he devotes to its climatic justification (contrast XV 7 with XVI 2–5, 8, 11–12). The distinction created by climate between master and slave is in the case of domestic slavery more deeply rooted in the nature of man—in the natural distinction of the species into male and female.

Domestic slavery has graver political effects than civil slavery because the mode of behavior among members of the family has a very great influence on the relationships among citizens. Civil slavery can be understood to have to do with persons who are outside of "our" community. The same cannot be thought of domestic slavery. Where habits and usages of freedom prevail in political life, it is difficult to maintain customs of slavery within the family. "The empire over women cannot be exercised so well there; and when the climate demands this empire, the government of one man has been more convenient." Montesquieu says of domestic, but not of civil, slavery that it "is one of the reasons why popular government has always been difficult to establish in the Orient" (XVI 9; cf. VII 9). A republic can tolerate civil slavery, but not domestic slavery.

The theme of Book XVII is this gravest effect of climate on man, the effect on the possibility of republican government and political freedom in general. After explicitly restating what had been shown in Book XIV, Montesquieu reveals that there is an additional and crucial factor necessary for the creation of conditions propitious to freedom. Besides the need for a cool climate, it is required that the inhabitants not be contiguous with the inhabitants of warm climates. Only in temperate regions such as Europe and perhaps North America will the Northerners not be corrupted by easy conquest of the Southerners:

> This is the great reason for the feebleness of Asia and the power of Europe, of the liberty of Europe and the servitude of Asia: a cause which I do not believe anyone has before remarked. (XVII 13)

Immediately following the books on climate, Montesquieu's train of thought once again becomes obscure. The first part of Book XVIII describes the effects of the nature of the terrain on the men who inhabit it. In the second part Montesquieu turns to a rather lengthy discussion of the way of life of primitive societies and especially of the early German tribes.[10]

We will understand what Montesquieu is about if we start from the fact that in Book XVIII he turns to a detailed consideration of the human situation in Europe. His first and heaviest emphasis is on the effect of climate and geography in the areas where they distort and limit human nature. But he is ultimately much more interested in the opportunities for political life in those temperate regions where climate least restricts the influence of human reason and will. Here the greatest opportunities for freedom and improvement exist.

When we focus our attention on the temperate regions we find that as the influence of climate recedes another natural factor makes itself felt: the character of the terrain. But the effects of the terrain are less powerful and restrictive than those of climate. Man remains far less determined by the natural environment in Europe than elsewhere.

This does not mean that European man remains unshaped and unmolded. For we have learned that even in the hostile climates it is not only nature which molds man into diverse national groups; man differentiates and shapes himself. Indeed, the characters of the many nations correspond only loosely to the diverse natural environments; sometimes widely differing nations are found in the same environment. The unique way of life of each nation represents the human *response* to the natural environment. The nation is a product of human making. This is the case in Europe above all. The same facts which led to the conclusion that man's humanity is radically shaped by the influence of the climate on the body imply that this humanity is subject to a less permanent but still profound reshaping by the conventions instituted in each nation.[11] If man does not become civilized or human because of a permanent tendency or end rooted in his nature, if man's humanity is a product of accident and response to accident, then that humanity will manifest a permanent variety of forms corresponding to the variety of accidents which in different times and places caused that humanity to come into being.

The conventions which constitute a national character may originate with all or only a part of a people. In the most important cases they originated in decisions made by "legislators," or rulers who gave comprehensive guidance to a people. The legislators responded to the needs of man and the exigencies of the natural environment with varying degrees of wisdom and error—with varying notions of what happiness is and of what can be hoped for in the given circumstances, and with varying prudential capacities for attaining what they sought. The freedom to err, the freedom to be more or less wise which is implicit in the exercise of human reason, is the principal explanation for the indeterminacy, unpredictability, and uniqueness of each national character.

In cooler regions like Europe, where a hot climate did not give the conventions an "immutability" (XIV 4), the conventional response to the environment developed through time. The manners and customs of a nation were repeatedly altered as new generations with new rulers reassessed the permanent elements in their situation and came to grips with new elements. To understand the conventional forces that have shaped European humanity, it is therefore necessary to investigate not only the present climate and customs but the history of the European nations. It is especially important to learn as much as possible about the earliest history of Europe, for it was then that much of the later development was determined. And it is in studying the early days, when the people were simple, that the impact of the climate and terrain can most clearly be seen (cf. XIX 4): the history of the origins reveals what in Europe is due to nature and what is due to convention. In Book XVIII Montesquieu moves away from the study of the static human situation in most of the world to a study of the dynamic human situation in Europe; away from the contemplation of the enslavement due to nature to a contemplation of the freedom due to man and reason; away from the concentration on nature to a new emphasis on history.

The survey of the primitive "hordes" is meant to be a sequel to the discussion of the state of nature in Book I. Our awareness of the way in which climate and terrain radically shape man makes us now realize that we need a supplement to the description in Book I of the typical emergence of man from the state of nature; we need to know to what extent the men of each nation were altered by their particular environments on their way to becoming civilized. Such a supplement is most needed in the case of European man.

At the same time, the study of the earliest Europeans sheds light on original man in general. These "nations which do not cultivate the earth" are so simple that they are all very similar. Since we have no records of man's natural state, our knowledge of it is based on deductions from what we see of man in civil society. These speculations are made more solid when they are based on the records we do possess of the earliest societies.[12] Montesquieu implies that what can be learned of these earliest societies confirms the view of human nature sketched in Book I. It is true that the description in Book XVIII begins with societies or "peoples"; it does not throw light on the difficult question of how solitary natural man was induced to form familial clans. However that may be, we find that "these peoples wandered and dispersed themselves in the pastures and the forests." Originally, not even the family existed as a stable unit:

> Marriage will not there be as stable as among us, where it is fixed by the dwelling, and where the woman belongs to a house; they can then more easily change women, have several, and sometimes mix with one another indifferently like beasts. (XVIII 13)

In some places tiny nations were formed (XVIII 11); but it is only where the forests were rather infertile, as they are in Europe as opposed to America, that men were forced to leave off hunting to become nomadic herders, and hence acquired more fixed usages of women and property (XVIII 11, 13).

Civil society comes into being for the sake of sustenance, but also for the sake of protection, for the scarcity of things creates a situation of constant war:

> These peoples . . . will have among themselves many subjects for quarrelling; they will dispute about the uncultivated earth. . . . Thus they will find frequent occasion of war, for their hunting, for their fishing, for the nourishment of their beasts, for the kidnapping of their slaves. . . . The weak people, in uniting, defend themselves against violence. (XVIII 12, 16)

The Obstacles to Freedom

If it is true that Montesquieu never mentions the term "social contract," it is also true that he practically describes it without naming it. In his description of the formation of civil society there is no mention of compassion, pity, or that "pleasure which an animal feels at the approach of another animal of his species" (I 2). The role of "humanity" in the creation of *civil* society is negligible; civil society is a product of fear and the need for collective security.

Despite the extreme hardships and the superstition prevalent among these primitive "hordes," the members of each tribe enjoyed equality and "a great liberty." Equality and liberty were the result of the simplicity of their needs and the natural limitations of their powers of repression (XVIII 14, 17, 18; cf. 31).[13]

After this account of the general character of the original civil societies, Montesquieu investigates the particular character assumed by the hordes in various natural environments. We immediately learn that in Asia the liberty of the hordes was considerably lessened not only for the reasons of geography presented in Book XVII, but also because of the terrain. In Europe the constant state of war among the tribes did not lead to conquest and political enslavement because the defeated groups could always flee into the forests, swamps, or mountains and find refuge; but on the vast plains of Asia such refuge was impossible (XVIII 19). It is in Europe alone that the natural environment promoted civil societies which were secure or free, civil societies which came near to achieving the purpose for which they were established.

And even in Europe, this freedom was not universal. Where the land is rich, the spirit of freedom is weakened. Men are less hardy where life is easy; they become accustomed to property and fear for its loss; their greater enjoyment of life makes them less capable of risking it. Barren land, on the contrary, forces men to be stronger and more predatory, gives them less to lose and makes life seem less precious (XVIII 1, 4). The consequence, Montesquieu suggests, is that the inhabitants of fertile lands were destroyed and their countries turned into desert by the marauding, warlike nations from sterile terrains (XVIII 3).[14]

It would seem then that the only peoples whose natural environment cultivated a free spirit were those who inhabited the barren lands of Europe. Such were "our fathers," the early Germans and Franks. But there is something seriously wrong with the freedom of these peoples to whom nature seems to have given the greatest chance for freedom. The freedom of the Germans is rather different from the "opinion of security." It is the bold, reckless, irrational liberty of ferocious warriors. It does bring victory, and therefore security, in warfare. And the free spirit of these independent warriors is reflected in the government, a "republic" where each man participates in the governing "assembly" (XVIII 27, 30). But this liberty also implies all the dangers inherent in constant bloodshed (cf. especially XVIII 29). Moreover, the warrior spirit is the source of the passions of pride and vanity that threaten the rational human search for security. Montesquieu seems to hold that the desire to display superiority originates in an extreme and perverted development of the pleasure men take in contemplating the personal power which insures their security.

The Obstacles to Freedom

The desire to see one's strength or dominance becomes divorced from the fear which is the true reason for that desire. Thus Montesquieu finds that fear is the true source of the "marvellous system of chivalry": "It was fear, which is said to have invented so many things, that made men imagine those sorts of prestige" (XXVIII 22 and context).

It is true that this proud and warlike spirit appears to be necessary in some measure as a precondition for any liberty. Montesquieu praises these barbarians as "the source of the liberty of Europe" (XVII 5): it was they who saved Europe from the despotism of Rome (XIV 3). Yet while the soft inhabitants of fertile lands lacked the courage necessary to protect themselves, they better understood the reason for such protection: "The fertility of a country gives . . . a certain love for the conservation of life" (XVIII 4). Inhabitants of fertile land are "occupied . . . with their own affairs" (XVIII 1).[15] The men who settled fertile lands became concerned with private property, wealth, trade, and money. Their preoccupation with material possessions "corrupted" them. Theft, ruse, and exploitation forced men to create good civil laws, and savage independence came to be replaced by legal liberty (XVIII 12, 13, 16). Rational political liberty requires some combination of the opposed spirits of these two kinds of peoples.

Montesquieu indicates how such a synthesis came about in his discussion of a third possible human development within the environment of Europe. When the land is neither rich nor so barren that vigorous and unremitting labor bears no fruit, a people can develop who combine a degree of military tough-

ness with a sturdy industriousness productive of material comfort (XVIII 3, 4). Such peoples have a better
chance for survival if they inhabit a protected
place—an island, or the middle of a swamp which
they have drained (XVII 5–7). These same conditions
are the ones most likely to lead to seafaring commerce
(cf. XX 5 with XVIII 1). The warlike peoples may
have freedom of a sort, but

> the countries which the industry of man has ren-
> dered habitable and which need, in order to exist,
> the same industry, are those which evoke moder-
> ate government. (XVIII 6)

> Just as destructive nations do evils which last lon-
> ger than they do, there are industrious nations
> who do good which does not end with them.
> (XVIII 7)

This third possible development is less a necessary
effect of the climate and terrain than are the first two
possibilities; moral causes here play a much greater
role than physical causes. Men achieve this situation
not as they achieve savage freedom, that is, "solely
by the good sense attached to the gross fibers of these
climates" (XIV 3), but rather "through their care and
through good laws" (XVIII 7). The productive altera-
tion of the land is "a good which nature has not at
all made, but which is maintained by nature" (XVIII
7).

The superiority of the mixture of the effects of barren and fertile terrain reminds one of Aristotle's praise
for the Greek climate, which mixes northern freedom
and southern reason (*Politics* 1327^b 18–36). But Montesquieu's mixture is predominantly northern; it

emphasizes the elements of vigor, industry, and free-dom, not sensitivity and leisured thought. Above all, the mixture praised by Montesquieu is due less to the bounty of nature and more to the labor of man.

As Montesquieu indicated in his earlier remarks on the "sickness" induced by the English climate, free civilization is a product of that natural environment which makes man the most uncomfortable, the most anxious (cf. XXI 3). The best region for man is one which induces neither slavish slothfulness nor careless and self-satisfied independence; the best situation is one which fills man with "care," which compels him to take up an actively negative or alienated posture towards his environment. This is perfectly consistent with Montesquieu's description of man's relationship to nature in Book I. Man achieves his humanity and the satisfaction of his needs only when he reacts against his natural state and transforms and overcomes the state of nature. It is tempting to say that nature's only kindness to man is the ferocity of her malevo-lence. Man can be thankful that in at least some regions of the earth his misery is originally so acute that it is literally unbearable.

Unfortunately, nature is niggardly even in her malevolence. In that part of the world where she is most favorable to freedom she tends to make men form nations whose sense of freedom leads to the spirit of war, honor, and vanity rather than to the anxious and insecure spirit of productive labor. These warrior men do not remain simply barbarous. Agriculture and commerce develop to a certain level, but the men who farm and who pursue commerce do not set the tone of society or control the government. There is a balance of powers, but it protects principally the warrior-nobles. For the emergence of countries like England, where the laboring and commercial classes possess power and security, the best situations seem to be swamps, islands, and seacoasts. It seems doubtful whether true political freedom can flourish even in Europe. The only hope would seem to lie in the possibility that human reason, imitating the "works of man" which made barren lands productive and free, might overcome or transform in some measure the tendency to barren vanity which is produced by nature's warping of the human spirit. Such a possibility emerges in the books which immediately follow.

But this possibility is not the first thing that strikes the reader in Book XIX. One's first impression is of additional obstacles to freedom. It appears that convention or history limits the legislator almost as much as climate.

Montesquieu begins by giving an explicit formulation of the teaching about national character which has been emerging in Books XIV through XVIII. This national character Montesquieu calls "the general spirit of a nation." As we have seen, it is a product of both physical and moral causes:

> Several things govern men: climate, religion, laws, maxims of government, examples of past things, customs [*moeurs*], manners; from which there is formed a general spirit which results from them. To the extent to which, in each nation, one of these causes acts with more force, the others give way to it. (XIX 4)

But it is only among savage peoples that physical

causes predominate; in general, "moral causes form the general character of a nation and decide more the quality of its spirit than do physical causes."[16] The general spirit is manifested above all in the customs or morals and manners (*les moeurs et les manières*—see the title of XIX), the "way of life" as we might say, of a nation. The things a nation values shape its perceptions, its sentiments, and its experiences; each person looks at the world through his nation's eyes. Every hope for political change must come to terms with the particular spirit of a nation. Any attempt to ignore or push aside this spirit, even for the sake of political freedom, leads to "tyranny" (XIX 3). The attempt to uproot deeply ingrained habits will require actual violence and forceful repression. But what is more, even if men are wrong in their sense of their own political liberty, liberty is an "opinion of security." A frontal attack on a nation's tradition will instill in all a deep feeling of oppression and fear—what Montesquieu calls a "tyranny of opinion" (XIX 3, 14, near the end). And tyranny is not the only evil likely to result from an attack on the general spirit. The general spirit provides the social bond of habit that welds men into a cooperative community. Its enfeeblement may lead to anarchy (XIX 12). To avoid tyranny or anarchy, it is therefore necessary that a nation's opinions be correct: "For the best laws it is necessary that the spirits be prepared" (XIX 12).

In his discussion of the things which shape the general spirit of a nation, Montesquieu is silent about the role of the nature and principle of the government. This seems to indicate a shift away from his earlier emphasis on the "supreme influence" of the political principles. The enumeration of formative influences (XIX 4) includes political actions, but they are not given marked preeminence. Indeed, Book XIX as a whole teaches the limited influence of direct governmental action on a society's way of life. Observations such as these lead most modern commentators to see here an implicit movement or even an unconscious drift away from the perspective of traditional political science toward the perspective of social science or sociology.[17] This interpretation is not altogether clear because among social scientists the meaning of "sociology" or "social anthropology" is unclear: the notions "society" and "the social" and their relation to "the political" are not well-defined.[18] But it is not a distortion to say that all versions of sociology are characterized by an agreement that the political sphere is not, in general, the source of a society's way of life. All agree that the political constitution is, if not merely a derivative "superstructure," then at any rate only one among many equal and independent elements of the "infrastructure," the real matrix of a society.

Doubtless Montesquieu's discussion of the general spirit of a nation supplements his analysis of the species of government. But it is an exaggeration to say that this implies a contradiction of his earlier emphasis on the political. In Book XIX the notions of "the political" and "the legislator" do not cease to be of central importance (see XIX 2, 5, 9, 11, 14–17, 19, 20, 21, 27). After all, Montesquieu never asserted that the political principle was the only influence on the laws. He limited himself to saying that it was the "supreme influence." In the very chapter where he spoke of this supreme influence of the four political principles, he also said that "it is a great piece of luck if the laws of one nation can suit another" (I 3). Beginning with Book XIV, Montesquieu makes clearer the fact that each principle of government is manifested in a variety of different nations, a variety created by the influence of nonpolitical as well as political factors. This in itself does not constitute a revision of Montesquieu's theoretical approach.

Nor does the depreciation of the influence of law and direct governmental action indicate a decisive change in orientation. To say as Montesquieu does that the political is fundamental is not to say that laws and institutions are always fundamental. By "the political" Montesquieu means the character and way of life of the men who rule, who actually possess power in a society. By the influence of the political constitution he refers to the "modification of soul" which is caused in every citizen by the nature of the government, the decision as to who shall rule. According to Montesquieu, the tone—the customs, manners, and morals of a society—is determined principally from the top, by the habits of those who hold power. Everyone in a society looks up to and emulates the human type represented by those who possess authority. The source of a society's spirit or character is for the most part not something hidden from human intention and consciousness; it is rather the open words and deeds of the politically powerful, that mixture of the freely chosen and the necessary in which the intended predominates over the unintended.

As an illustration, let us glance at Montesquieu's

Chapter Six

rather lengthy discussion of the general spirit of the French nation. This general spirit is largely formed by the habits of the aristocracy in its private, nonpolitical life. But these private habits exert a powerful influence precisely because the aristocracy has held and still holds actual political power. And the habits owe their character to the aristocracy's peculiar political situation as it has developed down through the ages. Despite the importance of the influence of Christianity, one can ascribe the character of the aristocracy above all to the fact that it originated in a bloody conquest of the soil of France and experienced a subsequent prolonged struggle for power against king and church, a struggle that finally left it in a position which combines certain kinds of dependence with certain kinds of independence (compare XIX 5–8 with Book XXVIII as a whole, especially chapter 22 and context).[19]

Recognizing the error of identifying Montesquieu's orientation with a sociological orientation, one must not fail to discern the important kernel of truth in this mistaken view. Although Montesquieu retains the belief in the preponderance of the political sphere, he goes farther than his predecessors—certainly farther than Aristotle—in qualifying that preponderance. This tendency is obvious in his treatment of "physical" causes. It is also evident in his treatment of "moral" causes. The very fact that the causes of society which proceed from the human will are called "moral" rather than "political" points to a tendency to qualify the preeminence of the political element.[20]

This shift in emphasis manifests itself in two ways, each of which has its roots in Montesquieu's theoretical innovations. In the first place, he is more open than Aristotle to the possibility that important aspects of a nation's way of life may find their source in human activities which are more or less independent of the actions of legislators and rulers. This openness follows from Montesquieu's more restricted notion of the natural scope of the state and civil society. Aristotle's emphasis on the determining power of the political principle is based on his view that civil society exists for the sake of (and therefore is essentially a conscious, cooperative effort for) the attainment of a life of happiness through the full use of faculties which cannot be exercised except in a political association. Every society represents some version of this effort, some groping toward this goal, however unenlightened. Hence every society is understood as defined above all by its political part—the part which consciously and intentionally tries to give comprehensive guidance to the whole (see especially *Politics* 1278^b 18–31, 1280^a 25–1281^a 8). For Montesquieu, on the other hand, civil society exists not for the sake of creating happiness but for the sake of protecting the means to happiness, or the means to each individual's avoidance of unhappiness. Civil society exists in order to secure or liberate good things which exist *prior to* civil society. The individual and his property, the family, its attachments, its customs, its morals and religion, predate the establishment of civil society (XVIII 13, 16; as to religion, cf. XVIII 31 with XXV 2 on the one hand and XXVIII 22 on the other). For the sake of securing these good things civil society transforms them to some extent; but in principle they remain to a considerable degree autonomous. The spheres of economic activity, of the family and private life, of religion, retain a greater independence than in Aristotle's analysis.

This is only a difference, not a reversal, of emphasis. Montesquieu chooses the English nation, the nation which embodies most perfectly the true principles of civil society, the nation whose government gives the greatest liberty to private life, as *the* example of a nation whose customs and manners are caused by the political life, the laws and constitution (XIX 26–27). Even the liberal society—precisely the liberal society—is created above all by the deeds and intentions of the men who found and maintain the constitution.

The de-emphasis of the political in Montesquieu stems not only from what one may call his liberal-pluralistic viewpoint, but even more from his new concentration on the role of history. Insofar as Montesquieu asserts that man is determined by his conventional past, he narrows the scope and lessens the influence of the deliberate activity of legislators and statesmen. He not only narrows the latitude of choice of each generation of rulers; he also makes more incontrovertible the unintended or unforseen consequences of their actions. He thus makes a nation more the product of a semiconscious development. With Montesquieu begins a tendency to see profound domestic conflicts over political principles and great battles for survival against foreign threats—the things which appear all-important to the statesman—as only the foreground of a nation's life, a foreground predetermined to a considerable extent by causes hidden in the past.[21]

Montesquieu's thought appears to be the beginning of a movement toward the view that actions of statesmen are determined by historical developments in economics, or religion, or art and thought. We are introduced to the possibility that a nation's "spirit" is the product not of its political history but of its economic, or cultural, or even linguistic history. And since the spirit of one nation seems clearly related to the spirit of other nations, there appears on the horizon the possibility that the development of each national spirit must be understood in terms of the development of a "world spirit." In other words, Montesquieu's teaching appears as the starting point for the emergence of the philosophy of history, which both in its universalistic version (Kant, Hegel, Marx) and in its particularistic version (the "historical school") tends to deny the practical autonomy and supremacy of political prudence.[22]

It is through this new emphasis on history that Montesquieu truly appears as the precursor of sociology. For sociology, as is well known, developed out of the philosophy of history.[23] And when one reflects on the considerations outlined in the two previous paragraphs it becomes intelligible how, by way of the turn to history, the conception of the science of man as *social* science could evolve from the conception of it as *political* science. Because Montesquieu represents only the first step in this evolution, study of his thought helps reveal to us the partly veiled intellectual sources and philosophical presuppositions of the sociological orientation. We become fully aware of the degree to which "social" science is a continuation, and not merely an outgrowth, of the philosophy

of history.[24] The new liberal political theory of the
state and society opens the way, but it is the subsequent turn to an emphasis on history that truly
initiates the intellectual evolution toward scientific
preoccupation with the "social" at the expense of the
political.

Nevertheless, for Montesquieu himself the discov-
ery of the historical dimension does not lead to a disavowal of the suzerainty of politics. The general spirit
of a nation is formed by its political history more than
by anything else. In this Montesquieu seems to antici-
pate Burke; yet he remains more faithful to the classical understanding of political history than Burke does.
Montesquieu does not characterize the state or the
nation as an organism: nations do not "grow"
(although cf. XXX 1). For Burke a nation's religion
is not necessarily derivative from politics and may
be as great a formative force as any political phenomenon;[25] Montesquieu indicates as clearly as he
dares that religion is largely the political product of
a human legislator (XIV 5, 11; XV 17, 18; XIV 7;
XIX 21; XXIV 6, 24; XXV 3; XXVI 14). But the
difference appears most clearly in Montesquieu's
teaching about the origins, the founding of nations
and societies. In his discussion of the history of the
French nation in the final part of *The Spirit of the Laws*,
Montesquieu shows that the nation did not simply
spring up or coalesce. It owes its origin to the deeds
and above all to the martial victories and defeats of
its political chiefs. "At the birth of societies, it is the
chiefs of republics who make the institution; and afterwards it is the institution which forms the chiefs of
republics" (*Considerations, Works*, II, 70). We should

never forget that the explicit purpose of *The Spirit of the Laws* is the education of the "legislator" (XXIX 1). In contrast to Burke, Montesquieu's emphasis on the individual legislators in the future as well as in the past marks his belief in man's capacity to reshape or create history in certain times and places—to use reason to revolutionize the established orders. This belief leads Montesquieu to assess every situation in a way that gives more power to human intention and prudence.

With this in mind, we will be in a better position to recognize that the principal purpose of Book XIX is not, as is often thought, to teach that the legislator must follow the general spirit. The teaching that the legislator is limited by the general spirit is only the first step. The aim of the argument as a whole is to show how and under what circumstances the legislator can alter or even overcome the general spirit in order to bring about the maximum of political liberty. Any attempt to state the intention of Book XIX is bound to be controversial, for this important book is perhaps the most obscure of all in its central or unifying argument. No one has claimed to explain the reason why each chapter is where it is. And we cannot fully remedy the situation. But we believe that the core of the argument in Book XIX can be understood in the light of the general line of argument of Books XIV and following. To restate this argument in brief: having presented the correct political principles through his analysis of England in Books XI through XIII, Montesquieu proceeds to show how these principles can be applied to political life elsewhere.

Chapter Six

Montesquieu himself warns the reader of the difficulties he will encounter in trying to comprehend Book XIX. This is the only book which begins with a brief chapter "on the subject of this book" and its mode of presentation. At the beginning of six other books whose theme is both important and somewhat obscure, Montesquieu helps the reader by devoting a brief opening chapter to the "general idea" of the book (Books V, VIII, XI, XII, XIV, XXVI; cf. also XX). Here one might expect the same help but, for reasons which will become apparent later, Montesquieu feels reluctant to be so explicit. Instead, he leaves it at warning the reader of the difficulty and giving him a hint as to how to proceed. After noting the "great extent" of the subject matter, he says that he "will be more attentive to the order of the things than to the things themselves." By this he seems to indicate that while it will be necessary for him to "wander to right and left" in order to find and bring together examples as evidence for his principles, his intention is to unfold an orderly argument which will reveal fully the general principles governing the relation of law to the general spirit. It is required, then, that we attempt to discern the precise order of Book XIX.

The book appears to be divided into five sections, corresponding to five stages in Montesquieu's argument:

Section 1 (chapters 2–4). In these chapters, which we have already commented upon, Montesquieu begins by stating the problem to which Book XIX addresses itself: in order to bring about the "best laws" it is necessary that the spirit, the "manner of thinking" of a people, be prepared to receive them. He then indicates more precisely what he means by this general spirit (chapter 4).

Section 2 (chapters 5–11). Having shown the limit or obstacle imposed by the general spirit, Montesquieu turns to an investigation of how the general spirit may sometimes be used by the legislator to bring about improvement, especially in Europe where political freedom is most possible. In four chapters he discusses the situation of a European monarchy (France) whose general spirit is not, despite first impressions, necessarily at a tension with correct "principles of government" (chapters 5–8). The reason this monarchy's spirit need not be radically "corrected" is that it is partially founded on a certain vice—vanity—which is capable of being used as the basis for political improvement. Montesquieu extends this principle in the next three chapters (9–11): vanity and other vices are conducive to work, industry, and commerce. Exactly why commerce goes together with political improvement is not yet made clear.

Section 3 (chapters 12–15). In the previous section Montesquieu showed how the legislator may use the existing general spirit, and especially the vices it contains, to bring about improvement. Now Montesquieu examines the situation where the general spirit by itself cannot lead to freedom, the situation in despotism. In order to bring freedom, the general spirit has to be changed, but it is usually dangerous to do so: in most despotisms (for example, China) no other form of order or tranquility is possible because of the climate and the established habits of the people. A change in manners and morals only leads to anarchy and an eventual new despotism (chapters 12–13). But sometimes the situation of a country, above all its climate and its proximity to Europe, makes freer government conceivable. The central chapter of Book XIX (chapter 14) deals with the proper way to create a new general spirit, to introduce new manners and morals, especially in such a despotism. The correct method proves to be similar to that by which the legislator uses the general spirit of monarchy: the liberation and use of the natural but immoral passion of vanity, especially feminine vanity (chapters 14–15).

Section 4 (chapters 16–26). Sections 2 and 3 dealt with the proper relation of law to general spirit. Now Montesquieu describes the improper relation, the mistake that legislators are especially tempted to make: the attempt to change manners and morals through law, through the fiat of the legislator. To thus wrench man's second nature into a new course does "violence" to man. It is a form of tyranny, and it requires harsh penalties and sanctions. This violence can be justified only in lands like China where climate makes fear and compulsion the only means to order; it cannot be justified in Europe (chapters 16–20). The examples Montesquieu gives of nations where this mistake was made are Rome, Israel, and above all Sparta, the "singularity" and fanaticism of whose institutions we remember from the last chapters of Book IV: "It is only singular institutions which thus confound things naturally separated: the laws and the morals and manners" (XIX 21; cf. IV 6).

Montesquieu teaches that the legislator in Europe must restrict his attempts at change to methods which follow the "natural genius," the passions and inclinations, of a people. Any attempt to change the general spirit of a nation must not try to restrain these passions; one must rather try to free them to pursue new objects. But this means that the legislator must not try to reform a people. The legislator is forbidden to try to create in a people who lack virtue or self-restraint a new regime founded on virtue. A virtuous republic is possible only where the "laws follow the morals," or where the virtue already exists. But how many civilized nations are naturally virtuous? A virtuous republic is possible only among a simple, poor, primitive people (chapters 21–26).

Section 5 (chapter 27). In the long concluding chapter of this book, Montesquieu at first seems to contradict the teaching of the previous section that the laws should never create, but should rather follow, the morals: "We have seen how the laws follow the morals: let us see how the morals follow the laws" (XIX 26, end). The apparent contradiction is really only a qualification. The legislation of morals can be appropriate where the morals are like those of England. The English way of life is based on the liberation of the petty selfishness of man (see our analysis above, pp. 146–60). The legislator need not act with violence and compulsion when he creates through law a way of life which follows the selfish bent of human nature. This does not mean to say that Montesquieu now abandons all his previous cautions about the importation of English law elsewhere. Chapter 27 must be read in the light of what has gone before. In most places natural environment and history prevent application of English institutions. But where a people

dwelling in a European climate have been able to partially break with their history, English law might
revise the morals. Montesquieu might well approve,
for instance, the application of English institutions to
some American colonies.

But the chief practical lesson of chapter 27 for the
European statesman is not so much the applicability
elsewhere of the laws of England, but the applicability
of a key part of the "customs," the "manners and morals," of England. The central feature of the English
way of life, and a chief purpose of its constitution,
is the free pursuit of commerce. The commercial way
of life produces comfort and security. And commerce
can be promoted by the power of vanity, especially
feminine vanity. Here we begin to understand Montesquieu's advice earlier in Book XIX about the proper
way to make use of the general spirit in monarchy
and how to introduce a new general spirit into despotism. Commerce is the solution to the problem of
liberty in Europe, if not elsewhere. Chapter 27 of
Book XIX is the introduction to Books XX through
XXII, whose theme is commerce. There Montesquieu
will spell out in more detail the way in which the
spread of commerce implies the spread of liberty, and
how this can be achieved.

We now begin to understand the sense in which
Montesquieu advocates respecting and preserving the
established order even as he teaches how to transform
it. A resolution of the paradox that first appeared in
the Preface has come to sight. Insofar as a national
spirit contains the possibility for the liberation of the
selfish passions of avarice and vanity, it has the potential for commerce and hence for vastly increased secu-

rity or liberty. That liberty will vary according to the degree to which a spirit of freedom is already embodied in the general spirit and the institutions.

Book XIX teaches that the legislator must not attempt moral reform. But Montesquieu goes far beyond classical restraint. He teaches that great progress *is* possible but only through moral corruption. Not for one moment does Montesquieu confuse or lose sight of the enormous difference between traditional virtue and vice. In full knowledge of what is implied, he teaches that a good political life for Europe depends on the cultivation of vice:

> I have not at all said this in order to diminish in the least the infinite distance which exists between the vices and the virtues—God forbid! I have only wanted to make it understood that all political vices are not moral vices, and that all moral vices are not political vices. (XIX 11)

We can now understand why Montesquieu is so reluctant to state openly and clearly the central practical teaching of *The Spirit of the Laws*. Part of the "moderation" which *The Spirit of the Laws* teaches the legislator is not only the necessity, but the beneficence, the charm, the power, of vice.

In England the free commercial way of life is a product of laws and a constitution embodying the principles of political freedom. The constitution is rarely transferable. But the commercial way of life is very transferable, and commerce brings freedom. In the elaboration of this teaching in the books that follow, Montesquieu makes more comprehensible many of the details of Book XIX.

7

COMMERCE AND THE CHARM
OF NATIONAL DIVERSITY

Most modern commentators fail to recognize the revolutionary significance of commerce in Montesquieu's political thought. Montesquieu's veiling of his plan is no doubt partly responsible for this lapse of interpretation. Yet he gives strong hints which should attract the reader's attention to the importance of Book XX. In the first place, this is the only book, except for Book XXVIII,[1] which is introduced with a classical poetic epigraph.[2] What is more, Montesquieu originally intended to introduce the book with a poetic invocation of the Muses written by himself. Although he was persuaded or compelled by a friendly proofreader to drop this invocation, it was preserved and has been restored in the chief editions printed since his death.[3] As a product of Montesquieu's fully matured presentation, it is worthy of note. Both epigraph and poem help us to understand the significance of commerce for Montesquieu.

The epigraph, "the things which great Atlas taught," would seem to characterize "the things" which are the subject of Book XX. In the original poem from which the epigraph is taken (Virgil's *Aeneid* I, 741), the reference is to "the things" about which a certain bard sings. These things comprise the study of nature and especially the study of the origins of heaven and earth and all the things in them, including man. By identifying the study of commerce with the study of the natural origins of things, Montesquieu links commerce with his teaching in Books I and XVIII about nature as a whole and the nature and true origins of man. The new understanding of man's origins leads to a new understanding of commerce as the answer to the natural human needs.

The meaning of Montesquieu's prose poem is somewhat more complicated. The first and most obvious implication of this invocation of the Muses is that the author believes himself to be commencing the most sublime part of his work. So sublime is the theme that Montesquieu now needs divine help to express it properly.

The difficulty of expression is not caused solely by the sublimity of the theme, however. Part of the difficulty is that Montesquieu himself is "overcome with sadness and weariness"; "charm and softness" have "fled far from" him. He presents himself as weighed down by his own elaboration of the obstacles to a happy political order. Prior to the introduction of the commerce theme, the outlook for human freedom is gloomy. But commerce will reintroduce sweetness and pleasure to our political reflections. Montesquieu knows that in order to speak properly of commerce he should have "charm and softness" in his heart. He therefore wishes the Muses to aid him in shaking off his depression and to enable him to speak of commerce in a tone of befitting happiness.

The third reason for Montesquieu's invocation, and the most important (or at any rate the one to which the most space is devoted), is that he wishes the Muses to help him adorn his writing about commerce. What

Montesquieu has to say now is not in itself entirely pleasing. Montesquieu "will announce new things." If we are to enjoy the benefits of commerce, we must abandon other interests and undergo the difficult labor of learning the new science of economics. And economics, if not a dismal science, is a prosaic one. Even the poem is a prose poem. Montesquieu is inspired "not with what they sing at Tempe with the flutes or what is repeated at Delos with the lyre," but with what is "according to reason." He wishes to make the study of commerce seem as attractive as possible by initially emphasizing the sweet rewards it will bring. He wants to hide the "work," the "reflection," behind a veil of "sentiment." Montesquieu hopes to make economics popular; he wants "all the world to read his book" and find in it "pleasure." Especially in the books on commerce Montesquieu intends his philosophy to be propagandistic.

The need for adornment arises not only from the inherent difficulty of the subject matter. As we have seen and will see again, the commitment to commerce is at odds with traditional morality. Montesquieu therefore needs to distract the reader's attention from traditional moral restraints. This is to be done through an appeal to "pleasure," and the pleasure appealed to will be not noble but soft and corrupting pleasure. Montesquieu indicates this too in his little poem. In a footnote he reveals that the opening line of his invocation is a paraphrase of a satiric invocation by Juvenal. That invocation ("Speak to me, Pieridian Virgins—and you should give me aid, in return for flattering you with the appellation of Virgins") is a sly reference to the lack of chastity in the Muses. Like Juvenal,

Montesquieu presents himself as making an appeal to Muses who are unchaste women amused or honored by graceful tongue-in-cheek flattery. Montesquieu leagues himself with certain morally questionable but powerful feminine deities (an alliance that reminds one a little of Socrates' alliance with the Clouds); as we have seen, an appeal to feminine vanity plays no little part in Montesquieu's political project. On the last page of Book XIX, the page immediately preceding this invocation, Montesquieu has said that England would produce many Juvenals who would write harsh satires on the society's vices (XIX 27, p. 583). Now he adapts a mock invocation which was used by Juvenal to introduce one of his harshest attacks on corruption. Montesquieu indicates that he agrees with Juvenal's assessment, but he praises and enjoys what Juvenal finds hateful. He transforms a bitter attack on corruption into a charming introduction to corruption.[4]

The first three chapters of Book XX are devoted to a discussion of the general character of commerce. Many of the key points were adumbrated in the previous chapter on the English general spirit (XIX 27). But in the discussion of England it was not altogether clear which aspects of the way of life were due to commerce alone and which were due to the combined influence of commerce and the constitution. Now Montesquieu focuses on commerce alone, showing us with more precision the benefits it will bring as well as the things which must be sacrificed to it. The outstanding benefit brought by commerce is that it enlightens and thereby "softens" men:

Chapter Seven

Commerce cures destructive prejudices; and it is almost a general rule that wherever there are soft ways of life there is commerce; and that wherever there is commerce, there are soft ways of life. (XX 1)

By this Montesquieu means, in the first place, that the experience of acquisition reveals to men their natural desire for security and property. It is with commerce just as with fertile land: it "gives, with ease, softness and a certain love for the conservation of life" (XVIII 4). Commerce brings its own "laws" and its own "spirit" (XX 1, 2). Men cease to seek satisfaction in devotion to the fatherland or king; they think of themselves. And they lose their taste for personal glory, or salvation after death; they look to their material affairs. They become hard-working, tolerant, and peace-loving.

The change in the way each man looks at himself goes together with changes in the way each man looks at others. Men are enlightened about their *common* insecurity and weakness. They no longer ignore their neighbors, as in despotisms, or consider them as almost belonging to a different species, as in monarchies, or look on them as responsible for almost infinite self-sacrifice and heroism, as in virtuous republics. They realize their need for others, and they see in others a corresponding need for them. Pity, humanity, is allowed to come to the surface in human intercourse. Compassion, or humanity, finds its source in the state of nature, in that mutual feeling of pleasure experienced when one of the lonely, fearful beasts encountered and recognized another frightened being akin to him. It is a sentiment men share with the animals, but seem to all but lose when they enter society and its state of war (I 2, 3). Despite its weakness, it is the only unselfish natural bond, except sex, that unites men and tends to bring peace and security. We remember that in the virtuous democracy there existed some humanity among the citizens (VI 15) but it was weakened by the sternness of virtue. The commercial regime is the only one which allows man's natural humanity to fully assert itself.

Through commerce man's humanity toward his neighbor extends also to foreigners. The communication commerce creates with foreign peoples brings knowledge of those peoples and their ways; this makes their differences seem less strange and forbidding. In becoming accustomed to a variety of modes of life, men become tolerant. They are inclined to see their own way not as the only way but as one among many ways, each of which pretends to be the true way. They begin to recognize the narrowness, the arbitrary and conventional character, of all particular ways, and tend to consider as true and serious only what is shared by all men. Men in commercial societies see in foreigners not creatures of a different species but men with passions and needs like their own. The treatment of all other men is softened as one becomes capable of identifying oneself with them. Earlier Montesquieu had praised the moderation in the conduct of modern war (X 3; cf. IX 1, XV 2, XXIV 3, XXV 13, XXIX 14, and *Considerations, Works*, II, 148). Now we can understand better why men have become more humane. The Christian religion is a factor, but it too must be further softened by "knowledge." The great factor is the new modern philosophy and its espousal of the commercial way of life:

One shouldn't be surprised in the least if our

morals [*moeurs*] are less ferocious than they were in earlier times. Commerce has made it so that the knowledge of the ways of all nations has penetrated everywhere: they have been compared to one another, and great good has resulted. (XX 1)

Knowledge renders men soft; reason brings humanity: it is only prejudice that makes men renounce humanity. (XV 3, see the context)

Now we can understand better the sense in which Montesquieu, despite his reservations about the popularization of philosophy, is nonetheless an advocate of enlightenment: "It is not a matter of indifference that the people be enlightened" (Preface). Montesquieu desires popular awareness of the desirability of security and commercial acquisition, and the knowledge and manner of thinking which follows from this commercial spirit. It is true that Montesquieu wishes to create through enlightenment a moderation of the passion for change (Preface, p. 230), but he also wishes to bring about change. He wishes to establish a popular understanding of the need for gradual, peaceful change. Both the desire for change and the caution will come from a pervasive consciousness of the one thing most needed—security.

Pacification comes about not only through a humanization but even more through a commercialization of the manner of thinking. Men who pursue private acquisition of property through trade are much less moved by motives of glory and conquest. Merchants who understand the ephemeral nature of riches acquired through pillage fix their eyes on more solid and permanent sources of wealth (XX 8). Commercial England is not warlike except in self-defense; it has acquired a reputation of unambitious independence (XIX 27, pp. 577, 579).

Furthermore, "the natural effect of commerce is to bring peace. Two nations that negotiate together render themselves mutually dependent" (XX 2). The dependence of all governments on international monetary exchange limits the violence or irrationality of each (XXII 13). The spread of trade does more than make nations interdependent; it "unites the nations" because it "founds them on mutual needs" (XX 2; cf. *Reflections on Universal Monarchy, Works*, II, 34). Nations grow similar to one another. Insofar as they all come to be preoccupied with riches they, "in this respect, constitute but a single State, of which all societies are members" (XX 23). The tolerance of all foreign ways goes together with a homogenization of ways, for all come to have the same desires and needs: "it is the nature of commerce to render superfluous things useful and useful things necessary" (XX 23). The worldwide spread and intensification of commerce is insidiously powerful. The establishment of the brotherhood of man comes about through the reduction of all differences to the lowest common denominator—the need for security and the desire for comfort.

Today one cannot help but find Montesquieu's hopes for world pacification through commerce overly sanguine. While his remarks on England's wars illustrate his appreciation of the fact that commercial countries may still be required to defend themselves against noncommercial powers, Montesquieu seems to have been insufficiently attentive to the potential

sources of war within the commercial spirit itself.[5]
He fails to give enough weight to the probability of
war arising from competition for scarce resources or
colonies, and he shows in remarks elsewhere an amazing blindness to the pernicious effects on armaments
of unlimited technological development.[6]

Montesquieu combines with his elaboration of the
benefits of commerce some further indication of what
must be given up for the sake of commerce:

> One can say that the laws of commerce perfect
> the morals [*moeurs*] for exactly the same reason
> that these very laws destroy the morals. Com-
> merce corrupts pure morals; this was the subject
> of the complaints of Plato; it polishes and softens
> barbaric morals, as we see every day. (XX 1)

At the beginning of *The Spirit of the Laws* Montesquieu
seemed to voice his own complaint against modern
political thought:

> The Greek political thinkers, who lived under
> popular government, knew of no force which
> could sustain it except virtue. Today's political
> thinkers talk to us only of manufacture, of com-
> merce, of finance, of riches, and even of luxury.
> (III 3)

And again in the present context Montesquieu
reminds us of the incompatibility of commerce and
ancient participatory republicanism, its virtue, its
liberty, and its great deeds. Citizens of such regimes,
he says,

> are poor only because they have disdained, or
> because they haven't known, the commodities of

life; and these men can do great things, because this poverty makes up a part of their liberty. (XX 3)

With the deepest possible awareness of the issue and of all that was at stake, Montesquieu sided unmistakably and intransigently with the moderns.[7]

It is not enough to say that the effect of commerce is to destroy political virtue; as we have seen in our discussion of the English way of life, commerce weakens the generous habits and sentiments which are called moral virtues:

> But if the spirit of commerce unites the nations, it does not unite individuals. We see in the countries where one is affected only by the spirit of commerce that one traffics in all human actions and all the moral virtues: the smallest things, the things humanity demands, are performed or are given for money. (XX 2)

One must then qualify the notion that commerce brings humanity. It brings only a part, or a certain sort, of humanity. All that part of humanity associated with generosity and greatness of soul disappears:

> The spirit of commerce produces in men a certain sentiment of exact justice, opposed on the one hand to brigandage, and on the other hand to those moral virtues which make it so that one doesn't always discuss one's own interests with rigidity, and that one can neglect them for the interests of others. . . . Among the Germans, says Tacitus . . . he who exercised hospitality towards a stranger went to show him another house where it would be exercised again, and the stranger was received there with *humanity*.

But, when the Germans had founded kingdoms, hospitality became a burden to them. . . . (XX 2; italics mine)[8]

Montesquieu implies that pure and generous morals, the morals praised by the ancients, go together with barbarism. Virtue and civilization are incompatible; the virtuous republic is perhaps necessarily barbarous:

The total privation of commerce produces on the contrary the brigandage which Aristotle places among the modes of acquisition. This spirit is not at all opposed to certain moral virtues: for example, hospitality, very rare among commercial countries, is found to an admirable extent among robber peoples. (XX 2; cf. *Politics* 1256ᵃ)

Good civil laws are born with the new means and diverse ways of being wicked. (XVIII 16; cf. XIX 22–23)

After his treatment of the "nature" of commerce, Montesquieu turns in chapter 4 to an analysis of its "distinctions" (cf. the title of Book XX), or of the different ways it may be carried on in different governments. Commerce requires security, and therefore some degree of moderate government. It will not spring up in despotism. On the other hand, the despotic taste for luxury provides fallow ground for the introduction of commerce by foreign traders (cf. XX 23 with VII 4). Once a taste for foreign goods is acquired, the despotic rulers may well be led to encourage more commerce in general, and the liberalizing and enriching effects of commerce will be felt to some extent throughout the country (cf. XXII 14). Of course, the degree to which these salutary effects are experienced will vary from one national situation to another. In particular, since hot climates produce sensuality and require the confinement of women, luxury will there tend to remain simple and voluptuous. Vanity will never promote that level of refined taste which is productive of commerce on the largest scale. It appears that this climatic effect on women and vanity creates the insuperable barrier which sets the limit to political progress. This would perhaps explain why the relation between climate and the confinement of women forms the theme of the central book of *The Spirit of the Laws*. Despite his failure to foresee the full effects of weapons technology and commercial imperialism, Montesquieu points to the fact that, within limits established by nature, commerce introduced from abroad will ameliorate despotism. For the improvement of the human lot in despotic as well as in moderate nations, the key is the fostering of commerce in the moderate nations—above all in European nations.

We know from our analysis of England that commerce is most at home in free, popular government. The most fully developed sort of commerce is named "the commerce of economy" by Montesquieu:

> This kind of traffic . . . is only founded on the practice of making a small profit, and even a smaller profit than any other nation, and not to reward oneself except by the act of continually gaining. . . . (XX 4)

It is therefore favored by and itself favors a country where a large number of people have power and a high degree of security for their lives and property:

"It is related to the government of a number of persons by its nature and to monarchy only occasionally" (XX 4).

But there is another kind of commerce—a kind which finds its home in monarchy. This is "the commerce of luxury": "Although it is also founded on real needs, its principal object is to procure to the nation which carries it on everything which can serve its pride, its pleasures, and its fantasies" (XX 4).

The commerce of economy is a superior form of commerce; its spirit is that which imbues the citizens with frugality, moderation, and the desire to work (cf. V 6), while luxury makes men "spend a great deal and see only great objects" (XX 4). Nevertheless, if we compare what Montesquieu says here in Book XX about the commerce of luxury with what he said about France in Book XIX, we recognize the great possibilities in the commerce of luxury. For while the spirit of luxury weakens the ascetic spirit of hard work, it vastly increases the number of objects desired and thereby stimulates a broader commerce. The commerce of luxury is based on an idle upper class animated by the freedom and appetites of women. Women and the men who spend their lives pleasing women are poor producers; but they are the most voracious consumers:

> One could restrain the women [in France], make laws to correct their morals, and limit their luxury; but who knows if one would not lose a certain taste which is the source of the riches of the nation, and a politeness that attracts to it foreigners? (XIX 5)

The society of women harms morals, and forms

taste: the desire to be more pleasing than others establishes ornamentation; and the desire to be more pleasing than one really is establishes fashions. Fashions are an important object: while rendering the spirit frivolous, they constantly increase the branches of its commerce. (XIX 8)

Luxury, vanity, *can* stimulate work and economic vigor:

Vanity is as good a spring for a government as pride is dangerous. In order to understand that, one has only to picture for oneself the countless benefits which result from vanity: from it come luxury, industry, the arts, fashions, politeness, taste. . . . Work is a consequence of vanity. (XIX 9)

The luxury of the idle nobles stimulates industry and commerce in the lower classes.

Montesquieu advocates for monarchies like France an economic system in which the commercial activity and the new way of life most closely resembling England's characterize the lower classes, while the nobles remain idle (cf. V 9). This does not mean to say that French society will exactly imitate English society at either level. Politically, the French common people will have less power; they will be less free, less secure, and therefore less enterprising. The spirit of luxury will in some measure penetrate all classes (VII 4). The tone of society as a whole will be set by the polished dalliance of the upper-class salons. France will preserve its unique general spirit, and this general spirit does not promote the most efficient commerce: "There is a hardiness in states which subsist by the commerce of economy which isn't found in monarchies" (XX 4). France may well be at a competitive disadvantage with regard to England and Holland, except in those aspects of commerce where quality and taste are preeminent factors.[9]

But we must not overemphasize the difference between France and England. The commercial development of France must be unique—but it cannot be simply unique. Commerce everywhere requires certain similar practices. Besides, the desire for acquisition that exists among the French merchants will necessarily have a great similarity to the acquisitive desire of English merchants, and the desire for luxury will grow in England:

> One commerce leads to another; the small to the mediocre, the mediocre to the great; and he who has had so much desire to gain a little puts himself in a situation where he has no less desire to gain much. . . . I don't mean that there is any monarchy which would be totally excluded from a commerce of economy; but it is less carried that way by its nature. I don't mean that the republics which we know are entirely deprived of the commerce of luxury; but it has less relation to their constitution. (XX 4; see also VII 6 and XXI 6)

Because Montesquieu believed the commercial way of life to be the most adequate response to the needs of human nature, he advocated its spread wherever possible, and he thereby consciously promoted a levelling of the differences among nations. But he understood that these differences even within Europe were such that the most efficient form of commerce was not suitable to most nations. Not a "commerce of economy," but a "commerce of luxury," which would perhaps eventually lead to some combination of the two, is the greatest hope for progress in much of Europe. This he makes clear in the chapter following that on the two kinds of commerce. After showing the superior efficiency of the commerce of economy, he asks what sort of peoples have carried on this commerce. We learn that,

> it has been seen everywhere that violence and vexation give birth to the commerce of economy, when men are forced to seek refuge in swamps, on islands, in the low places by the sea, in the sea's marshes even . . . fugitives found safety there. They had to subsist; they took their sustenance from the whole universe. (XX 5)

The commerce of economy is possible only where men begin with a relatively clean slate, in conditions of "vexation" and deprivation.

Montesquieu's wish to promote the progress of commerce within France was spurred by a sense of impending crisis. Like other intelligent observers, he recognized that the fulcrum of Europe was France —that the direction taken by France would determine the fate of Europe and, ultimately, of the whole world. And Montesquieu was fearful of the tendencies he saw in France. He feared the French monarchy's imperial designs, and tried to show that they ran counter to even the most selfish interests of a French king: neither his patriotism nor his friendship for Berwick prevented him from expressing relief at the outcome of the War of the Spanish Succession (IX 7; cf. IX 5–6, 8–10, X 9, 16). But he feared even more the internal decay which was the source of French imperialism. Throughout *The Spirit of the Laws* his discussions of despotism are partly intended as a portrayal of the evils toward which European monarchy was inclining. In his remarks on monarchy he draws attention to the contemporary growth of the king's power at the expense of the traditional countervailing powers of clergy and nobility (II 4). Not only did this centralizing tendency threaten the principle of honor and the institutional protections for the liberty of nobles and all others, but it also led to an increasing royal preoccupation with the "sick desire for a vain glory" and a corresponding neglect of the material prosperity of the citizens (cf. XIII 1 and context).

There is only one chapter of *The Spirit of the Laws* whose title begins with the word "danger": the chapter entitled "Danger of the Corruption of the Principle of Monarchy." There Montesquieu says,

> The inconvenience is not when the State passes from one moderate government to another . . . but when it falls and throws itself from moderate government to despotism.
> Most of the people of Europe are still governed by manners and morals [*moeurs*]. But if by a long abuse of power, if by a great conquest, despotism establishes itself at a certain point, neither the manners and morals nor the climate will restrain it; and in that beautiful part of the world human nature would suffer, at least for a time, the insults which are made to it in the other three parts of the world. (VIII 8)

Montesquieu foresaw that a continuation of the centralizing tendency would sooner or later result in despotism or the anarchic revolutions which always come to characterize despotism (especially in Europe where men of honor live: cf. III 9). In the *Persian Letters*, where Montesquieu could express himself more boldly and dramatically by using the veil of allegory, he speaks more openly of the danger of revolution. The bloody suicidal note which concludes that novel is a kind of prediction of the French revolution.

Montesquieu was opposed to the status quo because he thought its principles were not good in themselves and because he saw that it was not really a status quo but an accelerating decay. He trembled at the growth of monarchic power, but he "trembled" at least as much at the violent republican reaction which might come later.[10] He seems to have foreseen and detested the possibility of a Robespierrean republican moralism, a crazy attempt to reestablish virtuous Roman republicanism. *The Spirit of the Laws* as a whole, and Book XIX in particular, is the greatest modern attack on political moralism. Montesquieu detested this moralism because of its total inappropriateness, its complete lack of roots in France and the French people; at a deeper level, he believed, as we have seen, that it went against the grain of human nature itself. And Montesquieu opposed Lockean doctrinairism as much as he opposed moralism, for he recognized that a simple transferral of English principles would also result in a tyranny and insecurity that would destroy all possibilities for decent government. He therefore tried to show France and Europe another way, another path to progress.

Montesquieu wished to persuade the French

monarchs that they could better realize their aspirations to national grandeur through commercial expansion than through military conquest. France's preeminence, her superiority in wealth and population, the dominant influence in Europe of her way of life, her opportunity for various forms of colonial hegemony, could be retained through commerce at the same time as the mass of her citizens were made secure, prosperous, and content.

Beyond that Montesquieu hoped to teach the nobles and the bourgeoisie their common interest in the promotion of commerce based on luxury. The merchant class should recognize the encouragement given to commerce by the nobility's way of life as well as the importance of the aristocracy for the balance of power. The nobles, on the other hand, should realize that the growth of commerce and the power of the commercial interests was less of a threat than might at first appear. Besides the beneficent effects of increased commerce, the recognition of mutual interests on the part of bourgeoisie and nobles may well provide the basis for a cooperative reinvigoration of the system of countervailing political powers within the monarchy.[11]

It is helpful to pause for a moment in order to view Montesquieu's thought in a somewhat broader context. According to Hobbes, the natural tendency of pride and vanity is bad: these passions lead to self-destructive belligerency (*Leviathan*, chaps. xi, xiii). The only safe or consistent foundation for civil society is the fear of death prudently channelled. As much as possible, pride and the way of life founded on pride must be expunged. Or to use the formulation of

Hobbes's great successor, Hegel, between the master morality and the slave morality there exists a radical contradiction, solvable only by means of a "synthesis" which in fact requires the eventual destruction of the master morality through the French Revolution and the Napoleonic Wars. Montesquieu tries to show that the contradiction can be resolved without the destruction of the master morality, by a kind of domestication of pride.

In addition to the wish to forestall the chaos of violent revolution and provide for the peaceful spread of commerce, there is a second motive underlying Montesquieu's desire to preserve the unique French national spirit. We recall the grayness of English life, the emptiness of a life dominated by the purely commercial spirit:

> This commerce is a kind of lottery, and each is seduced by the hope of a black ticket. Everyone loves to play; and the wisest men gladly play, when they don't recognize the appearance of a game, its unpredictability, its violences, its dissipations, the loss of time, and even the loss of a whole lifetime. (XX 6)

But France has "a joy in life." In England men are stingy; in France there is "an openness of the heart . . . generosity." In England men are withdrawn; in France they have a "sociable humor . . . a facility in communicating their thoughts." The French are "lively, agreeable, playful, imprudent, often indiscreet." They "do frivolous things seriously and serious things gaily." Above all, they possess "taste" (XIX 5–8; cf. above, pp. 150–60). Montesquieu wished to preserve and foster that kind of society devoted in some measure to nonutilitarian pleasure, including the contemplation of beauty and grace for their own sake. In modern times the only possibility for this kind of tone lay in the preservation of the leisured aristocracy of France.

Montesquieu compares France to Athens:

> The Athenians . . . were a people who had some similarity to our people. They brought a certain gaiety into affairs; a trait of raillery pleased them on the podium as at the theater. That vivacity which they brought to their councils, they continued in their execution of them. (XIX 7)

Athens was a commercial republic; it represents a combination of commerce and taste. The example of Athens shows that taste is compatible with commerce and even promotes it: "What a cause for prosperity for Greece [were] the taste and the arts . . ." (XXI 7). At the same time, the example of Athens reveals that the cosmopolitan intercommunication of peoples produced by commerce can foster taste and may well be the precondition for the most refined taste. In Athens, we find "taste and the arts carried to such a point, that to believe them surpassed will always be not to know them" (XXI 7). Athens foreshadowed England in its commerce of economy (V 6; XX 4; XXI 7). But in Athens there existed something which qualified and even curtailed the single-minded and narrow commercial spirit (cf. XXI 7, p. 611), something which promoted a "sociable humor" with its gaiety and grace. In this respect it is France which is the heir to Athenian greatness. Montesquieu seems to hope for a Europe where the dominant French and

English ways of life can coexist and complement one another.[12] It would seem that Montesquieu hoped for a recreation of Athens, or at any rate for the closest possible approximation within the modern context.

Considerations such as these might lead one to the conclusion that Montesquieu espouses the cause of commerce at least as much because it promotes culture as because it promotes security and comfort.[13] But in fact these considerations convey only a partial, and therefore a misleading, picture of Montesquieu's intention. The full picture emerges when one reflects on the fact that Montesquieu devotes rather scant attention to Athens or to that whole dimension of Greek republicanism represented by Athens. It cannot be said that Montesquieu holds up Athens as the model of a good political order. If he had seen the fostering of art and taste to be the paramount goal of politics, he would have had to explore thematically the relation between politics and the arts in republican Athens. It is not sufficient to leave it at a discussion of this theme in relation to monarchic France. Whatever similarities France and Athens possess, the art and taste of Athens is different from and superior to the art and taste of France (XXI 7; "On the Gothic Manner," *Works*, I, 970–71). The general spirit of Athens had little to do with the freedom and power of women which is fundamental to the general spirit of France. And it is this all-powerful influence that seems to be at the root of the relative inferiority of French art and taste. For all its delicacy and sensitivity, the taste of France, when compared to that of Athens, appears both artificial and frivolous. On the one hand the corruption of women and the decay of

family life causes the educated to lose their appreciation of some of the most lovely sentiments of natural
affection (*Pensées*, nos. 916 and 1217; cf. XXVIII 22).
On the other hand, and more serious in its consequences, in France the audience for art is truly idle,
in contrast to the audience in republican Athens.
When the audience that judges is not dominated by
men who are active in serious affairs, art ceases to
be preoccupied with the grandest and most compelling
themes of war and politics:

> I was asked why there is no longer a taste for
> the works of Corneille, Racine, etc. I replied:
> 'This is because the things for which *esprit* is
> required have become ridiculous. . . . One can
> no longer abide any of the things which have
> a determined object: men of war can no longer
> abide war; men of government can no longer
> abide government; so it is with other things. . . .
> It is the commerce of women which has brought
> us to this. . . .' (*Pensées*, no. 860; "On the Gothic
> Manner," *Works*, I, 971; cf. XXVIII 45, near the
> end, XIX 27, p. 582, and XIX 2 at the end)

The French taste is similar to the Athenian in gaiety
and vivacity; but it does not share the profundity
of Athenian taste.

Had Montesquieu been fully serious in his concern
for the cultivation of the arts, he would have examined
much more fully what has to be combined with commerce to produce a general spirit like that of Athens.
At the least, he would have had to take the first steps
in the train of thought sketched by his predecessor
Shaftesbury: to ask whether the political life of the
polis is not the most fertile soil for the growth of that

rare combination of passion and perceptivity which is the precondition for the highest art and taste. According to Shaftesbury, the creation of participatory republican regimes in Greece gave birth to the art of speaking in public and in private discussion: "Persuasion must have been in a manner the mother of poetry, rhetoric, music, and the other kindred arts." As a result, the citizen body as a whole developed a profound habituation to clarity and beauty in language. It was above all this political experience that fostered the delight in language and thought for its own sake.[14]

Reflections such as these would have induced Montesquieu to reconsider the possible superiority of the polis to all other forms of political society. Moreover, Montesquieu would have been led to give more weight to the value of the aristocratic element in the classical republic. It is true that the full flowering of taste and the arts in Athens and other cities seems to have occurred at the time of the breakdown of the aristocratic order, but that flowering nevertheless seems to have depended on the release of the talents and energies built up by the aristocratic order. It depended on the influence of a class devoted to both political rule and proud aspiration to individual excellence in taste and thought. This entire dimension of Greekness, expressed so clearly and unforgettably by Nietzsche,[15] is left obscure in Montesquieu's analysis of republican antiquity. Montesquieu and his student, Rousseau, were led to neglect this part of the polis because of their intransigent desire to understand equality and freedom rather than excellence and thought as the true core of the ancient city.

Chapter Seven

Despite his respect for the art and taste of Athens, Montesquieu never really reconsidered his understanding of the ancient virtuous republic in the light of the possible political relevance of these things. He could remain satisfied with, he could even prefer the art and taste of France, because his own comprehensive thought about man led him to believe that the whimsy and frivolity characteristic of French culture reflected more accurately the true place in human life of nonutilitarian pleasures. The very tone in which Montesquieu discusses taste and the arts reveals his light and playful posture toward them.

In order to understand fully the reasons for this posture it is necessary for us first to take up the question which has not yet been raised in our discussion of taste and the arts: what is the source of these pleasures in human nature, according to Montesquieu? A difficulty is immediately apparent. If man is by nature an anxious animal seeking security, what basis is there, except in convention and distorted passions, for the pleasures of taste and art? By what right can we, for the sake of such things, attempt to place any more than the minimal prudential restraints on man's acquisitiveness?

The reason is to be found in additional implications of the notion of *history* in Montesquieu's thought. For the significance of history goes beyond the negative or contributory role on which we focused in chapter 6. History provides more than a framework which surrounds and channels the permanent core of human need; in some sense history adds new needs which alter that very core itself.

From the very beginning, the animal man must have

had the capacity to perceive and experience various pleasures. Given the impoverishment and terror of the original situation, this capacity was left almost undeveloped until a more secure social life emerged. But once this stage had been reached, the human faculties for knowing and loving used in the state of nature almost exclusively for mere survival and occasional sex, became to some extent independent of these original objects. As we have seen, the history of each nation represents a process of socialization through which the human passions found new objects of attraction and aversion. In the course of this process some of man's passions were diversified and modified to such an extent that there was practically a change in kind, a development of new passions. In society, the "natural pleasures" are mixed with and modified by "others . . . which are founded on the bents and prejudices which certain institutions, certain habits, have made the soul acquire" ("Essay on Taste," *Works*, II, 1240–41). Hence history presents us with the picture of the development of a pleasing variety of national spirits, each with its unique culture and taste.

This understanding of the source of our ideas of the sensibly beautiful leads Montesquieu toward a point of view which looks on all the national tastes, all the notions of beauty, as not only impermanent but as relative or incomparable with each other. Yet two considerations allow him to continue to maintain some permanent standard of ranking. In the first place, the desires for self-preservation and for the preservation of the family remain the fundamental human passions; any national tastes which unnecessarily threaten personal security or the family are unnatural (consider, for example, the case of Japan: VI 13; XII 14; XXIV 14; XXV 14). But in addition to or beyond this minimal qualification, the tastes of the various nations and their cultures can be ranked as better or worse, as more or less refined, according to the degree in which the "acquired taste," the changing conventional "bents and prejudices" develop and exploit the "natural taste," the full range of the human potential for sensitivity or pleasant perception (cf. *Works*, II, 1242). A strict ranking of all national tastes may be impossible; but some cultures can be said to possess taste to a high degree and others to a much lesser degree. French taste is supreme in modern Europe although there have been nations in the past and there may well be nations in the future with different but equally or even more refined tastes.

It is especially with regard to nations such as France that, as we have noted, Montesquieu almost says man develops a second nature, a "national" nature. He can speak of the general spirit of such a nation as "our natural genius"; he ascribes to "nature" the vivacity which helps produce French polish and taste (XIX 5, 6). Man is above all impelled and guided by the longing for security. But in a nation where the developing pleasures do not thwart, but only modify, the search for security, they should be taken into consideration as guides for political life. This is part of what Montesquieu means when he says:

> The legislator should follow the spirit of the nation, when it is not contrary to the principles of government; because we do nothing better than what we do freely, in following our natural genius. (XIX 5 and context)

In Montesquieu's discussion of France there comes to sight then a modification or, more precisely, an expansion, of the meaning of liberty. "What we do freely" is not only what we do in security but also what we do "in following our natural genius." Liberty is secondarily the protection or even the fostering of harmless national diversity.

It might be said that Montesquieu has in mind what we have come to call human creativity. The creativity he speaks of is principally a creativity of nations and not of individuals; but the French general spirit praised so highly by Montesquieu is one which promotes "the singularities of individuals" as well as the "love of change" (XIX 8; cf. 12). The pleasures of the most refined taste go hand in hand with the maximum development of ordered variety, individuality, and change (*Works*, II, 1243–51, 1253–58). Although taste is not simply relative or subjective, although Montesquieu is not exhilarated by limitless variety for its own sake, he does take the first great step toward replacing man's original and permanent nature as the standard for politics with a new standard based on the pleasures man discovers or creates in and through history.

But Montesquieu himself does not carry through this momentous transition from nature to history. In order to do so he would have had to speak more emphatically of the character of taste at its highest in his great work, *The Spirit of the Laws*, instead of relegating his thematic discussion to a far less significant essay which seems almost an afterthought. He would have had to make it clear that security, humanity, and compassion exist in the final analysis for the sake of something higher. More concretely, he would have had to indicate a theoretical, if not an immediately practical, preference for France with its aristocratic and tasteful society over England with its egalitarian, humane, and more purely commercial society. Montesquieu indicates the opposite preference. He knows that the English commercial spirit with its cosmopolitan power poses a threat to all that aristocratic France stands for. He tries to show how that threat may be softened, but not for one minute does that threat make him an opponent of England. On the contrary, Montesquieu is the most influential foreign champion that England ever had. His reservations against England on behalf of France are never more than reservations; he wishes to ease the tide of the commercial spirit, but he never shows a desire to stem it. Taste and the arts are the product of a considerable modification of the commercial spirit. Montesquieu was not willing to go very far in advocating such a modification because he was still too impressed with the contrast between the changeability of the passions depending on convention and the permanence of the passions stemming more directly from nature.

As we have indicated in chapter 4, the classical tradition had a very different interpretation of the pleasures involved in the apprehension of visible or sensible beauty. The classics understood these pleasures in the light of the notion of a permanent hierarchy of beauty solidly based in nature. According to the classics, the leisured gentleman's intellectual pleasures are a reflection or intimation of the truly fulfilling pleasure the philosopher finds in the contemplation of the truth.[16] They could claim that the contemplation of the truth completes the gentlemanly love of beauty and fully satisfies man's natural desire for pleasure because they held that the truth is beautiful and therefore supremely pleasant to behold—that the whole is constituted by what Socrates called the idea of the good, an eternal and beautiful thing (*Republic* 508^d–509^a).

Montesquieu's new understanding of the status of the gentlemanly intellectual pleasures goes together with, and is ultimately based on, a new interpretation of the relation of the beautiful to the true and a new interpretation of philosophy. From Montesquieu's understanding of the source of taste, it follows that our pleasurable experience of the beautiful is not the experience of something beautiful or good in itself, independent of and beyond our human apprehension of it. The truth—nature—is neither beautiful nor ugly. "Beauty" is a specifically human interpretation of certain parts of the truth; and this human interpretation is in turn the product of the accidental development and refinement of our physical and mental organism. Through history some nations have developed greater awareness of some of the range of things which can strike this human organism as pleasant, and it is the pleasure of seeing these things and not other things which is the experience of the beautiful. In short, beauty is derivative from human pleasure, human pleasure is not derivative from the beautiful:

> It is the different pleasures of our soul which form the objects of taste. . . . The sources of the beautiful, the good . . . are then in ourselves.

. . . Our manner of being is entirely arbitrary; we could have been made like we are, or differently. But if we had been made differently, we would have sensed differently; an organ more or less in our machine would have given us a different eloquence, a different poetry. . . . I know well that the relations which things have among themselves would have remained the same; but the relation they have with us would have changed . . . [and] there would be required a change in the arts. . . . ("Essay on Taste," *Works*, II, 1240–42; cf. 1245, bottom).[17]

According to Montesquieu, the decisive flaw of classical philosophy is its misapprehension of the relation between the perception of beauty and the perception of truth:

The terms beautiful, good, noble, great, perfect, are attributes of objects which are relative to the beings which are considering the objects. It is very important to keep this principle firm in one's mind; it is the sponge that erases most prejudices. This is the destructive error [*fleau*] of all ancient philosophy, of the physics of Aristotle, of the metaphysics of Plato; and, if one reads the dialogues of this philosopher, one will find that they are only a tissue of sophisms caused by the ignorance of this principle. . . . (*Pensées*, no. 2062, *Works*, II, 1537. Cf. *Pensées*, no. 2093, *Works*, I, 1546; *Persian Letters*, no. 17; and above all the "Essay on Taste," *Works*, II, 1556)

If the beautiful is not founded on the truth, if the truth is not intrinsically attractive or lovable, it becomes doubtful whether contemplation of the truth is intrinsically pleasant. It becomes questionable whether philosophy carried on for its sake alone can be said to make a man happy. And the political claims advanced on behalf of philosophy, or on behalf of its reflection in the gentleman's love of the beautiful, are drastically weakened.

It is undeniable that in the "Essay on Taste" Montesquieu speaks emphatically of "pleasures which the soul has independently of the pleasures which come to it from the senses, pleasures which are proper to the soul . . . in the nature of the soul . . . because they belong to every being which thinks." But it is immediately shown that these pleasures do not come from a delight in the things known. They come rather from curiosity, from the charm of variety, or, above all, from the awareness of our own continued existence and strength:

> If our soul had not been united with a body . . . it appears that it would have loved what it had knowledge of; in our present state we love almost only what we do not know.

> [Pleasures of thought itself are] such pleasures [as] those which give the soul curiosity, ideas of *its* greatness, of *its* perfections, the idea of *its* existence, opposed to the feeling of nothingness [*neant*]; the pleasure of embracing all of a general idea, that of seeing a great number of things, etc., that of comparing, of joining and separating ideas. ("Essay on Taste," *Works*, II, 1241; italics mine)

The pleasure of thinking is not the joy of contemplating something beloved; it is rather the satisfaction of the restless need to sense the exercise of our power and to flee the "feeling of nothingness." Insofar as we experience a pleasure beyond these pleasures, a pleasure derived from the character of the thing we perceive, it is because we are attracted to the thing by the "feeling" which constitutes our "taste": "for, although we oppose idea to feeling, nevertheless when the soul sees a thing, it feels it; there is nothing which is so intellectual that the soul doesn't see it or believe that it sees it, and consequently there is nothing that it does not feel" (*Works*, II, 1243).

The classical tradition which held that the whole is beautiful or good misapprehended the whole; one could say that it saw the whole as if under the influence of a myth. Like those who believe in myths, the ancient philosophers believed that the whole is animated by beautiful and good immortal beings. Accordingly, Montesquieu can without too much exaggeration identify the contemplative life of the ancient philosophers with the religious life: "The diverse sects of philosophy among the ancients can be considered as kinds of religion" (XXIV 10; the first editions of *The Spirit of the Laws* had "were" in place of "can be considered"). Montesquieu's only thematic treatment of philosophy and contemplation occurs approximately in the middle of the book on religion, "considered in its practices and in itself." Here in the chapter "On Contemplation" (XXIV 11) Montesquieu makes explicit his rejection of the contemplative life. Having identified ancient philosophy with religion in the chapter immediately preceding, Montesquieu opens this chapter by saying:

> Since men are made to preserve themselves, to nourish themselves, to clothe themselves, and to

perform all the actions of society, religion ought not to give men too contemplative a life. (XXIV 11; cf. XIV 5)

By this Montesquieu teaches in the first place the common-sense principle that, for most men, religious, and especially Christian, otherworldliness is destructive of prudent and necessary attachment to life on earth. But he never qualifies this attack on contemplation. It holds not only for most men, but for all men. In raising man "above" political life, philosophy does not perfect man: it makes him "savage" (IV 8; XXI 20; XXIII 21). In this context Montesquieu discusses the "Stoic sect," the single apparent exception. He makes it clear that he prefers it to all other "sects" of classical philosophy because, as he understands it, it led the philosopher to devote himself totally to political life.[18]

But our demonstration of Montesquieu's rejection of the primacy of contemplation is incomplete without an understanding of how he accounts for his own philosophic activity. In Montesquieu, philosophy ceases to be contemplation of the beautiful and takes on a new meaning and a new justification. This new meaning and justification are difficult to discover because Montesquieu speaks very rarely about himself or his own doing. But his praise of the Stoics gives us an entrance into his self-understanding. The Stoic public-spiritedness Montesquieu praises is not the same as the political virtue which he analyzed in Books II through VIII. The Stoics were good citizens; but they were much more. The Stoics whom Montesquieu praises most highly were emperors. These Stoic emperors are the exceptions to the "eternal experience

that every man who has power is led to abuse it"
(XI 4)—the experience which must usually guide our
assessment of absolute rule. The Stoics were not only
patriotic, they not only cared for Rome; they felt in
themselves "a kind of favorable providence which
watched over mankind." Montesquieu's description of
the universal benevolence of the Stoic emperors
reminds one immediately of his description of his own
activity as the "practice of that general virtue which
comprehends the love of all";[19] the publication of *The
Spirit of the Laws* is an act intended to benefit mankind
as a whole (Preface).

Montesquieu thus seems to identify his spirit with
the spirit of the humanity of the Stoic emperors.
Philosophy is not contemplative but benevolently
active. Yet what is the source or justification of this
benevolence? Can it be sufficient to trace it to a vastly
magnified sense of humanity? Or are we not entitled
to wonder whether Montesquieu's description of his
motives in the Preface is not made with a view to
self-defense? For the Stoics, the source was their
"belief" that "a sacred spirit," a "kind of providence"
or "destiny" was "within them" (XXIV 10). But Montesquieu is stubbornly silent about this theology or
metaphysics which was the core of Stoicism. Stoicism,
like all "the diverse sects of philosophy among the
ancients, can be considered as a species of religion."
Montesquieu praises and accepts Stoic practice, the
effect of Stoic metaphysics; he cannot praise or accept
that metaphysics itself. Initially one cannot help but
be baffled by the apparent disproportion between
Montesquieu's egoistical interpretation of human
nature and his indications about the benevolence

which motivates the philosopher. And one finds nowhere in *The Spirit of the Laws* a thematic treatment of this question—a coherent account of Montesquieu's reasons for writing this book.

Yet Montesquieu does make Delphic but not wholly impenetrable allusions to the reasons for his literary activity. In the Preface his account of himself includes more than an explicit statement of motive: in the concluding paragraphs he makes some revealing remarks about his actual writing of *The Spirit of the Laws*. And in the course of these remarks he gives three illuminating literary references. In addition, there are the hints provided by Montesquieu's other literary allusions: the epigraph to the whole work, the epigraphs to Books XX and XXVIII, and the quotation from the *Aeneid* which ends the whole work. All of these quotations or references are in Latin except for one in Italian; all are from poets or artists. None are in Greek, none are from philosophers. None, therefore, immediately remind us of ancient political philosophy. The spirit of all these allusions is the same as the spirit of Montesquieu's remarks at the end of the Preface, where he emphasizes his creative originality. No classical political philosopher lays so much emphasis on originality. This was not because the classics thought justified boasting was distasteful, but rather because they did not place as high a value on originality as Montesquieu does. Why originality should be so important becomes clearer from consideration of Montesquieu's other hints.

The epigraph to the whole work is a line from Ovid: "a child created without a mother" (*Metamorphoses* ii 553).[20] By these words Montesquieu indicates in the

first place his sense of both originality and proprietorship. His work is like a child who is more his own
than any natural child. This impression is
strengthened by the second of the poetic quotations
in the Preface: "twice the hand of the father failed"
(see *Aeneid* vi 33). By these words Montesquieu compares himself to Daedalus, the most famous human
artist of antiquity, in the act of sculpting an image
of his own son. Since the epigraphs to Books XX and
XXVIII are not directly connected with the work as
a whole, they are of less significance for us now, but
both are lines referring to what is said by poets, one
a character in Virgil, one Ovid himself. In the Preface,
after referring to the *difficulties* he had while writing
by identifying himself with a Roman, or an ancient
Italian artist, Montesquieu refers to his successful
completion of his task by identifying himself· with
a modern Italian painter, using his words: "I too am
a painter." Montesquieu is a creator like the ancient
artist, but his creation is modern.

Montesquieu's modern creation is not merely the
book he has written. The book, if it succeeds, will
help men; it will bring about a change in political
life. Montesquieu's creation is, then, a new mode of
political life throughout the world. In his first quotation in the Preface, Montesquieu identifies his writing
with the writing of the Cumaean Sibyl (see *Aeneid*
vi 75). Montesquieu is a prophet; he is a prophet
as well as a creator because his creation is a remaking
of the future. The Cumaean Sibyl showed Aeneas
his future—the obstacles he would face and how he
would overcome those obstacles to become the
founder of Rome. *The Spirit of the Laws* ends with the

shout which went up from Aeneas and his companions when they sighted the new land which was to be theirs: "Italiam, Italiam . . ." (see *Aeneid* iii 523). Montesquieu is the prophet and the creator, the educator, of the founders of a new Rome, a new order of things for mankind. As we have noted, Montesquieu states in Book XXIX that the purpose of his work is the formation of legislators. But at the end of the same book he indicates that it is the philosophers who are *the* examples of legislators (XXIX 19). The philosopher, as the teacher of legislators, is himself the legislator par excellence. Whereas according to the classics the political philosopher could never fully assume the role of legislator because he could never be pursuaded to take political things seriously enough,[21] for Montesquieu the philosopher almost becomes identified with the legislator.

Montesquieu's benevolence to man is the benevolence of a father, a maker of men; it is like the benevolence of a god. The epigraph to the whole work identifies Montesquieu with Hephaistos, the only god who succeeded in creating a son (the hero Erichtonius) by himself, because of, or despite, his unconsummated pursuit of the goddess of wisdom.[22]

The Stoic emperors were benevolent because they "believed" they had to give themselves up to a god who worked through them. They disdained ordinary pleasures and pains, hopes and fears, because of their religion. Montesquieu is benevolent and can share their disdain, because he can become like a god. In the philosophic creator of a new political order there exists the fullest possible harmony between self-interest and public spirit. The principal motive for the philosopher, as for his legislator-students, is only a supremely powerful manifestation of the strongest motivation all men feel—the interest of proprietorship, a sublime self-preservation which combines glory and the perpetuation of oneself through one's lasting work or product.

In Montesquieu perhaps more than in any other modern philosopher, we are made aware of the amazing, nay, the astounding paradox of the attempt to explain the highest human activity as some form of the desire for self-preservation. Throughout Montesquieu's work one senses always an exquisite taste and a passionate love of the truth. The harmonious combination of urbanity, wisdom, and humanity remind one more than once of what one finds in the Platonic dialogues; the description of the *homme d'esprit*, which is no doubt a self-portrait, reminds one immediately of Socrates. But whereas the Platonic dialogues are devoted to the understanding of such a man and of the whole of human life in light of the possibility of such a human type, in Montesquieu taste and philosophy are truly subordinate themes, and the attempt is made to understand them almost exclusively in the light of the rest of human life.

> Plato thanked heaven for the fact that he was born in the days of Socrates; and I, I thank heaven for the fact that it made me born in the government where I live, and that it wished me to obey those whom it made me love. (Preface)

Plato was most thankful for the blessed chance that gave him a philosophic teacher and friend; Montesquieu is most thankful for the chance that gave him a secure political order which provided an opportunity for his political enterprise.

We have seemed to stray from the theme of commerce, but we were inevitably led to do so by our need to fathom what was implied in Montesquieu's praise of the French way of life in contrast to the English way of life. We now understand better the exact status and limits of what is implied in this praise of France.

In the rest of Book XX Montesquieu investigates in detail what political practices are most conducive to the increase and extension of commerce. While of great practical importance, these recommendations are in general simply the consequences of what has already been stated. We will confine ourselves to an explanation of the order of the chapters and the general thrust of the argument.

After making even clearer the superior efficiency of the commerce of economy and of the commercial practices of England in particular, Montesquieu shows that nations which lack a commerce of economy should try to profit from nations which possess one, rather than attempting to frustrate those nations (XX 6–8). All nations, even those with a commerce of luxury, should try to emulate the universality of English international trade: Montesquieu advocates not "free trade" but floating tariffs carefully geared to the encouragement of greater trade (XX 7, 9). Some advantageous commercial institutions like large banks, trading companies, and free ports are not possible in monarchies because the structure of government cannot permit such power in the hands of individuals from the lower classes (XX 10–11); but wherever possible, all nations should imitate the freedom of movement of persons and goods practiced in England and other commercial republics (XX 12–18). After these chapters on the salient beneficial practices of the commerce of economy and how they may be applied in monarchies, Montesquieu devotes four chapters to explaining how to avoid the greatest danger to commerce in monarchies: the stifling of free competition by the prince and nobles (XX 19–22). The book concludes by delineating the extremely rare cases in which commerce may be bad for a country: here Montesquieu opposes the notion that a country which is rich need not become commercial, for no country is ever prosperous enough (XX 23).

In Book XXI Montesquieu turns from contemporary practices to study the history of commerce and of the relation between commerce and politics. Throughout *The Spirit of the Laws* Montesquieu draws lessons from history, but commerce is the only topic whose history merits a separate book. This is due not only to the inherent importance of commerce. With regard to commerce even more than criminal law (cf. XII 2) the significance of history is not limited to scattered examples of helpful practices. The world history of commerce reveals a faltering and yet ultimately progressive development. Book XXI makes more explicit the fact that *The Spirit of the Laws* foreshadows a universalistic philosophy of history. Montesquieu does not imply that all human history possesses a meaning which makes it rational; but he does imply that in the course of history something which has meaning has been developing. Montesquieu takes the first step in the direction of the teaching that world history has a nontranscendent meaning or pattern. The problem of human nature is solved not by nature but by man; and not simply through man's "figuring it out" at one time but through the collective effort of men and nations down through the ages. Up to now the progress in the knowledge of commerce and economics has been largely unconscious, and much of the knowledge acquired has been forgotten. Through his historical study and his implicit encouragement of further research, Montesquieu wishes to make men conscious of this process and thus lead them to a full recovery of what has already been learned.

The intention of Book XXI, then, is to found the discipline of economic history. This explains what at first appears to be excessive scholarly zeal. By economic history Montesquieu means neither economic determinism nor useless pedantry, but rather the conventional study of political history informed and animated by the desire to learn about commerce and economics.

Montesquieu begins the book by showing what history reveals to be the relationship between "physical causes" and commerce. We thus learn what kind of trade can be expected between different parts of the world, depending on the varying needs of peoples and levels of civilization in different climates (XXI 1–4). Within this general physical setting, commerce has varied with the *political* activities of man. The rest of the book follows those activities in strict chronological order. The chief general lessons are: the importance of the development of technology, especially naval technology (XXI 6, 9, 10, 11, 22); the way in which luxury encourages commerce in monarchies and despotisms but discourages the full growth of commerce in republics (XXI 6, 16); the fact that Rome, which has been always considered justly admirable and emulated as a political regime, is from the point of view of commerce in no way admirable and not to be emulated (XXI 13–17); and, finally, the danger to commerce of traditional philosophic and theological speculation, which turns men from material to spiritual pursuits (XXI 20).

Montesquieu closes the book with a chapter on the evil consequences of the contemporary Spanish thirst for gold. Spain is the extreme case of the preoccupation with false theories about the relation between money and wealth. This error is widespread in one form or another: what we today refer to as "mercantilism" was a powerful and often pernicious economic doctrine in Montesquieu's time. In the following book he therefore turns to a lengthy dissertation on money and finance.

We will not follow the largely technical arguments of this book. With only minor exceptions, Montesquieu's economic theory is an endorsement of laissez-faire economics *avant la lettre* (see esp. XXII 10, 15; cf. XX 7ff., and XXI 21–22). One of the most widely ignored facts of the history of thought is that Montesquieu shares with Adam Smith, his successor by a generation, the honor of being the founder of modern economics. As Alain Cotta has remarked, "the study of economic thought, with a few rare exceptions, has not been seriously undertaken except for authors whose work dates subsequent to 1789".[23] And this ignorance about the origins of modern economics has led to ignorance about economics itself. It is not well enough understood that modern economics is not the necessary and inevitable view of man's commercial activity in the world, but the product of a specific revolution in political philosophy which justified and created the freeing of man's unlimited desire for acquisition.

The books on commerce are followed by a book investigating the conditions, practices, and laws which foster population growth. As d'Alembert remarks, "population and the number of inhabitants have an immediate connection with commerce," for prosperity and commercial growth are dependent on an adequate and increasing supply of men to produce, transport, and consume goods.[24] Today we are likely to be somewhat perplexed at the fear of underpopulation. We seem to have learned that commercial prosperity brings gigantic increases in population without any special efforts. But Montesquieu, together with many of his contemporaries,[25] saw a constant tendency in temperate climates toward a dearth of population, and a consequent threat to the growth of commerce. While it is certain that Montesquieu gravely mistook the nature of the problem of population, we can see that his concern is not entirely misplaced when we recall the fact that, in the time since, France has been constantly plagued with a problem of decline in relative population. Montesquieu states the nature of his concern and the reason for it in the opening chapter. He begins Book XXIII by quoting at length the hymn to love with which Lucretius opens his *De Rerum Natura*. Whereas Montesquieu began the book on commerce with his own poem, he salutes love through someone else's poem. This implied subordination and perhaps denigration of love is further emphasized by the source he uses: Lucretius understood love as the sexual propagation engaged in by all animate material beings. It is in this light that Montesquieu now looks at human love. He is here interested almost exclusively in the sexuality which increases population growth and which at the same time fosters the sweet natural pleasures of family life, the pleasures which have been part of man almost from the very beginning (XXIII 10).

The great obstacle to human propagation in the family is the fact that women oppose it for the sake of certain ideas they have—principally ideas of vanity and of another, romantic, sort of love. Montesquieu's underlying aim throughout this book is the reestablishment of the interest in creating a family in opposition to these and other conflicting interests. In the light of the danger of underpopulation, Montesquieu is led rather far in opposing the spirit of France and its freedom for women. We remember that England is unromantic, but has a good family life. France must in this respect become more like England; the pleasures and charms of gallantry must give way, in some measure, to the commercial need for population growth. We see here one of the clearest indications of Montesquieu's preference for the spirit of England over the spirit of France.

In the first nine chapters Montesquieu discusses the institutions of marriage and the family with a view to determining the best conditions for propagation (XXIII 2–10). He then turns to the effect on propagation of extrafamilial influences. He begins by stating the general principle that harsh government, like all other harshness, is an obstacle to propagation (XXIII 11). In the chapters immediately following, he investigates the relation of the physical environment of civilized peoples to their propagation (XXIII 12–15). The last series of chapters, and the most important, is devoted to the ways the legislator can influence propagation, especially to increase it (XXIII 16–19). Characteristically, Montesquieu focuses on the European situation.

In the transition to this theme Montesquieu notes that some climates create conditions which lead to adequate propagation and even to a problem of overpopulation. In such areas as China the encouragement of abortion and infanticide are grim political necessities. This is not, however, the case in Europe where the problem seems to be underpopulation.

But Montesquieu immediately shows us that this is not always the case. There are certain forms of government which create a problem of overpopulation even in Europe. These are the virtuous republics of Greek antiquity. The effect of these republics on population seems at first a sign of their excellence: they created conditions of peace and prosperity which favored population growth. But the growth they could accommodate was limited. Given their poverty, the idleness of the citizens, and their strictly agrarian economic foundations, they were unable to deal with the natural results of the peace they established. Here, as in China, abortion and infanticide and perhaps even homosexuality must be encouraged; but here it is a result of the political institutions. This is by no means the first time that Montesquieu has drawn our attention to the similarities between life in despotic China and life in virtuous republics (cf. VIII 21; XIX 16–21). Montesquieu ends his chapter on the population policies of these republics with the famous remark, "There are countries where a man is worth nothing; there are some where he is worth less than nothing" (XXIII 17). One of the consequences of the fact that the Greek political thinkers talk only of virtue, while modern political thinkers talk only of commerce, finance, riches, and luxury (III 3), is that "the Greek political thinkers talk to us always of the great number of citizens who wear away the republic, [while] today's political thinkers talk to us only of the means to augment the number of citizens" (XXIII 26). Modern, commercial political life will have room for every human being.

Most of the rest of the book is devoted to the key theme—the population policies of Rome and how they may be applied to France and modern Europe. Rome is most instructive and helpful because she faced the same problem that modern France and Europe face. Rome was underpopulated, and the luxury of the empire made men and women reluctant to raise families. Montesquieu praises those Roman laws which encouraged propagation through appeals to feminine vanity, through material rewards and honors for both fathers and mothers, and through some mild reinvigoration of public supervision of family morality. But there was a great and ultimately insuperable obstacle to the success of these laws in the Roman empire. And this obstacle is also present "among us." Vanity, luxury, and the opinions these give to men and women can be overcome; they are not the greatest enemies of population growth. The real enemy is Christianity, which makes honorable and even profitable a life of celibacy.

Christianity's effect on population is pernicious not only because it removes the men and women who are priests and nuns from the available supply of propagators. In addition, the denigration of the holiness of marriage encourages a general indifference to marriage:

> The principles of religion are extremely influential on the propagation of the human species: sometimes they encourage it, like among the Jews, the Mohammedans, the Guebres, the Chinese; sometimes they oppose it, as they did among the Romans who became Christians. (XXIII 22)

Christianity forestalls the possibility of laws which discourage childlessness through penalties and dishonor: "When celibacy has preeminence, there can no longer be honor for marriage . . ." (XXIII 22). In addition, Montesquieu suggests that one cannot expect men to practice true celibacy—the public encouragement of celibacy leads to adultery and childless sexual indulgence:

> It is a rule drawn from nature that, the more one diminishes the number of marriages which can be made, the more one corrupts those which are made; the fewer married men and women, the more infidelity in the marriages; just as when there are more robbers, there are more robberies. (XXIII 22)

Here Montesquieu's criticism of the effects of Christianity goes beyond its direct effect on marriage. He speaks of the general tendency to idleness, laziness, and retreat from affairs engendered by Christianity among the Romans. Christianity, adopting and magnifying certain tendencies in pagan philosophy, encouraged a forgetting of all the activities required for producing populous, prosperous peoples. It did this in the name of a "perfection attached to all that leads to a speculative life" (XXIII 21). Book XXIII thus introduces us to and sets the tone for Montesquieu's extensive treatment of religion in the two books that follow.

It should come as no surprise to us that Montesquieu concludes his treatment of commerce with a lengthy examination of the relation between the laws and religion. The commercial political order envisioned by Montesquieu stands or falls with the pervasive awareness of the need for security through private acquisition encouraged by the freeing of vanity and the tastes of luxury. The greatest enemy to this attitude of mind is the belief spread by the Christian religion that men must restrain these passions for the sake of an immortality far more secure and enjoyable than any earthly benefit. This belief makes men fearful of fully indulging the selfishness required by commerce and incapable of the great efforts needed to make it flourish. Montesquieu's project cannot succeed unless he can show the way to a destruction or emasculating transformation of Christianity. The endorsement and promotion of commerce leads inevitably to a confrontation with Christianity.

8

RELIGION

Religion in general, and the Christian religion in particular, advances an authoritative claim to give guidance in all spheres of human life. Anyone who reflects in a comprehensive way about politics and who gives any credence to this claim must accord to religion a paramount place in his reflections. Montesquieu shows at the very outset, by the place of the word "religion" in the full title of *The Spirit of the Laws*, that he does not accord it this paramount place. He indicates that the relation of the laws to religion will be treated only after several other important relations have been treated. We have indicated the grave doubts that are cast on his orthodoxy by his reflections about God in Book I. Nevertheless, we might have gathered from the title that religion would occupy a place of considerable importance, coming prior to commerce and other topics.

In fact the relation of the laws to religion is the last particular relationship discussed.[1] Montesquieu turns to a thematic discussion of religion only after he has presented the bulk of his teaching; in the twenty-three preceding books where that presentation has been made, religion has played a very minor role. These observations suggest that for Montesquieu religion does not contribute substantially to an understanding of what good political life requires. They might even suggest that, except in the virtuous republic and in despotism, religion is of little practical use. It would then seem that religion must be treated at some length only because "belief " stands as a massive political fact which we cannot ignore but which cannot much help us: "The prejudices of superstition are superior to all other prejudices, and its reasons to all other reasons" (XVIII 18). In the case of what Montesquieu calls "today's" Christian religion, the remarks to which we have drawn attention in the pages immediately preceding seem to show that the fact of widespread belief in this religion's particular "prejudices" poses a considerable obstacle to sound politics and economics.

Montesquieu's presentation of the relation of the laws to religion is divided into two books. In the first his intention is to show which *dogmas* are more advantageous; in the second, he discusses what are the best arrangements of religious *institutions* within a state. The teaching of the second book is largely a consequence of the first.

The manner in which Montesquieu introduces his reflections on the advantages and disadvantages of the various religious beliefs and practices confirms our impression that religion makes no contribution to political theory. Montesquieu says that in this work he will not discuss theology. Although he is aware that "there may be things which would not be entirely true except in a human manner of thinking," he has not "considered them in their relation to more sublime truths." The likely possibility of a contradiction between rational and revealed political truth is unimportant. Religion is to be judged by standards derived from "human thought" and "the happiness in this life" (XXVI 1).

This posture might well seem to imply a "ceding of the interests of true religion to the interests of politics" (XXVI 1). Anticipating or drawing attention to this difficulty, Montesquieu denies such a consequence. But he can make this denial only by implicitly contradicting himself and denying the possibility he mentioned previously of a divergence between human and "sublime" truth. His assertion that the political principles following from Christian teaching are identical with the principles of rational political science is supported only by the argument that since Christianity wants men "to love one another," or to be charitable, it must "without a doubt" also want the best laws among men. The uncharacteristic rhetorical phrase "without a doubt" would not be needed were the demonstration truly indubitable; Montesquieu's argument, of course, simply begs the question of whether Christianity does not call for a sacrifice of some "happiness in this life" for the sake of "felicities of the other life" (XXIV 1). Montesquieu shows by his contradiction and by his inept argument that despite his explicit claim to the contrary he does in fact "cede the interests of the true religion to the interests of politics." What *is* true, however, is Montesquieu's claim that he wishes to "unite" the two interests. In these two books on religion, in contrast to the preceding books, Montesquieu does no more than allude to the threats Christianity poses to propagation and commercialism; having already pointed to these threats earlier, his policy here is one of reinterpreting

Christianity so as to make it harmless. Montesquieu proceeds to show what are acceptable or beneficial religious dogmas from a purely political point of view and then assumes that Christianity holds those dogmas and no others. By this he seems to show through example what should be the policy of a legislator in a Christian country who wishes to follow his teaching.

After his introductory chapter, Montesquieu enters the subject matter by piously defending all religion against the famous, or notorious, argument of Pierre Bayle. Bayle was the first political philosopher who openly advocated the possibility and desirability of an atheistic society. By defending religion, Montesquieu lends respectability to his own position. At the same time, and more important, he seems to show that the inference we were led to by his earlier silence about religion is wrong: for Montesquieu religion almost always serves a beneficial political function. What Montesquieu emphasizes most, however, is the advantage of religion in principalities where it can check the power of the supreme ruler. We remember his earlier remarks on the importance of religion in despotism and on the role of the clergy in the monarchical balance of powers (II 4; IV 10; V 14). One would have to say that Montesquieu is at least less emphatic about the value of religion in well-balanced political systems. And he does admit that "religion is sometimes abused"; he is therefore unwilling to take on himself the task of proving that every man and every people should have religion:

> The question is *not* to know whether it would
> be better that a certain man or a certain people

should have no religion at all, rather than abuse
the one it has. . . . (Italics mine.)

We are at this point led to wonder whether no religion
may not be preferable to a bad religion among certain
peoples, especially well-governed peoples (cf. XXIV
14, 15, 19, 22; note especially the word "pernicious"
in the title of XXIV 19). It becomes important, then,
to know what constitutes bad religion, or an "abuse"
of religion. And after having seen Montesquieu's
defense of religion in general, we expect him to show
us next the relative merits of various religions, starting
from the best or most advantageous as a standard.

In the next chapters he does indeed turn from a
discussion of all religions, including idolatrous ones,
to a praise of Christianity. But this praise is at first
rather weak. Christianity is praised only as preferable
to the modern alternative, Islam, and especially
because of its restraining effect in despotic regions.
Christianity moderates absolute rule better than Islam
because of the "softness" of its teachings (XXIV 3–4).

We are thus kept in suspense as to whether Christianity is an advantageous religion in all regimes. In
chapter 6 Montesquieu finally answers our doubts,
praising highly the contribution Christianity makes
to good citizenship. His praise is framed as an answer
to another impious attack by Bayle. Again his role
as defender of the faith gives him respectability; but
at the same time his introduction of the objection of
Bayle, "this great man," serves to introduce serious
doubts about the political soundness of Christianity.
His method of answering these doubts shows his
essential agreement with them. In order to refute
Bayle, Montesquieu shows himself compelled to radi-

cally reinterpret the traditional distinction between the "laws" of the Christian religion and its "counsels." The laws, which alone are absolutely binding, include everything conducive to good citizenship, and nothing more. Everything pertaining to "perfection," to the other world, to "the heart," everything which cannot be applied to "the universality of men," must cease to be considered a "law" and be relegated to the status of a "counsel" which is by no means absolutely binding (XXIV 7). Thus understood, Christianity is advantageous and forms the standard for judging the political advantage of all other religions.[2]

The chapter praising and redefining "Christianity" is followed by a chapter praising a "false" pagan religion because its precepts were devoted to the "laws of morality" (by which Montesquieu here seems to mean the principles of reciprocal justice necessary for any society). Montesquieu follows this with a brief chapter implicitly praising a Jewish sect on similar grounds; finally, he turns to a praise of the pagan Stoics (including the apostate Julian) and a condemnation of the contemplative life. It becomes clear that what constitutes a good religion is merely its enforcement of the rules necessary for maintaining a social bond within a regime, and no more. Both "religion and the civil laws ought to tend *principally* to make men good citizens . . ." (XXIV 14). This understanding of religion implies that insofar as the laws and customs of a people are politically sound, religion should simply reinforce adherence to them; where the political institutions are defective, the ruler should emphasize those elements of the religious prescriptions which can remedy the defects; where religion itself promotes antisocial behavior, the laws must try, without contradicting the religious teachings, to substitute motives for useful behavior (XXIV 14, 18). In addition, religion, as an institution of "the legislator" (XXIV 6, 24), should, like all other political institutions, conform to the physical environment (XXIV 24–26).

In his praise of non-Christian religions, Montesquieu makes no more than vague allusions to their specific doctrines about divinity. Two of them deny any after-life (the religion of the Essenes and of the Stoics); the third (that of Pegu), which seems to have instilled as much "softness and compassion" as Christianity, was extremely undogmatic and tolerant. Montesquieu seems by these examples to teach that the less doctrine about divinity the better. In the best case, religion will de-emphasize all but moral-political precepts. In later chapters Montesquieu discusses how various transcendent or spiritual doctrines may be interpreted so as to bring them into harmony with the needs of men, who are "made to conserve themselves . . . and to do all the activities of society" (XXIV 11). The general principle governing these chapters is that "it is less the truth or falsity of a dogma which renders it useful or pernicious to men in the civil state than the use or abuse one makes of it" (XXIV 19).

Montesquieu thus indicates the lines along which Christianity is to be reinterpreted in order to make it harmonize with the needs of the commercial republic. Like Locke, Montesquieu promotes a new understanding of the "reasonableness of Christianity."

Chapter Eight

Nothing reveals more clearly Montesquieu's refusal simply to bow to the "general spirit of a nation" than his opposition to the religion so deeply entrenched in the manners, morals, customs, and traditions of every European nation.[3]

The reasons for Montesquieu's policy of "uniting" politics and religion rather than opposing religion openly as Bayle had done include more than a concern for his own safety and the respectability of his work. In the next book, when discussing the reasons for tolerance of religion by government authority, Montesquieu takes up thematically the question of how best to "change religion." He argues at first that it is bad to change or destroy the dominant religion because such a radical change in the way of life will unsettle men's opinions about everything and create the threat of revolutionary upheaval (XXV 11). But in the next chapter he implies that this prudential prohibition applies only to changes carried out swiftly and through force or violence. The proper way to change religion is by tempting men:

> A more sure way to attack a religion is by favor, by the commodities of life, by the hope of wealth; not by what drives away, but by what makes one forget; not by what brings indignation, but by what makes men lukewarm, when other passions act on our souls, and those which religion inspires are silent. *Règle générale:* with regard to change in religion, invitations are stronger than penalties. (XXV 12)

Christianity will be overcome by making men "forget" everything which is at a tension with securing "the commodities of life." All that is required on the part of "political writers" like Montesquieu is to show the way to an understanding of Christianity which is not in conflict with devotion to commerce and comfort; the inherent attractions of these things will do the rest.

Montesquieu's discussion in Book XXV of the proper institutional place of the religious "cult" within the political order follows strictly from this understanding of the proper dogmas. He begins by drawing our attention to the effects of two extreme postures toward religion: both the pious man and the atheist are preoccupied with religion, the one because he loves it and the other because he fears it. The purpose of Book XXV as a whole is to combat both extremes, to make men neither pious nor atheistic but simply "lukewarm" or indifferent. All Montesquieu's recommendations tend toward reducing to a minimum the role of religion in the life of the citizenry.

He speaks first of the motives which attract men to religion. One must understand these motives in order to know how to placate them, how to limit religion to what is necessary to it and keep from it what is not necessary. According to Montesquieu, men are led to religion primarily by "hope and fear," that is, by the passions which are the primary motives for all human activity. Vanity is often the motive which leads men to choose one religion over another. But men are also attracted by a certain universal love of morality (XXV 2, 3). Montesquieu is silent about motives of gratitude or awe or recognition of beauty and order; neither does he mention the motive of anger or revenge (contrast Plato *Laws* 886[a], 887[c]–888[a]). However that may be, the motives Montesquieu does recognize imply that religion requires a rather considerable external cult, including property and splendid adornments (XXV 3–4). The wealth of the church can and should be kept within limits; the legislator best achieves this through "indirect means" (XXV 5).

Besides restrictions on the material wealth and power of the church, the other most important limitation is the enforcement of toleration and the discouragement of proselytizing. But toleration should be extended only to existing religions; religious freedom is not itself the aim of toleration. Peace, freedom from religious strife and discordant preoccupation with religion, is the proper end of the legislator (XXV 9–10).

Montesquieu's treatment of religion becomes somewhat bolder in Book XXV.[4] On the one hand his discussion of the institutions of religion induces him to speak more concretely about the Catholic Church. On the other hand, and more important, he contradicts his original disavowal of an intention to enter on any theological speculation: he goes so far as to suggest that the argument for limitations on gifts to the church can be based on the "natural light," the natural theology, of the pagan philosopher in Plato's *Laws* (XXV 7; cf. 13). In the book which follows (Book XXVI), Montesquieu will go still further, entering into a discussion of the central theme of Christian political theology, the relation between divine, natural, and human law. Despite the initial pretense of avoiding theology, it in fact proves impossible to speak comprehensively about politics without confronting Christian theology: this theology has a widespread influence on the political practice of all Europeans. From Montesquieu's point of view, the two worst effects of this influence are first, the belief that Christians are subject to a universal divine law and, second, the belief that man everywhere is so constituted by his nature that he is subject to some of the rules of divine law, prior to any revelation, through natural law. Throughout *The Spirit of the Laws* Montesquieu has wished to combat the universalism or doctrinairism of previous natural law teachings. We have emphasized his opposition to Hobbesian and Lockean natural law. But that opposition extends a fortiori to Christian natural law, which placed universal demands on men considerably more stringent than those imposed by Locke or Hobbes. In the next book Montesquieu will bring this implication into full view. The systematic statement of Montesquieu's own understanding with regard to natural and divine law is therefore intended in large part as a continuation of his attempt in Books XXIV and XXV to protect political life from the pernicious effects of Christianity.[5]

9

NATURAL LAW AND THE PRUDENCE OF THE LEGISLATOR

Montesquieu presents his systematic account of the relation between human, natural, and divine law within the context of a general consideration of all the different "orders of law." The variety of legal orders is a reflection of the variety of relationships existing among men and between man and God. Each of these relationships has its own goals and hence its own realm of "right," comprising rules aimed at achieving those goals. For example, a man's belonging to a political community subjects him to political and civil law; his belonging to a church subjects him to canon law; his belonging to a family subjects him to domestic law. According to Montesquieu there are nine such orders of law. Eight of these comprise laws promulgated to a community by some authority: these range from the most general and broad, the divine law given by God to all men, to the most narrow and particular, the domestic law given by the head of a family. But the first and apparently most general order, natural law, would seem to have a somewhat different origin. It comprises the rules deducible from the relation men have to one another prior to, and underlying, any established community. The intention of Book XXVI is to teach the legislative authority in each kind of community the extent to which his order of law should or should not be guided by and subject to other orders of law.

Natural Law and the Legislator

Montesquieu hints at the very outset that he hopes to replace the traditional legal teaching with a new teaching that restricts the scope of universal divine law and gives greater latitude to the statesman's prudence. When he mentions political law in the list of orders of law, he says that it "has for its object that *human* wisdom which has founded *all* societies" (XXVI 1; italics mine). This book which deals with divine law is the only book whose first chapter begins (and ends) with the word *hommes* (men). But in order to make the replacement acceptable, in order to cause as little shock as possible to entrenched opinion, Montesquieu makes the new appear in the outward trappings of the old. This is the reason for the obvious stylistic peculiarity of Book XXVI and, to a lesser extent, of its sequel, Book XXIX: these are the only books most of whose chapter titles are in that wordy, hortatory, and doctrinal style so characteristic of scholastic treatises on law and duty.

The new teaching about the correct relation between human law and higher law represents the "sublimity of *human* reason" (XXIV 1; italics mine); Book XXVI seems a fitting culmination and conclusion of Montesquieu's theoretical argument as a whole. And yet why does Montesquieu wait until almost the end of his work to state systematically his position on a question of such importance? Book XXVI is in great part a continuation of Book I; we now learn the politically applicable natural laws which can be deduced from the description of human nature and natural law given at the beginning of the work. In the intervening books these laws have been mentioned, but very infrequently. Indeed, one gets the impression that Montesquieu is reluctant to state fully his teaching about natural law, and that he does so only when compelled by the need to combat Christian political theology.

The reason for this reluctance appears when we remind ourselves of the place of natural standards in Montesquieu's thought as a whole. While the satisfaction of the needs natural to man is the aim of politics, it has appeared very questionable whether the heterogeneity of political life permits the formulation of any universal rules showing how this goal is to be achieved. As it turns out, there are some such rules, but their scope is very limited. By not stating them systematically until almost the end of the work, and there in the context of a subdued attack on Christian thought, Montesquieu both indicates his fear of their being misinterpreted and at the same time forces the reader to see them in the context of the complexity of political life as shown in the preceding books.

Montesquieu begins by discussing in the second chapter the relation between divine and human law. Divine law aims at "the best," or perfection. Political life aims at "the good" (XXVI 2). Since perfection is by its nature always the same, divine law has an unchangeable character. But there are many earthly "goods," or what is good takes many forms in many different circumstances. Sometimes the good is merely the prevention or reparation of the bad. Political or human law must therefore be innovative and adaptable. Preoccupation with divine law tends to make one indifferent to these lower goods; in case of a conflict it makes one refuse to sacrifice what is always needed to achieve the best, for the sake of what may temporarily be needed to achieve the good. Montesquieu therefore states by implication the principle that divine law should be restricted in its application to the sphere of the individual in his private relations with God (cf. XXVI 9). Only in a despotism does Montesquieu seem to recommend a great scope for divine law, where it has the advantage of limiting the pernicious caprice of the tyrant (compare Aristotle *Politics* 1349^b 39ff.).

Montesquieu does not yet make explicit the bearing of this discussion on Christian divine law. By now we begin to expect the worst with regard to Montesquieu's estimation of Christianity. But, after all, Montesquieu has just previously tried to persuade us that it is only the "counsels" of Christianity, not its precepts or laws, which are concerned with "perfection": the precepts or laws of Christianity were said to be in harmony with good citizenship (XXIV 6–7). In fact, however, Montesquieu proceeds gradually to reveal the falseness of this understanding and explicitly apply the principle of chapter 2 to Christianity as well.

The natural law as Montesquieu formulates it in chapter 3 is simply an adaptation of the natural law presented in Book I. Natural law is identified with "natural defense," primarily of oneself and secondarily of one's family. Civil society is a means to natural defense, and in all times and places human law must obey natural law or contradict and eventually destroy itself.

The second part of natural defense, the part pertaining to the family, is not as simple in its application or as purely natural as the first, and so Montesquieu devotes more space to explaining it. There are two reasons for this complexity, derivative from the nature of the family. First, the family is neither as clearly defined nor as permanent as the individual. The problem is indicated by such situations as divorce, children born out of wedlock, and marriage alliances made prior to puberty. The law must intervene with conventions which help stabilize and preserve the family. Second, whereas almost everyone can be counted on to care for his own preservation, it is not so certain that everyone will care for his family's preservation. The law must therefore intervene here also to enforce such care (XXVI 3–5).

After stating his own understanding of natural law, Montesquieu refutes a false understanding in chapter 6, immediately following. He denies the notion that natural law demands that fathers bequeath their property to their children (XXVI 6). He thus emphasizes the very limited demands of natural law. At the same time, by indicating that the error in question stems at least in part from the influence of St. Augustine, Montesquieu points to the way natural law has been extended or distorted under Christian influence. The extension of the part of natural law applying to the family leads to dangerous political consequences because it restricts the arrangements men may think suitable for the succession to monarchies.

Chapter 6 is the introduction to a series of eight chapters on the tension between religious and civil laws (XXVI 6–14). Here Montesquieu moves step by step to show that the principle of chapter 2 must be applied to the Christian law. Indeed, he reveals that this is especially necessary with Christian law because of the especially pernicious character of this religious law. Clearly Montesquieu must proceed with caution; it is much easier and safer to speak in a general way about the need for separating divine and human law than it is to show concretely that the laws of France and Europe should not be guided by precepts of Christianity.

After having implied in chapter 6 that natural law should not be understood in terms of Christian precepts, in chapter 7 Montesquieu turns to a discussion of the possibility of direct conflict between "precepts of religion" and the natural law demanding preservation or defense of the community. His examples, which illustrate the necessary precedence of the natural law, are all non-Christian. Montesquieu never explicitly shows a conflict between natural and Christian law. In the next chapters he ceases, temporarily, to speak of natural law and shifts his attention to possible conflict between *civil* and religious law. He shows first the need to keep Christian canon law separate from civil law (XXVI 8); then he proceeds to a chapter whose title states that only "rarely" should civil affairs be governed even by "principles" taken from religious law (XXVI 9). Actually, his examples do not show *any* case in which the influence of religious law is good. And the examples now are Christian, although all are from ancient Roman days. Only in the chapter after this is Montesquieu willing at last to spell out the implications of this teaching for present-day experience, and then only with regard to a practice in nations which have recently been converted to Christianity (XXIV 10).[1]

After this elaborate approach calculated to de-emphasize his boldness as much as possible, Montes-

quieu finally attacks a European Catholic nation for
allowing its civil law to be guided by ideas of penitence
and perfection taken from Christian precepts. Even
at this point he ventures to attack only a practice
which was rather generally frowned upon in France,
the Spanish Inquisition (XXVI 11–12). His specific
example is more cautious than the principle it implies
or exemplifies. The movement of the argument of
these chapters is arrested at this point. The reader
is left to take the argument further in the direction
indicated—toward the goal of recommending the creation of a civil law which is oblivious to Christian law.

But even a more or less total separation of civil and
religious law (the apparent implication of Montesquieu's argument) is not to be considered an absolute
rule. Characteristically, he presents in the next chapter (XXVI 13) an example of how this separation may
sometimes be imprudent. Given the importance and
fragility of marriage, it is wise to enlist the aid of
religious law in solemnizing it. When religious law
"adds to" but does not "contradict" civil law, it may
be encouraged. In thus qualifying the separation of
church and state, Montesquieu merely follows the
spirit of his treatment of religion throughout these
three books. Wherever advisable, religion is to be used
to support the necessary social bond.

Montesquieu concludes his account of the higher
law which governs political life with a chapter devoted
to the limitations on incest (XXVI 14). This discussion
serves to epitomize his treatment of the relationship
of natural and divine law to civil law. Having shown
the pernicious effects of the belief in the applicability
of Christian religious law, Montesquieu now ceases

to speak of it and returns to speaking of natural law. While he still prudently avoids any mention of a contradiction between natural and Christian law, he makes it clear that natural law is far less strict with regard to incest, and would allow things which are anathemas to Christians. What marriages are to be forbidden depends strictly on what would endanger the family. While some relationships are always dangerous and therefore seem to fall under absolute prohibitions, there are other intrafamilial marriages, those between in-laws or first cousins, whose danger depends on circumstances which vary from one society to another. And even within marriage-relationships considered always dangerous, there are degrees of danger and therefore degrees of unnaturalness. Montesquieu goes so far as to imply that in some societies marriage between father and daughter may not be unnatural.

In short, religious law ceases to be a guide for the civil law. The only higher law is the natural law, and this is of a very limited scope. Natural law is similar to the "relations of justice prior to positive law" (I 1) in that it seems to demand only what almost all civil authorities must necessarily do in order to avert anarchy. Yet the demands of natural law are more limited—being confined to "natural defense"—and they are also stated more absolutely.

At this point the question at once arises, if natural law does no more than set the lowest requisites, or the distant outer bounds, for political and civil law, what principle guides the myriad decisions that must be made in formulating law within those bounds? In the chapters that follow Montesquieu shows the need for distinguishing between the various "orders" of man-made law without any further reference to natural law. To some extent what he says is based on simple common sense; but to no small degree Montesquieu must go beyond common sense, and it is this part of his discussion which reveals the character of the underlying principles. The most helpful section is the one immediately following the nine chapters on higher law. Here he discusses the necessity of a distinction between "political" and "civil" law (XXIV 15–18).

In order to understand the proper scope of the law governing civil society, Montesquieu is compelled to speak of the origin of civil society. The general character of a state's laws should be guided by the principle of liberty or security, which was and is their purpose. It is this principle which dictates the fundamental distinction between political and civil law.[2] Political law is the law which constitutes and preserves the civil society as a whole, the law which determines the ruler or the authority who makes laws regulating all members of the society. From the point of view of political law each individual must surrender completely his independence to the "empire of the city." But this surrender to "political law" should lead to the creation of a "civil law" which gives back to each individual, within the confines of the rule of law, a private sphere of security, and above all the use and enjoyment of the private property which is essential for maintaining security and comfort.

In the formulation of law, then, the civil authority should take its bearings by a principle originating in the nature of man. But this guiding natural principle of justice does not have the character of a "law." A law is a universal and unchangeable rule. This principle has rather the character of a goal or end. The goal cannot be stated as a rule or law because the degree of its realization changes and is dependent on the constantly varying political circumstances. The possibility for civil liberty changes from place to place and from time to time. Free regimes are frequently impossible. Even where they are possible, one cannot find rules which can be applied to all free regimes. There is a variety of free regimes, suited to varying circumstances, and what is possible in one is not possible in another. To take the example Montesquieu gives here, a virtuous republic requires the institution of ostracism, which temporarily deprives a man of all civil liberties solely because he is too talented (XXVI 17; cf. 18). Nor is it even possible to formulate a rule for any one kind of free regime, a rule demanding some given degree of civil liberty. For even in regimes where property is most fully protected it must sometimes be seized for political needs. One can recommend that there always be indemnity; but there may be times when the state cannot make recompense. Recommendations of this kind must be stated not as "laws" but only as "maxims" or "general rules" (*règles générales;* cf. II 2, 3, 4; V 4, 7, 8, 18; XII 5; XVI 15; XXVI 6). And the maxims must not be stated as clear-cut rules, for then they will only be violated some day and brought into contempt. One must limit oneself to saying something like this:

> Let us then pose as a maxim that, when it concerns the public good, the public good is never that one deprive an individual of his property,

or at least that the least possible part is to be taken away by any law or political regulation. (XXVI 15)

Even the preservation in free regimes of at least *some* separation between political and civil law cannot be made a natural law. On the one hand this rule is too general to be called a law: it does not tell us what precisely falls under the categories "political" and "civil." And on the other hand, there may be times when every law, except one, must be confounded or brought into question in order to preserve the society from destruction: "THE SAFETY OF THE PEOPLE IS THE SUPREME LAW" (XXVI 23: Montesquieu's capitals).

The only absolute rule deducible from nature is the law dictating the bare, minimal achievement of security for individuals and families. This is indeed absolute. Montesquieu makes it clear that in this respect his teaching about natural right is more absolutist than Plato's (XXVI 3). But what is to be done to achieve comfort, security, and liberty beyond this minimum cannot be dictated by a law. It is up to the statesman to strive to achieve the most that the circumstances allow. The statesman should not usually be guided by the ugly exigencies of extreme situations; he should always keep in mind the ultimate goal. But no rule can guide the choice of means to that goal, for unique situations are constantly appearing and extreme situations may occur at any time.

The discussion which shows the relationship of political and civil law to higher law leads to the conclusion that good political life depends not so much on higher law as on the prudence of the statesman, the "man on the spot." The book on the orders of law therefore serves as an introduction to the true conclusion and culmination of *The Spirit of the Laws*, the book devoted to the legislator and his prudent "composing" of the laws (Book XXIX).

At the very beginning of Book XXIX, Montesquieu states that the intention of the work as a whole has been to prove what should be the spirit of the legislator. In a sense, then, the description of the legislator is implicit in the teaching of all the earlier books taken together, where the problem of political life has been presented and certain solutions indicated. But it seems that Montesquieu's teaching would have been incomplete if he had not distilled from the earlier books the special character of the human being and the activity which bring these solutions into actual being. The students of *The Spirit of the Laws* need, if not a model, then at least some more than implicit description of the spirit and the mode of operation of the legislator. This need is especially acute in a world where, as Montesquieu believed, the reigning tradition subordinates prudence to the exaggerated preeminence of theory and legalism.

Montesquieu begins the book by describing the proper "spirit," or habitual attitude of mind, of the legislator. That spirit should be one of "moderation." The moderation of which Montesquieu speaks has much in common with the moderation and prudence the classics called for in statesmen and legislators. Indeed, the emphasis on prudence represents in the first place a return to the political science of antiquity.

Chapter Nine

But when we reflect on *The Spirit of the Laws* as a whole, as Montesquieu indicates we should in trying to understand all that is implied in this moderation, we recognize that he means to include something that goes beyond the classical spirit. For the ancients the activity of the lawgiver must be characterized by moderation principally because there is almost always a radical disproportion between the high aim of all political life and what is possible in most expectable situations. Moderation is the necessary toleration of or resignation to serious imperfection. Montesquieu certainly retains the notion that there is a great need for adaptation of goals to circumstances. But the more important meaning of the legislator's moderation involves something different.

That the character of the highest political virtue is different in Montesquieu and in the classics is not surprising. The virtue of deliberation is bound to be affected by the nature of the ends toward which it is directed. And for Montesquieu the goals of politics are much lower than they were for the ancients. The spirit of moderation, as Montesquieu emphasizes in chapter 1, is intimately connected with the realization that "liberty" or "security" is the true goal. Or in other words, the moderation of the legislator is the same as that of the "moderate" regimes. As we know from Book XIX, this goal requires not merely the tolerating but even the fostering of certain kinds of vice. What the classics tolerated as a necessary evil, Montesquieu welcomes as a good in itself. Here in chapter 1 he imitates Aristotle in speaking of the moral good as a mean; but for Aristotle this signified a mean between two vices, whereas for Montesquieu it signifies the mediocrity of virtue itself.

Natural Law and the Legislator

In addition to this change in general moral orientation, there are other more particular elements included in Montesquieu's notion of the legislator's moderation, and these are illustrated in the two examples he now gives us. In both examples we find something reminiscent of the classical spirit and at the same time something alien to it. The opening example teaches in the first place that the legislator should measure every particular improvement in its relation to his overall goal. With this sound advice the classics of course would have agreed. But Montesquieu goes further. His example is judicial procedure—a practice directly aimed at securing the liberty of the citizens. The sound general advice takes on a special significance. Montesquieu implies that the legislator should keep in the foreground the fact that his aim is providing the citizens with a sphere of private liberty and that therefore he must avoid pushing the means to this protected sphere so far as to invade and destroy it. The aim of government is in a sense simply letting the citizens alone. Governmental restraint or moderation is not just a response to the intractable complexity of politics; it is a part of the goal itself.

Through the second example, in chapter 2, Montesquieu shows that "moderation" includes a certain mellowness, softness, or humanity. Legal penalties should avoid becoming "atrocities." The difference between Montesquieu and the classics here is one of emphasis. He manifests a greater concern for the physical discomfort and the fears of the citizens. It is no accident that his example of "the cruelest laws" is drawn from antiquity.

After this discussion of moderation Montesquieu takes up what he, following the tradition, calls "prudence" (XXIX 5, 7)—the capacity to adapt goals to particular circumstances. The key circumstance to be considered is the nature of the regime for which the laws are to be given; the legislator must adapt his general understanding of the needs to be satisfied to the way those needs appear in his own political order (chapter 3). And the circumstances to be considered include not only the preexisting ones, but the very law to be instituted. The legislator must reflect on how the law will change the circumstances; he must try to foresee the indirect as well as the direct effects of a law (chapters 4–5).

We have seen that there can be no law or strict rules for the guidance of political societies beyond the minimal law of nature. This means that the legislator in his adaptation to circumstances must depend on experience. Since his own experience is necessarily limited, he is led to turn to the experience of other lawgivers in other times and places. The study of political history is a key part of the statesman's education. It has been a paramount feature of *The Spirit of the Laws* itself. But the same reason that renders general rules questionable makes the prescriptive character of history questionable: no two situations are really alike. Much can be learned from political history, but only if it is approached with appropriate subtlety and precaution. Montesquieu therefore devotes a number of chapters to showing by means of examples what must be taken into consideration when comparing two laws, or when investigating the applicability of any former law to new circumstances. These lessons serve at the same time to show through concrete instances the variety of factors which go together to give a law its character and effect.

Natural Law and the Legislator

In order truly to understand a law, we must know the precise difficulty it was intended to solve (XXIX 6); the wording of the law, or its precise mechanism (XXIX 7); the "motive" of the lawgiver, including the deeply held opinions and beliefs of the people to which the lawgiver responds (XXIX 8–10, 13); the connection of the law with other laws (XXIX 11, 14); and, in criminal law, the relation of the law to its penalties and to the penalties instituted by other laws (XXIX 12). A difference in any of these respects between two laws or situations may make them differ entirely. On the other hand, similarity in all these respects, or in those which are most relevant, makes laws and situations similar even if they appear otherwise (XXIX 10).

After having shown the complex considerations required in order to understand each situation requiring a law, Montesquieu turns to a discussion of the principles of style, tone, and form which should govern the actual composition of law. Here we gain an understanding of the full magnitude of the problem confronting the lawgiver. For while his deliberations about what law is best for the given situation must be complex, wide-ranging, adaptive, and subtle, the law itself cannot explicitly reflect any of this subtlety. Law must be concise, simple, and clear, possessing as few qualifications and being as little subject to change as possible. In addition, it should usually be given without reasons or explanations, and it ought always to be naive, or "innocent" (XXIX 16). The nature of law is to be always a crude, oversimplified, and inaccurate reflection of reality, and the lawgiver must know how to speak in this kind of language.

Men living together in a political community

require such distortion or reshaping of the human reality because all men lack the time, and almost all lack
the intelligence, to carry out or even to follow the
complicated reflections of the lawgiver. The vast
majority of men would only be confused by hearing
the reasons that stand behind laws. In their simplicity,
most men identify the good and true with the uniform:
"There are certain ideas of uniformity which . . .
infallibly captivate [*frappent*] little minds" (XXIX 18).
Men are to the legislator like children: the laws "are
not at all an art of logic, but the simple reason of
a father of a family" (XXIX 16). Law must for this
reason be not only simple but also in conformity with
the moral prejudices, "the ideas of honor, morality,
and religion," of the people for which it is enacted.
Any attempt to change those prejudices must be very
gradual and go almost unnoticed.

> Men hold prodigiously to their laws and to their
> customs; these make the happiness of each nation;
> it is rare that they are changed without great
> upheavals and a great spilling of blood, as the
> history of all countries makes evident. (XXVI
> 23)

The lawgiver's task is to make the best compromise
possible between the true complexity of things and
the simplicity of men's understanding. Legislation
requires a "genius" (XXIX 16, 18; Preface), a mind
which combines the subtlest eye for detail, the nicest
and most learned judgment, the most intricate and
sophisticated moral sensibility, with the capacity for
the simplest, clearest, and most naive expression.

Montesquieu began Book XXIX with a discussion
of the virtue of the legislator; he concludes with a

discussion of the vices most tempting to the legislator. Exemplifying the spirit of moderation, Montesquieu leaves as the last and strongest impression on the reader a warning against what is most difficult to avoid rather than encouragement about what is most to be hoped for.

The first vice is one whose likelihood is increased by the universality of law itself: the tempting attraction the lawgiver may find in "certain ideas of uniformity." The danger Montesquieu speaks of here is not so much the possibility of misapprehending the heterogeneity of man and things. It is rather the mistaken belief that one can or ought to overcome or at least ignore that heterogeneity in imposing uniform laws. A nation may embrace many individuals, or several peoples, who have different ways of life. Here at the conclusion of the book on legislation, Montesquieu returns to the theme that appeared in his discussion of the French way of life: in creating security and comfort the legislator must as much as possible avoid the suppression of the natural diversity which has developed among men and peoples. In order to achieve this goal, the legislator may even have to create different laws for different groups within the nation: "When the citizens follow the laws, why is it important that they all follow the same laws?" (XXIX 18).

This individuality natural to man is reflected in the legislator himself, and gives rise to the other very tempting vice of legislation. The individual humanity of the legislator always creates in him certain unique, personal passions and prejudices which tend to give a bias to all his thought. No man is free of some such personal weakness; Montesquieu indicates its inescapability by taking examples from the most rational and objective of all legislators, the philosopher-legislator (Aristotle, Plato, Machiavelli, More, Harrington): "The laws encounter always the passions and prejudices of the legislator. Sometimes the latter pass through the laws and only tincture them; sometimes they stay and are incorporated" (XXIX 19). It would seem that the best that can be hoped for is that the legislator be aware of this weakness and try to take steps to counterbalance it.

By using as his examples in the concluding chapter "On Legislators" only political philosophers, Montesquieu, as we have seen, blurs the distinction between philosopher and legislator and thereby points to the new politicized understanding of philosophy implied in his allusions to his own activity. But at the same time that he indicates the intimate connection between philosophy and legislation, Montesquieu reveals by his rather exaggerated attack on the objectivity and motives of some of the outstanding previous political philosophers (XXIX 19) a certain distrust of philosophy and theory in general. He implies that the philosophers have been abstract and have lacked objectivity because they have been insufficiently aware of the limitations inherent in all theorizing. This attack, like so many other elements of Montesquieu's thought, foreshadows Burke. But unlike Burke, Montesquieu's distrust of abstract reason does not lead him to part company with theory in general. He continues to believe in the importance of the legislator, and the legislator is not necessarily limited to making laws for "his own" nation (XXIX 16). The need for legislators who are prepared for all possible circumstances in all nations will require theoretical speculation, but theory of a new kind. His attack on the philosophers, like the remarks on the tempting vice of uniformity, is intended as a warning which will lead to a reform of philosophy and legislation.

The legislator's theoretical knowledge must be accompanied by a knowledge of the variety of particular national characters and above all of the "general spirit" of the people for whom he gives laws. It is this kind of knowledge which is the antidote to all errors of abstraction. It is to be derived from a study of the history of peoples. "To transport into long-ago centuries all the ideas of the century in which one lives, that is the most fertile source of error" (XXX 14).

The need for the study of history seems to be part of the reason for the books which form the background or context for the book on legislation (XXVII–XXVIII; XXX–XXXI). We have of course taken some liberty with the true order of *The Spirit of the Laws* in our interpretation of Book XXIX as the immediate sequel to Book XXVI. In fact, Book XXIX is inserted in the middle of four books, one giving an historical analysis of the laws of inheritance in Rome and three others giving a lengthy and detailed analysis of the origins of the laws of France. From the title page of *The Spirit of the Laws* we are led to think that these books are "additions," or appendices of a kind, to *The Spirit of the Laws* itself. But the fact that Book XXIX is placed in their midst, together with Montesquieu's assertion that he "would have believed that there was an imperfection in the work" if he had not added the material in Books XXX and

XXXI (cf. XXX 1), indicates they have a far greater importance than the typical appendix.

And we can now recognize a principal reason for their importance. These books serve as examples of the kind of research necessary for the lawgiver to undertake. That this is indeed the principal reason for Book XXVII seems indicated by a passage which Montesquieu originally wrote as an introduction to Book XXVII but which he later removed.[3] Montesquieu's teaching about the influence of the "general spirit of a nation" is complemented by these examples of the method of learning the general spirit. By his use of minute historical research here and throughout *The Spirit of the Laws*, Montesquieu encourages and implicitly calls for a widespread cultivation of scientific history as the indispensable aid to wise legislation.

As we have indicated in our remarks on Book XIX, the historical studies which conclude *The Spirit of the Laws* make crystal clear the fundamentally *political* rather than sociological character of the "general spirit of a nation." The historical study Montesquieu presents is a study of political, rather than economic, social, or intellectual history.[4] It is true that he emphasizes the development of political institutions rather than the deeds of individuals; but where deeds of individuals become decisive for institutional development, he does not hesitate to focus on them (cf. XXVII at the beginning; XXVIII 29, 37–39, 42; XXXI 1, 3, 11, 18–23). Indeed, Montesquieu's approach to history seems in part merely a return from the chronicles of the Middle Ages and the Christian approach to history represented by Bossuet, to the sober political-constitutional history epitomized in Aristotle's *Constitution of Athens*.

Natural Law and the Legislator

But Montesquieu goes beyond Aristotle in estimating the formative power of a nation's past political history. This is one reason for the fact that whereas Montesquieu makes his examples of historical research a part of his treatise on politics in general, the *Constitution of Athens* is not even an appendix to the *Politics*. The other reason for this difference is that Montesquieu is, as we have emphasized, much more intent on improving contemporary political life than is Aristotle. Montesquieu's extensive treatment of the early history of the French "constitution" is therefore considerably more than an example of the historical study required for legislation in general; this particular historical study has a direct connection with Montesquieu's plans or hopes for French reform.[5] And as we have seen, his hopes for French reform are at the core of his political project as a whole (see chapter 7 above, page 215ff.).

Montesquieu begins his study of the roots of the French general spirit with a book devoted to the origin and development of civil law (XXVIII). We remember that in Book XII he seemed more insistent on the necessity and possibility of other nations imitating the libertarian spirit of English civil law than he was on their imitation of the English constitution. Since Book XII we have learned of the limits to any such imitation imposed by the general spirit peculiar to each nation. But now Montesquieu tries to show that the formative early history of civil law in France (and in northern Europe in general) reveals a closer similarity to English civil law than might appear from an examination of the contemporary situation only. This fact was adumbrated in Montesquieu's portrayal in Book XVIII of the earliest French history, with its spirit of independence and freedom. Now he shows the considerable extent to which this spirit was maintained through the later centuries of the development of the nation.

The civil law brought by the Salic Franks who invaded Gaul, and revised by their "sages," combined an "admirable simplicity," a "natural candor," and a "judiciousness" with a great respect for the honor, independence, and safety of each individual. There were no painful or "afflictive" penalties—all were monetary. At least among the Salic Franks, there was originally no trial by combat and no "negative proofs" by holy oath (XXVIII 1, 2, 13, 14). Above all, Montesquieu says that originally "among the Germans, in contrast to all other peoples, justice was rendered in order to protect the criminal against the one he had offended" (XXX 20). It was precisely the warlike and ferocious nature of these men that forced them to create a legal system protective of the criminal while giving satisfaction to the victim of the criminal. For if the legal system failed to do either of these things well, the individuals were all too willing to resort to private war.

There are two powerful legal influences which have from the beginning threatened the free civil procedure that stems from the Germans: the church, with its canon law, and Roman law. Montesquieu tries to show the tension that has existed and still exists between these kinds of law and the original spirit of French law, while at the same time attempting to resuscitate and make more respectable that original spirit.

The danger of the influence of church law is only

another example of the danger of Christianity in general. Church law tends to demand too much of men and relies too heavily on divine sanction or support (cf. XII 4–6; XXIV 7, 14–15; XXVI 9–12 with XXVIII 1, 13–14). Montesquieu shows that the original "character" and, as a consequence, the civil law of the Germans who settled France, as opposed to that of the Visigoths who settled Spain and Italy, remained fundamentally independent of the clergy's influence (XXVIII 1, 3, 4). The fact that the ancient spirit of the laws was not preserved among the Visigoths who occupied Spain is one of the chief causes of the abuses that arose during the Inquisition:

> The Visigoth kings refounded the laws and had them refounded by the clergy. The bishops had an immense authority at the court of the Visigoth kings. . . . We owe to the code of the Visigoths all the maxims, all the principles, and all the views of today's Inquisition; and the monks only had to copy, to use against the Jews, the laws made in those early days by the bishops. (XXVIII 1; cf. XXVI 10–12)

But despite the French freedom from direct legal control by the clergy, the pernicious influence of church law gradually made itself felt. The church was able to introduce the legal practice of defending oneself in any civil dispute by means of an evangelical oath sworn in a church. Once such an oath was sworn, it could not be challenged. This practice, convenient to all malefactors, spread quickly: "The ecclesiastics were pleased to see that, in all secular affairs, recourse was had to the churches" (XXVII 18). In reaction to this there arose the practice previously used only by the non-Salic Franks (and only sparingly by them): trial by combat. The only way an evangelical oath could be challenged was by a test of endurance—combat, boiling water, fire, and so on—which seemed to give proof of veracity to God himself (XXVIII 14, 17, 18): "The law of combat was a natural consequence, and the remedy" (XXVIII 14). The Franks themselves adopted this barbaric and irrational usage only with reluctance: "It wasn't known what to do. The negative proof had its inconveniences, and so did proof by combat" (XXVIII 18). The barbarization of Frankish law was a result of the pernicious effect of church law. And the settling of all judicial disputes by combat was "the principal cause" which, when added to illiteracy and dispersion of the populace, brought about the "loss" of the ancient Frankish law (XXVIII 19; cf. 9–12). Civil law decayed into a mere code of regulations for duelling.

Nevertheless, what survived of the judicious and free spirit of Frankish law made the institution of trial by combat less irrational than might be thought. The regulations were attentive to the honor and "rights" of the combatants; for example, care was taken to protect those incapable of fighting. Besides, the institution was not wholly ill-suited to the fair settlement of disputes and punishments of crime in a warrior-nation where cowardice was the root of most vice. Montesquieu paints a picture of the liberal spirit of Frankish law struggling valiantly through the centuries to overcome the irrationality and tyranny of Christian influence (XXVIII 17).

The development and refinement of the civil law based on trial by combat continued down through the centuries until the epoch of St. Louis, who did his best to abolish the system and reinvigorate Roman law as represented by the newly recovered Institutes of Justinian. The result was a melange of Roman law, local customary law, and the remnants of the ancient Frankish law. Montesquieu speaks of St. Louis's work as a "chef-d'oeuvre of legislation" (XXVIII 29). By this he refers as much to St. Louis's method of introducing the new ways as to the new ways themselves:

> He did away with the evil by making the good felt. . . . To invite, when it is not necessary to constrain, to conduct, when it is not necessary to command, this is the supreme ability. (XXVIII 38; also 39)

St. Louis tried to show the way to a more reasonable kind of civil law. He was partially successful: although "the judicial forms introduced by St. Louis ceased to be used," the law based on combat gradually disappeared, the influence of Roman law spread, and the codification and rationalization of local customary law brought more order into French law as a whole. It is this mixture of Roman law, canon law, and codified local customary law which has ever since constituted French civil law.

Unfortunately, the introduction of Roman law prevented a full reinvigoration or preservation of the liberal spirit of Frankish law. "Roman law" meant the law of the empire, not the law of the republic (XXVIII 38). This imperial law lacked some of the key safeguards for liberty and honor which were present in German law. Judicial process ceased to be public and became secret (XXVIII 34). Roman law lacked any provision for trial by a jury of peers (referees in the procedure of trial by combat). This, combined with the complicated, dull, and technical character of·the Roman law, led to the gradual disappearance of trial by peers (XXVIII 27, 42–43), and finally to the loss of control over the judiciary by the local nobles. A centralized "Parlement," composed of men appointed by the king, at first from the nobles but eventually from the bourgeoisie, became the final court of appeal and the supervisor of the court system (XXVIII 39, 41). Centralization went hand in hand with Romanization (XXVIII 42–43).

At the same time, the renascence of Roman law was connected with a strengthening of the influence of canon law. Canon law had from the beginning retained much of Roman law. The ecclesiastics "received no prejudice from it, and it was moreover convenient for them, since it was the work of Christian emperors" (XXVIII 4; cf. 6, 11). So, "in abandoning the established judicial forms, those of the canon law were adopted rather than those of Roman law," for "one had always before one's eyes the clerical tribunes . . . and one knew of no tribunal which followed the forms of Roman law" (XXVIII 40). There resulted a new struggle, a new "flux and reflux of ecclesiastical and lay jurisdiction," which, fortunately for France, led to the victory or predominance of the lay judiciary headed by the Parlement (XXVIII 14). Still, although the Parlement dispensed with the worst "abuses" introduced by a "murky ignorance," it had "adopted in its form of proceeding everything that was good and useful in the procedure of the clerical tribunals" (XXVIII 41). The indirect influence of canon law remained strong.

The influential combination of canon and Roman law was generally more reasonable than either the canon law itself or the preexisting system of trial by combat. But it was not unqualifiedly so, for it was in many cases inapplicable to circumstances in France. In the book on legislation, which immediately follows the book on French civil law, Montesquieu reveals by examples a particular concern with the limited applicability in France of many Roman laws and usages (XXIX 6, 8, 10, 12, 14, 16, 17). This same concern may be part of the reason for Book XXVII's discussion of the unique spirit of certain Roman civil laws. Not only is Roman law unreasonable because to some extent inapplicable, but the fact that it contradicts or overlaps what has been preserved of Frankish customary law means that it has introduced into French law an unfortunate excess of complication and formalities. Montesquieu has a principal character in the *Persian Letters* say of the influence of Roman law in France:

> This abundance of laws adopted and, so to speak, naturalized, is so great that it weighs down both justice and the judges. . . . These foreign laws have introduced formalities of which the excess is the shame of human reason. (Letter no. 100; cf. no. 129)

It is partly this difficulty which Montesquieu has in mind in the example he gives at the beginning of the next book (XXIX 1).

The prudently subdued suggestion of Montesquieu's historical study is the possibility and necessity of a rather thoroughgoing revision of French civil law which would return to the original spirit of the laws of the Franks and oppose the later accretions of canon and Roman law. The revision should follow the methods of the highly praised St. Louis, who "invited rather than constrained" by giving "an example which could be followed" rather than a "general law." Montesquieu implies that the change should be slow, and carried out by means of the gradual introduction of new practices:

> When one sees in one's tribunals . . . a manner of proceeding more natural, more reasonable, more in conformity to morality, religion, public tranquility, the safety of person and property, one adopts it and abandons the other. (XXVIII 38)

Montesquieu himself has followed the procedure of St. Louis. Without insisting on innovation, he has presented in Book XII a glowing picture of the English civil law, and here in Book XXVIII he has demonstrated the kinship between that civil law and the deepest spirit of "our" French civil law. An introduction of some kind of imitation of the English civil usages will be made possible not only through the softening and humanizing effects of the spread of commerce, but also by recurring to the true foundations of the present legal system, a practice accepted as a natural, legal procedure. In addition, by his elaboration of the importance of the general spirit of a nation, Montesquieu has given theoretical foundation for such a use of early history. Montesquieu does not, however, simply identify the old with the prescriptive. Legal reform must be based on "our own" history, but we are to be discriminating about "our own"; we are to be guided by "our own" insofar as it is "good." We are to effect a meeting of our own and the good. Our history is prescriptive insofar as it conduces to liberty. Montesquieu never suggests a simple return to barbarian civil law: after all, the barbarians lacked commerce and therefore all civil procedures necessary to commerce. He rather shows that much of the "spirit" of ancient custom is "admirable" and therefore is to be imitated and honored. This same posture characterizes his approach to the origins and development of the "constitution" or "political law" of France.

Montesquieu's intimations about constitutional reform in France are both more momentous and more dangerous than his intimations about reform of civil law. For in raising the question of political reform, he challenges the foundations of the highest earthly powers.[6] Just as the historical study in Book XXVIII reinforced and expanded the implications of his earlier discussion of civil law in Book XII, so the historical study in the concluding two books enlarges on the even more cautious indications about French political reform given before now. In order to understand what Montesquieu is about in Books XXX–XXXI, it is therefore necessary to summarize briefly these earlier indications.

In the early books of *The Spirit of the Laws* Montesquieu showed that the moderate character of the French monarchy was due to the structural balance of intermediary powers and the proud passion of honor which animated that structure. Both these crucial elements require above all the independence of the nobility. In Book XVIII Montesquieu indicated that these elements find their source in the impetus to freedom which was given in the original days of France by the climate and terrain, which shaped men of warlike and proud temper who lived in free and independent "republics." Finally, we learned from Book XIX that this fierce spirit has been to some degree softened and transformed into a kind of vanity that fosters a sweet, pleasing civilization, and that this transformed version of the original spirit is conducive to the spread of commerce, with its security, humanity, and prosperity.

From all this we have gathered that Montesquieu's intention with regard to France in particular is threefold. First, he wishes to preserve the balance of powers and principle of honor that makes the nation "moderate." Second, he wants to preserve the charms of the French way of life, the tone set by the leisured aristocracy. Third, he wishes to extend the beneficent influence of commerce through a type of commerce that is in harmony with and dependent on that tasteful aristocratic tone; he hopes to persuade the French to move toward the imitation of English commercial politics within a French context. All three of these aims go together and assist one another. But the first is the absolute prerequisite for the latter two, and indeed, for any decent political order in France. As we have remarked, Montesquieu has indicated cautiously but unmistakably that this most basic structure and principle is threatened by the tendency to centralized despotism in France. It can therefore be said that equally urgent, although perhaps not as important in the long run as the spread of commerce, is a reinvigoration in France of the now disappearing structure and principle of monarchy. It is to such a reinvigoration that Montesquieu hopes to contribute in the two concluding books, by taking up again the account of the development of the general spirit begun in Book XVIII and showing how the original spirit of independence and balance of powers maintained and even improved itself through centuries of French history (cf. VI 10). Montesquieu demonstrates that the political liberty of the original "republics" was a feature not only of the origins but of much of the subsequent formative history of France.

Although these books are a continuation of what was said in Book XVIII, it would have been improper for Montesquieu to include them as part of that earlier book. For there he was concerned with developing fully the problem of how the security and comfort found in England could be brought to the rest of Europe through the spread of commerce. His brief sketch of the origins of the French spirit was sufficient for his purposes there; a longer discussion aimed at the more pressing but ultimately less momentous problem of reviving the balance of powers would not have been germane. Besides, the "mortally boring" (XXX 15) historical detail which Montesquieu thinks necessary would have interrupted the argument. Such detail is better left to a kind of appendix—not to mention that it is safer to relegate to a seeming appendix the discussion which comes closest to casting doubt on the legitimacy of some features of the reigning political order.

In order to grasp the full significance of Montesquieu's argument in these concluding books, it is necessary to have some understanding of the great though muted constitutional debate which was in progress when *The Spirit of the Laws* appeared. Ever since the suppression of the Fronde, that last open attempt by the nobles to reassert their traditional power against the encroachments of the monarch, there had been growing in France an intellectual movement fostered by the nobles which attempted to show by historical-legal research the illegitimacy of centralized monarchical power. Despite public suppression of all such studies, unpublished manuscripts circulated and served as a kind of rallying device for underground aristocratic politicking. During the relaxation of censorship following the death of Louis XIV, some of these manuscripts began to appear in published form. The highpoint prior to Montesquieu was Boulainvilliers' *Mémoires historiques sur l'ancien gouvernment de France* (published in 1727; see XXX 10, 25).

In response to this movement, apologists of the monarchy issued their own historical researches. These culminated in the work "of great art," representing the "endless erudition" of "that great man," the Abbé Dubos: *Histoire critique de l'établissment de la monarchie française dans les Gaules* (published in 1734; see XXVIII 3; XXX 10, 23–25).[7] It is this subdued but profoundly influential dispute which Montesquieu explicitly takes up and transforms (XXX 10).

We are indebted to Carcassonne for providing some important details of the opposing positions which are not made clear by Montesquieu himself. Boulainvilliers, in his wish to establish the precedence of the nobility, started from the claim that the Franks entered Gaul as conquerors and at that time permanently enslaved the inhabitants (XXX 5, 10). Beginning from the conquest, all Franks belonged to a single, racially distinct ruling caste. This caste developed directly into the feudal landholding aristocracy, the forefathers of the modern nobility of the sword. The nobility is therefore not only of a superior class but of a purer racial stock than the bourgeoisie. The monarch was originally and by right only first among equals, elected by his fellow conquerors and acting only as chief administrator. The democratic assemblies of the Frankish nobles, the origin of the present Parlement, shared national rule with their elected chief. The aristocratic title to land arose from the original conquest and appropriation by the forefathers of the nobles and is in no way derivative from the monarchy (XXX 5).

The gradual deprivation of the equal political authority of the nobles and of their independent title to land was a result of a policy of deceit and usurpation carried out by the successors of Charlemagne. The monarchs illegitimately raised the power of the bourgeoisie and freedmen in order to combat the power of the nobles. The Parlement, which rightfully is an institution of nobles, was transformed into an institution of the "nobility of the robe," the magisterial nobility artificially created by royal appointment of men from the Third Estate. These men were and still are merely the creatures and tools of the monarch.[8]

The Abbé Dubos, more erudite and subtle but less candid than Boulainvilliers, drew from a more thorough study of the evidence conclusions exactly contrary. There was no original conquest in France (XXX 24). After generations of gradual intermingling, the Franks were practically assimilated with the Romans and Gauls; they became polished and civilized, lost their barbarian freedom, and adopted Roman law. They were "the best friends of the Romans" (XXVIII 3). The Frankish king Clovis was made viceroy by the emperor when the empire became too weak to preserve its control over Gaul (XXX 24). Clovis, the first king, replaced the emperor by right and by custom. The Frankish people was no more privileged than the other peoples subject to the king (XXX 12–25). The nobility arose through grants given by the king; by right all title to land is derivative from the monarch (XXX 12). Although the monarch may have consulted advisors among the nobles, his authority was virtually independent (XXX 14–15, 17). On the other hand, the cities derived from Roman law a certain degree of local autonomy; the bourgeoisie has always been at least as independent as the nobility.

The usurpation was on the part of the nobles, who in the centuries following the reign of Clovis took advantage of weak kings and a general decay of law to wrest illegitimate autonomous power from the central authority and from the shrunken bourgeois class (XXX 14, 15). The modern renascence of the power of the monarch and a "nobility of the robe" chosen from the bourgeoisie is a return to ancient legitimacy.[9]

Montesquieu elevates the scholarly character of this dispute by calling for and carrying out a meticulous and objective research into the available legal documents and original contemporary accounts. What results is a more sober and far more solidly based version of Boulainvilliers' thesis. Montesquieu agrees with Boulainvilliers on the fundamental point: France originated in a bloody conquest, not a peaceful cooperation between Germans and Romans (XXVIII 3; XXX 12). "This point once marked, it is easy to see that the whole system of Abbé Dubos falls apart" (XXX 24), for Roman law and the political order derivative from that order were victims of this conquest. The authority of king and nobles is then derived from their roles in the German political order. The noble class of Franks finds its source in the companions of the warlord-kings (XXX 3, 25); they gained their landed fiefs as payment for their freely given services in war (XXX 3, 4, 12). These nobles gained, along with the land, local sovereignty—an independent power of taxation and independent judicial authority (XXX 12–13, 15, 18, 20, 22). They sat with the bishops in a national assembly which shared power with the king (XXVIII 9).

On the other hand, "Boulainvilliers has missed the capital point of his system: he has not at all proved that the Franks made a general regulation which put the Romans in a kind of slavery" (XXX 11). After the horror of the original conquest, there was a restoration of order, and the conquered peoples were allowed and encouraged to abandon their Roman law and become members of the German nations, subject to German law (XXVIII 2, 4; XXX 5, 11). Cities retained the autonomy derived from Roman law (XXX 11). In short, the Third Estate was not debased.

In addition, from the very beginning in Germany the monarchy was of considerable importance and power. The royal family was hereditary, the new king being chosen from among the eligible sons of the deceased king by his noble companions in war (XXXI 16–17). The fiefs were grants by the king, although in payment of debts; these grants were not at first inalienable (XXX 3, 4, 12). Finally, the king ruled directly over the numerous "free men" throughout the kingdom who were not serfs of the nobles. There existed everywhere parallel systems of feudal and "political," or royal, rule (XXX 18; XXI 7, 8, 24, 28).

Montesquieu then transforms the historical basis of the dispute by showing that the theme of French history is neither the supremacy of the king nor the total independence of the nobles. Boulainvilliers and Dubos, he says, "each created a system, the first of which seems to be a conspiracy against the Third Estate, and the second of which a conspiracy against the nobility" (XXX 10). In fact, the spirit of French history is a continuing struggle, a more or less balanced competition between king, nobles, and a third power, that of the clergy. At various times the struggle has become uneven and the nation has suffered; but the greatest epochs, above all the epoch of Charlemagne, have been characterized by "such a temperament in the orders of the state, that they were counterbalanced, and he [the king] remained the master" (XXXI 18; cf. 21, 24; XXVIII 41; XXX 1; and especially XI 8). Montesquieu recognizes that Boùlainvilliers' instinct is correct: at the present time the greatest danger to this balance is the eclipse of the nobility by the monarch. But Boulainvilliers' "noble simplicity" has led him to distort the full truth for the sake of present need (XXX 10).

Natural Law and the Legislator

Even more important, Montesquieu transforms the overall meaning of the dispute by giving a new theoretical significance to French history. What had been a legalistic quarrel about precedent and legitimacy, a quarrel which to some extent merely served as a mask for the rallying of dissident opinion, takes on new dimensions in the light of Montesquieu's teaching about the importance of the "general spirit of a nation." Early French history is far more important and relevant than either Dubos or Boulainvilliers had realized. The study of our history is important not so much because we may discover the correct titles to land and authority; rather from our early history we learn of the principles and institutions of government, the habits, customs, and usages which are the formative source of our second nature, our "manner of thinking" as Frenchmen. We become fully conscious of what we are and what our potential is by our knowledge of what we have been made into by our past, especially our most formative earliest past.

Just as in his discussion of civil law, Montesquieu does not imply here that we should simply allow that past to prescribe our future. We must reinvigorate and build on what is good in the past; we must oppose as best we can what is bad in full knowledge of the limits on such opposition. The admirable spirit of liberty and independence of those early times went hand in hand with a "bloody spirit"; our fathers belonged to a "ferocious and barbaric nation": "these princes were murderous, unjust, and cruel because the whole nation was so" (XVIII 29; XXI 2). Paradoxically, respect for our past must go with gratitude for our progress away from that past and respect for the forces which have created that progress. The balance

297

and separation of powers, and the spirit of individual liberty, must be judiciously integrated with the commerce, pleasant security, and humanity of the present in an attempt to overcome the ferocity and the myths of pride and religion which comprise a large part of our heritage.

It is then not only for reasons of prudence that Montesquieu's study of early French history does not lead directly to recommendations for present reform. The general prescription is clear: a revival of the balance of powers and spirit of liberty. But one has to put this together with Montesquieu's earlier, scattered discussions of modern France in order to begin to see how the general prescription is to be applied. By this study of French history Montesquieu has sharpened and made somewhat more convincing his adumbration of the fact that the French monarchy has the same origin as the much praised English constitution (XI 6, 8). There is a possibility in France for some kind of imitation of England. It would seem that any imitation would have to give much more power to the nobles and much less to the Third Estate than is the case of England. The injustice and disadvantage of practically excluding the commoners from direct participation in power would be balanced by the fact that France would not have to undergo the period of "despotism" which England endured in the days of the Tudors (XIX 27, p. 580; XII 10, 22; XXVI 3), or run the risks which England still does as a result of her drastic weakening of the intermediate powers of the nobles and clergy (II 4).

But there are clear indications that Montesquieu goes beyond the suggestion of a constitutional system including only the original factions of king, ancient nobility, and clergy. Montesquieu is well aware that the ancient nobility is unfitted by disposition and training for the complexities of modern administration. It has "a natural ignorance, . . . an inattention, a contempt for civil government" (II 4). In addition, the growth of commerce requires more power and protection for the bourgeoisie. Montesquieu is therefore led to give a very important place to the "nobility of the robe," that nobility originally appointed from the bourgeoisie by the monarch to carry on most of the functions of the judiciary and some of those of the administration. The key institution of this "nobility of the robe" is the Parlement, above all the Parlement of Paris, a body which serves as the highest court and as the "depository" of the laws, or as a kind of reviewer of all laws and administration (II 4; V 10; XX 22). Montesquieu indicates that it is this class, with its training and institutional base, which can most directly keep the monarchy in check and maintain the crucial separation of the judicial power. At the same time, through access to this class by appointment, especially by appointment combined with purchase, the merchants can participate in rule and have an incentive to industry: "The acquisition which one can make of nobility for the price of money encourages the merchants very much" (XX 22; cf. V 19).

Yet there is a danger that this nobility of the robe, left to itself, will fail to perform a balancing role. Insofar as it is merely an extension of the Third Estate it lacks a tradition of independence and pride; and it may feel its interests are, as they have been traditionally, at least as close to those of the king as to those of the old nobility. This fact combined with the king's appointive power threatens to make the nobility of the robe his tool.

The key to independence for the nobility of the robe is the strengthening of its connection with the old nobility. The old "nobility of the sword" will keep alive the principle of honor and independence which will seep down and animate the new nobility (see especially XX 22). To the extent that the old, higher nobility is accessible, especially through marriage, to the most honorable and wealthiest members of the nobility of the robe, it may to some extent control the lower by giving to it its own aspirations and objects of emulation. The nobility of the sword can thus continue to exercise its balancing power indirectly. The kinship between old and new nobility will be strengthened by, and will itself strengthen, the growing realization on the part of the bourgeoisie that their commerce in France depends on the luxury and independence of the old nobility.[10]

In sum, Montesquieu seems to suggest, without going into too many details, that France should move toward a constitutional arrangement in which the old nobility would participate in the national government only indirectly, balancing the monarch's power through its influence on the nobility of the robe. Given the fact that the commoners lack direct access to governmental power, the old nobility has much less need of a separate, protective parliamentary institution such as it has in England. The direct governmental role of the old nobility would seem in the main to be limited to an increased participation in local government and in a decentralized judiciary (cf. XXVIII 41)—some vastly diluted version of the original feudal power.

In meditating on Montesquieu's plans for reform, one cannot help being led to wonder whether he satisfactorily comprehended the forces he sought to shape or control. It is of course unfair to blame Montesquieu for not preventing the French Revolution. As has been indicated, he seems to have fully foreseen such a possibility; he is surely not to be held responsible for the fact that the French nation was too selfish and shortsighted to adopt the program he thought was needed to forestall the debacle. But one can wonder if the advice or project itself is thoroughly sound. Montesquieu hoped to create a harmony between what he himself called a "wholly warrior nobility" (XX 22) and a commercial bourgeoisie. As we have seen, he insisted on prohibiting the nobility from engaging in commerce. Yet if the luxury-loving nobles are to be cut off from the source of the vast new wealth, will not a relative as well as an absolute impoverishment overtake them? This was a process which was well under way in Montesquieu's own time, and he alludes to it (XX 22).[11] According to Montesquieu, "when [the nobility of the sword] is ruined, it gives place to another which will again serve with its capital" (XX 22). We can then look to a continual replenishment of the nobility of the sword. But from where? Can we not expect a slow but sure replacement of the old families with families who arise through the nobility of the robe from the commercial bourgeoisie, and will this not mean the dilution and

eventual desuetude of the character of the old nobility?
And will not the change of character be hastened by
the growing national concern with commercial
acquisitiveness? The reader is compelled to wonder
whether it will not be the bourgeoisie which will eventually give the tone to the aristocracy rather than the
other way around. It would seem that France must
inevitably become a wholly bourgeois or commercial
regime, that it must undergo, at a perhaps accelerated
pace, all the risks that England ran in the course of
its development. In the long run, France too seems
to face the danger of becoming a large nation that
is "a popular state, or rather a despotic state" (II 4).

These doubts about Montesquieu's plans for France
are more than doubts about his prudence, or about
one application of his principles. For Montesquieu
dwells on France: he seems to make of France a kind
of test of the proposition that it is possible to introduce
into other European countries government based on
the principles of modern political philosophy, the
principles which underlie the English constitution.

Montesquieu accepted the fundamental modern or
liberal premise—the idea of a system based on the
institutional balance and manipulation of competing
selfish interests, with the whole nation dominated by
the desire for security and the commercial spirit of
acquisitiveness. But more than any other modern
thinker, Montesquieu felt compelled to emphasize the
problem of the applicability of that fundamental premise. He was too wise and too humane to be tempted
for one moment to trust in the idea that decency and
security are likely to emerge from the blood and ashes
of violent revolution. He attempted to show how the

egalitarian commercial principles could be actualized without such bloody revolution—without obliterating the heterogeneity essential for a balance of powers as well as for so much of life's charm, and without uprooting that "general spirit of a nation" that is so deeply ingrained in men that it cannot be destroyed without a loss of the sense of security and a disappearance of the social bonds that tie men to one another.

But the difficulties in the Montesquieuian proposal for a solution to the political problem in France cast doubts on the Montesquieuian solution to the political problem in general. One is led to wonder whether a political order based predominantly on the passion for security or liberty can come into being without the impairment of that security—that is, whether such an order is not self-contradictory. We today can continue to hope that Montesquieu's overestimation of the durability of the safeguards to liberty provided by the old nobility and the general spirit it sustained is made up for by his underestimation of the capacity of men, in the English-speaking world at least, to replace the balance of class interests with an institutional channelling and balance of the conflicting interests of a classless popular state.

And yet, in the long run, is this sufficient? Can all the "interests" be "balanced"? May not the suppression of the decent, aristocratic love of honor and individual preeminence leave us unprotected against the vicious desire for prestige and the degrading search for individuality? This question leads to and is overshadowed by a more general question: does not Montesquieu's political program, aimed at making life secure, eventually threaten to create a way of life no longer lovely or enjoyable enough to be seen as worth securing? Is it possible that at the root of the practical difficulties is the unalterable nature of man, animated by needs and longings that cannot be harmonized with the desire for security and equality?

The apparent failure of Montesquieu's attempt to respond to this possibility—his attempt to explain and create a solid political foundation for the higher human faculties by supplementing the modern understanding of nature with a new conception of history—seems to foreshadow the failure of his illustrious successors. Perhaps then the study of Montesquieu can be only the beginning, if the all-important beginning, of our enterprise. A relearning of what Montesquieu teaches about the necessity for diversity, and the preconditions for the beauty of tasteful diversity, may be only the first step in our attempt to solve the problem of liberalism. Perhaps the source of that beauty and charm must be rethought, not in the light of man's historicity, but in the light of his unchanging capacity to know. This would lead toward the core of the philosophical debate between the ancients and the moderns to which Montesquieu so clearly directs us.

The concluding books of *The Spirit of the Laws*, by focusing on France and by compelling one to reflect on the requirements of French reform, complete the general development of thought which Montesquieu has introduced in the work as a whole. Beginning from a consideration of the universal principles governing human nature and the principles of the great alternative forms of government, he has moved to a consideration of the particular situation in "this" country, in "our" time. This progression of thought, completed in the last books, exemplifies Montesquieu's theoretical innovation. More than any previous thinker, Montesquieu teaches by precept and by example that political philosophy must be presented not only in the form of a philosophic treatise but simultaneously in the form of a tract for the times. More than any previous thinker, Montesquieu teaches that political philosophy must become historical philosophy; that it must come down to this earth, to this nation here and now, and learn how to make all men at home within it. Philosophy must learn to look away from the dazzling light of eternal or unchanging nature and come to see that light only as it appears when dimly reflected in the pleasing variety of temporal human things.

NOTES

Notes to Chapter One

1. Hanna Pitkin, ed., *Representation* (New York: Atherton Press, 1969), p. 5.

2. Georg Lukacs, *History and Class-Consciousness*, trans. Rodney Livingstone (Cambridge, Mass.: The MIT Press, 1971), pp. 228–29.

Notes to Chapter Two

1. Voltaire, "Lois (Esprit de)," *Dictionnaire philosophique*, ed. Perroten (Paris: Farne, 1847), pp. 34–40. Cf. Voltaire, "Dialogue entre A, B, et C sur Grotius, Hobbes et Montesquieu," *Oeuvres complètes*, 13 vols. (Paris: Firmin-Didot, 1876), VI, 670–77. See also Antoine Destutt de Tracy, *Commentary and Review of Montesquieu's Spirit of the Laws* (Philadelphia: William Duane, 1811), pp. 1, 143, 146, 197; Albert Sorel, *Montesquieu*, trans. M. S. Anderson and E. P. Anderson (Chicago: A. C. McClurg and Co., 1888), pp. 15, 91–92; Courtenay Ilbert, *Montesquieu* (Oxford University Press, 1904), pp. 20, 24–25; Joseph Dedieu, *Montesquieu* (Paris: Alcan, 1913), pp. 37ff., 84–85, 88, 125; Raymond Aron, *Les grands doctrines de sociologie historique*, 2 vols. (Paris: Centre de documentation universitaire, Sorbonne, n.d.), I, 18; Isaiah Berlin, "Montesquieu," *Proceedings of the British Academy*, XLI (1955), 274; Werner Stark, *Montesquieu, Pioneer of the Sociology of Knowledge* (Toronto: University of Toronto Press, 1961), p. xi; Georges Benrekassa, *Montesquieu* (Paris: Presses universitaires de France, 1968), p. 21.

One of the best-known exceptions is Barkhausen. But in his attempt to show the "obvious" plan of *The Spirit of the Laws* he refuses to see most of the real difficulties, and is therefore of help only in some details. See H. Barkhausen, *Montesquieu, ses idées et ses oeuvres* (Paris: Hachette, 1907), pp. 1, 49, 219ff., 254, 257–63.

2. Lawrence Levin, *The Political Doctrine of Montesquieu's Esprit des Lois: Its Classical Background* (New York: Columbia University

Press, 1936), p. 12; cf. p. 1. See also Stark, pp. 87, 144; Dedieu, pp. 3, 119–21, 304–5.

3. D'Alembert, *Oeuvres complètes*, 5 vols. (Paris: A. Berlin, 1821), III, 450–51. Compare David Lowenthal, "Book One of the *Spirit of the Laws*," *APSR* LIII (1959), 485–87.

4. *Works*, I, 1228. Cf. *Defense of the Spirit of the Laws, Works*, II, 1161.

5. *Defense of the Spirit of the Laws, Works*, II, 1121.

6. "Discourse on the Motives Which Ought to Encourage Us toward the Sciences," *Works*, I, 53.

7. *Defense of the Spirit of the Laws, Works*, II, 1136.

8. *Pensées*, no. 2097, in *Works*, I, 1546–47.

9. Ilbert, p. 23. Cf. d'Alembert, pp. 452–53; Destutt de Tracy, p. 144; Sorel, pp. 54–55; Barkhausen, p. 136; Gabriel Loretti, "Montesquieu et le problème, en France, du bon gouvernement" in *Actes du Congrès Montesquieu* (Bordeaux: Imprimerie Delmas, 1956), p. 225; Ira Wade, *The Clandestine Organization and Diffusion of Philosophic Ideas in France from 1700 to 1750* (Princeton, N.J.: Princeton University Press, 1938).

10. Hippolyte Taine, *The Ancient Regime*, trans. John Durand (New York: Henry Holt & Co., 1876), IV i 4, p. 260.

11. *Pensées*, nos. 851, 868 in *Works*, I, 1232, 1237.

12. Taine, p. 260.

13. Voltaire, "Dialogue," p. 672.

Notes to Chapter Three

1. Cf. Hobbes, *Leviathan*, at the very end.

2. Cf. Benrekassa, p. 35; Mark Waddicor, *Montesquieu and the Philosophy of Natural Law* (The Hague: Martinus Nijhoff, 1970), p. 40; Nannerl O. Keohane, "Virtuous Republics and Glorious Monarchies: Two Models in Montesquieu's Political Thought," *Political Studies* XX (1972), 384, 396.

3. *Defense of the Spirit of the Laws, Works*, II, 1124. Cf. "Discourse on the Cause of the Echo," *Works*, I, esp. 11; "Discourse on the Use of the Renal Glands," *Works*, I, esp. 16–17; "Discourse on the Cause of the Heaviness of Bodies," *Works*, I, 27; "Discourse on the Motives Which Ought to Encourage Us Toward the Sciences," *Works*, I, esp. 53, 55; "Discourse on Cicero," *Works*, I, 94. See also Robert Shackleton, *Montesquieu, A Critical Biography* (London: Oxford University Press, 1961), pp. 25, 60, 258.

Notes

4. Cf. Descartes, *Meditations*, III, near the middle.

5. Cf. Plato *Laws* 732^e, 739^{e-e} and Rousseau, *Contrat social*, III 4, at the end.

6. It is true that man's intelligence, as opposed to God's, is said to be "finite" (p. 234). But this in the context applies to man's initial "ignorance" and his capacity for "error" and "forgetting"; man's potential knowledge is not said to be less than that of God. This is especially true in the case of "the philosophers" and "the legislators."

7. See *Defense of the Spirit of the Laws*, "Première Objection" and "Réponse," "Seconde Objection" and "Réponse," *Works*, II, 1122–24. It is helpful to contrast, as Lowenthal does, Montesquieu's treatment of God and law with the traditional Thomistic treatment. See David Lowenthal, "Montesquieu," *History of Political Philosophy*, ed. Leo Strauss and Joseph Cropsey (Chicago: Rand McNally, 1963), p. 470; see also William Mathie, "Montesquieu's Conception of Natural Right" (M.A. thesis, University of Chicago, 1965).

8. Lowenthal, "Book One," p. 487.

9. This remark makes it obvious that Shackleton is wrong when he tries to explain Montesquieu's natural law as "descriptive" but not "normative." See Shackleton, pp. 250–51, and Benrekassa, p. 31. Durkheim recognizes that Montesquieu does not make this distinction between "facts" and "values," and criticizes him for not doing so. But Durkheim is so unshakably convinced of the validity of this distinction that, instead of really joining the issue, he ascribes Montesquieu's failure to a "confusion" arising from "a throwback to an earlier tradition." See Emile Durkheim, *Montesquieu et Rousseau* (Paris: Marcel Rivière et Cie., 1966), pp. 45ff., 50ff., 92–94. Durkheim would have profited from a real attempt to refute Montesquieu, for Durkheim's own understanding of the issue is so confused that he claims that social science cannot dispense with the notion of "the normal form of social life" and the concomitant idea that "everything normal is healthy" (p. 35). And he later goes so far as to criticize Montesquieu for not including the concept of "progress" in his social science (pp. 105–9).

10. Cf. John Locke, *Essay Concerning Human Understanding*, II xxviii 7–13, and Hobbes's reference to "the old moral philosophers" in *Leviathan*, chap. xi, at the beginning.

11. See VI 13, 20; X 2, 3; XV 7, 12, 17; XXIV 6; XXVI

Notes

3, 4, 5, 6, 7, 14. I disregard the note added to the second edition at the behest of the censor (XIV 12). Shackleton's list of the references to natural right in *The Spirit of the Laws* is incomplete and somewhat misleading (Shackleton, p. 250).

12. XXVI 3, 4, 5, 6, 7, 14.

13. Lowenthal, "Book One," p. 494.

14. Plato *Laws* 631^a–632^a, 641^b, 643^d–644^b; *Republic* 353^d, 441–42. Aristotle *Politics* 1252^b 28ff., 1253^a 30–39, 1280^b 5–15, 1323–1325; *Ethics* 1097^b 25–1098^a 20, 1099^b 30–35, 1129^b 11–1130^a 13. Polybius *Histories* VI v 10–vii 1. Thomas Aquinas *Summa Theologica* I ii 94. Grotius, *De Jure Belli ac Pacis* Proleg. 6, 7 (esp. note 6), 16, 19–20; I i 11. Pufendorf, *De Jure Naturae et Gentium* II i 4–5, ii 1, 3, 4, 9. Burlamaqui, *Principes du droit naturel* I iv 11; also I iv 3; II iii 6, iv 11–15, 24; and *Principes du droit politique* I iii 26–27.

15. It is sometimes suggested that Montesquieu, despite his later protestations to the contrary, follows Spinoza (rather than Hobbes) in his teaching about natural law. If this were true, our concentration on Montesquieu's confrontation with Hobbes might be faulty in its emphasis. It is surely the case that Montesquieu incorporates elements of Spinozism in his account of natural law. But the Hobbesian influence seems to us to be predominant. It is not possible to do more here than allude to one or two decisive observations. Although Montesquieu moves away from Hobbes toward Spinoza by making natural law comprehend all of nature and not only the human state of nature, yet with respect to human natural law, that is, in the key political respect, Montesquieu joins Hobbes and opposes Spinoza: there is no natural right or law of the human passions in general. There is only a natural right or law of the passions conducive to peace (especially fear of death and the desire for security). As a direct consequence, Montesquieu agrees with Hobbes, in opposition to Spinoza, in asserting that outside of the civil state contracts made under the compulsion of fear are obligatory. Cf. XXVI 20 with Spinoza, *Theological-Political Treatise*, in *Chief Works*, trans. R. H. M. Elwes, 2 vols. (London: George Bell and Sons, 1887), I, xvi, esp. p. 203, and Hobbes, *Leviathan*, chap. xiv. Cf. Leo Strauss, *Spinoza's Critique of Religion*, trans. E. M. Sinclair (New York: Schocken Books, 1965), chap. ix.

Notes

One might therefore tentatively characterize the relationship of Montesquieu's natural law teaching to that of his two predecessors as follows. Montesquieu wishes to effect a synthesis, combining the thoroughgoing naturalism of Spinoza, which is more consistent with modern natural science, with the Hobbesian doctrine of the natural primacy of the passions conducive to peace, which is more acceptable from the point of view of political theory. The desire to make this synthesis would then be an additional reason for Montesquieu's insistence on de-emphasizing the naturalness of human aggressiveness and desire for domination.

16. Compare especially *Leviathan*, chap. xiii, where Hobbes refers to the state of nature as follows: "But there are many places where they [men] live so [in a state of nature] now. For the savage people in many places of America, *except the government of small families* . . . have no government at all; and live at this day in that brutish manner." (Italics mine.)

And consider chapter x: "Germany, being anciently, as all other countries, in their beginnings, divided amongst an infinite number of little lords, or masters of families, that continually had wars with one another. . . ."

And chapter xxx: "Originally the father of every man was also his sovereign lord, with power over him of life and death; and that the fathers of families, when by instituting a commonwealth. . . ."

17. Rousseau, *The First and Second Discourses*, ed. and trans. Roger Masters (New York: St. Martin's Press, 1964), p. 107.

18. Cf. Dedieu, pp. 119–21: "Ces premises semblarent annoncer un traité conforme à la méthode des Grotius, des Pufendorf, des Richer d'Aube, où l'auteur s'appliquerait à déterminer d'abord les conditions absolues du juste, afin de montrer ensuite comment les lois positives s'en éloignent ou s'en approchent. De ce traité, Montesquieu n'écrivit que la première partie."

Shackleton, p. 253, quotes the following remark by Monclar, an eminent contemporary magistrate of Provence: "On trouve dans l'auteur de *L'esprit des lois* l'homme de génie, le philosophe, l'historien; on n'y trouve point assez le jurisconsulte, nourri des principes du droit public."

See also Paul Janet, *Histoire de la science politique*, 3d ed., 2 vols. (Paris: Alcan, 1887), II, 330–31.

Notes

19. See Aron, I, 18, 54–55; Dedieu, pp. 37ff., 40, 196–97; Barkhausen, pp. 53–54; Shackleton, p. 265; Durkheim, pp. 55, 68–69; Berlin, p. 277.

20. Durkheim, pp. 26, 28, 36–37; Aron, I, 14, 20–21, 39, 40–41, but see 54–55; Stark, pp. 77, 86, but see pp. 93ff., 103ff., 117.

21. Durkheim, p. 81; Georges Gurvitch, "La sociologie juridique chez Montesquieu," *Revue de Metaphysique et de Morale* LXVI (1939), 624–25.

22. Cf. Hobbes, chap. xxi: "The *greatest* objection is that of the practice: when men ask where and when such power has by subjects been acknowledged." (Italics mine.) See also chap. xxxi.

Notes to Chapter Four

1. D'Alembert correctly remarks: "Not that there are in the universe only these three kinds of government; . . . most governments are mixed or shaded the one with the other" (*Oeuvres*, III, 467).

2. As David Lowenthal puts it, "political structures [are] means for repressing social strife" ("Montesquieu," p. 472).

3. *Works*, II, 239, n. 1. Cf. Janet, pp. 343–45.

4. Hobbes, chap. xix.

5. David Lowenthal gives a helpful account of how the various institutional arrangements mentioned or implied by Montesquieu might fit together ("Montesquieu and the Classics" in *Ancients and Moderns*, ed. Joseph Cropsey [New York: Basic Books, 1964], pp. 259–62).

6. Part of Aristotle's justification of the democratic mixed regime is that it is composed of citizens who have enough money, leisure, and breeding to cultivate a part of moral virtue, that is, courage at the least. Montesquieu does not feel required to make such a justification of democracy. See *Politics* 1279^a 40–^{b} 5, 1295^a 25–1296^a 23, 1297^b 1–6.

7. Cf. Lowenthal, "Montesquieu and the Classics," pp. 276–79.

8. On two occasions, Montesquieu refers to something he calls "true honor" (III 7; V 19). Like his reference to "moral virtue," these allusions are never explicitly amplified. But consider pp. 233–39 below.

Notes

9. Contrast *Ethics* 1117^b 7–22 and 1124^b 7–9: according to Aristotle, the truly proud man is not warlike.

10. Lowenthal has pointed out the peculiarities of these three chapters and has given an interesting interpretation with which my account should be contrasted ("Montesquieu and the Classics," pp. 268–80).

11. Cf. *Considerations, Works*, II, 148: "The Romans, accustomed to playing with human nature in the persons of their children . . . could scarcely comprehend that virtue we call humanity. . . . When one is cruel in the civil state, how can one expect softness and natural justice?"

12. See Montesquieu, *Considerations on the Causes of the Greatness of the Romans and Their Decline*, ed. and trans. David Lowenthal (Ithaca: Cornell University Press, 1968), p. 18.

13. By this distinction between "political" and "civil" law, Montesquieu refers to a distinction, familiar in his time, between that part of law constituting the state, the form of government, and all that follows from it with regard to citizenship; and that part of law within the political order so constituted which governs the relation of the state to the individual and of the individuals to one another. In this division criminal law is part of civil law (VI 5, 9, 15; X 14; XI 6; XII 1, 2). However, Montesquieu sometimes uses the term "civil law" in its narrower sense, more familiar to us, of law governing relations between individuals to which the state is not directly a party (VI 1). See "Civil Law," *Encyclopedia of the Social Sciences* (New York: Macmillan and Co., 1935), III, 502–9; Rousseau, *Contrat social*, II 12; also Barkhausen, pp. 267–72.

14. Destutt de Tracy, p. 143.

15. Cf. XIX 16: "Lycurgus, whose institutions were harsh, did not have civility for his object when he formed the manners. . . . People always correcting, or always corrected, people who are both simple and rigid, will exercise virtue towards one another more than they will have regard for one another."

16. When discussing the principles of the various regimes in Book V, Montesquieu makes a two-chapter digression about the "nature" or structure of monarchy when he wishes to describe the "excellence" of monarchy (V 10–11).

17. IX 1–3: The outstanding examples of federation are Hol-

Notes

land and Lycia. Holland was clearly very commercial; one cannot be sure from the scanty descriptions in Strabo, Montesquieu's source, but the mention of Lycia's "fine harbors" which were "not used for piracy" indicates that Lycia was also commercial. Cf. Strabo *Geography* XIV iii 2–9. And consider Montesquieu, *Works*, II, 1006.

Notes to Chapter Five

1. Cf. Barkhausen, p. 258.
2. Cf. Durkheim, p. 64.
3. See, among others, Durkheim, p. 62; Barkhausen, pp. 64, 86, 258; Dedieu, pp. 84–86; Levin, p. 1; Janet, pp. 349ff.

Hegel has given the correct interpretation in his remarks on Montesquieu in the *Philosophy of Right*, section no. 273: "Here again, as in so many other places, we must recognize the depth of Montesquieu's insight in his now famous treatment of the basic principles of the form of government. To recognize the accuracy of his account, however, we must not misunderstand it. As is well known, he holds that 'virtue' is the principle of democracy since it is in fact the case that that type of constitution rests on sentiment. . . . But Montesquieu goes on to say that in the seventeenth century, England provided 'a fine spectacle of the way in which efforts to found a democracy were rendered ineffective by a lack of virtue in the leaders,' and again he adds 'when virtue vanishes from the republic, ambition enters hearts which are capable of it and greed masters everyone. . . .' These quotations call for the comment that in more mature social conditions and when the power of particularity has developed and become free, a form of rational law other than the form of sentiment is required, because virtue in the heads of state is not enough if the state as a whole is to gain the power to resist disruption and to bestow on the powers of particularity, now become mature, both their positive and their negative rights . . . [and] the fact that Montesquieu discusses 'honor' as the principle of monarchy at once makes it clear that by 'monarchy' he understands not . . . the type organized into an objective constitution, but only feudal monarchy."

Hegel, *Philosophy of Right*, trans. T. M. Knox (Oxford University Press, 1942), pp. 177–78. See also Shackleton, p. 287 n. 4;

Notes

Keohane, pp. 393, 395–96; and the essays of David Lowenthal already referred to. Consider, above all, Leo Strauss, "On the Intention of Rousseau," *Social Research* XIV (1947), 458–60.

4. Aristotle *Politics* 1297ᵇ 35–1301ᵃ 15.

5. Polybius *Histories* VI xi 11–xiv.

6. Cf. Walter Berns, "Milton," in Strauss and Cropsey, eds., *History of Political Philosophy*, pp. 397–412.

7. There are several reasons for Montesquieu's new understanding of the nature of the three functions of government. The reasons are difficult to distinguish because they are interconnected and because Montesquieu's wish to persuade men of the necessity of his new understanding leads him to de-emphasize somewhat its innovative character. We will try to articulate the reasons one by one as they appear.

8. XI 13, especially the third, sixth, and seventh paragraphs.

9. Montesquieu does not suggest a combination of the English system and a republican federation. While federation might promote representative government (XI 8), there would remain a grave tension between the spirit of monarchy and the spirit of small republics. Compare Montesquieu's comment on Holland in XI 6, pp. 406–7.

10. XI 6, p. 401; II 4. Cf. David Hume's letter to Montesquieu of April 10, 1749, in *Correspondance de Montesquieu*, ed. François Gebelin, 2 vols. (Paris: Champion, 1914), II, 170; see also *Works*, I, 884.

11. A revealing statement of the intention of the American Founding Fathers in this regard is found in Madison's remarks in the Convention against enlarging the Senate: *Records of the Federal Convention*, ed. Max Farrand, 4 vols. (New Haven: Yale University Press, 1966), I, 151–56 (debate of June 7, 1787).

12. It is in the emphasis on the separation of the judicial power that Montesquieu's discussion differs most markedly from Locke's. Locke is practically silent about the separate judicial power, and has much less than Montesquieu to say about "civil liberty," the theme of Books VI and XIII. On the other hand, Locke emphasizes much more than does Montesquieu the "supreme power" of the legislature (*Second Treatise*, chaps. xi–xiv). Paradoxically, Montesquieu speaks much less about the natural rights of the individual than Locke but much more about the institutions

providing for the security of the individual in civil society. This is due to Montesquieu's clearer understanding of the complexity and fragility of the machinery of government needed to translate natural rights into enforceable rights.

13. Letter to Montesquieu of April 10, 1749, in Gebelin, *Correspondance*, p. 176.

14. Cf. Herbert J. Storing, "The Problem of Big Government," in *A Nation of States: Essays on the American Federal System*, ed. Robert A. Goldwin (Chicago: Rand McNally, 1961), pp. 80–82. See also Locke, *Second Treatise*, chaps. xii, xiv.

15. The restraint on the prudence of both the legislative and the executive branches will become more serious if the legalistic ethos which animates the system should lead, as it did in the American version, to a more powerful and more truly political role for the judicial branch of government. It suffices here to recall the effect the United States Supreme Court has had in the great political crises of the American regime: the slavery dispute (the Dred Scott decision), Reconstruction (the Slaughterhouse Cases), the civil rights movement (the Civil Rights Cases), and the transformation of capitalism (the rise of substantive due process). This is not to deny that the Supreme Court, replacing to some extent the effect of the House of Lords and the monarch, has made an immeasurable contribution to the deliberativeness of the American system. This is only meant to point to the difficulty created by the peculiarly legalistic character that deliberation is forced to assume in this Montesquieuian system. In fairness to Montesquieu, it must be remembered that he does not recommend that the judiciary assume such a role (see especially *Works*, II, 401, 405, 575).

16. *Discourses*, I xx–xxi; cf. *Politics* 1287 [b] 19ff.

17. See, for example, Dedieu, p. 88; Jean Brethe de la Gressaye, ed., *De l'esprit des lois*, 4 vols. (Paris: Société des Belles Lettres, 1950–56), I, cxv; David Spitz, "Montesquieu's Theory of Freedom," in *Essays in the Liberal Idea of Freedom* (Tucson: University of Arizona Press, 1964), pp. 29, 34; Franz Neumann, "Introduction," in Montesquieu, *The Spirit of the Laws*, trans. Thomas Nugent (New York: Hafner, 1949), pp. xxix–xxxi, xlvi–xlvii.

18. There is a textual error at this point in the Pléiade edition. For "il n'y auroit plus d'esprit que de goût," read "il *y* auroit

Notes

. . . ." See the critical edition of Brethe de la Gressaye, ad loc.

19. Compare *Pensées*, no. 1434, in *Works*, I, 1337: "*The Difference Between the English and the French*—The English live well with their inferiors and cannot stand their superiors. We get along well with our superiors and are unbearable to our inferiors."

20. It is sometimes helpful to supplement one's study of Montesquieu's completed and published works with examination of his incomplete and unpublished writings, including the *Pensées* (which were found among his papers at his death and published by his heirs only within the past century). But in using these materials it is necessary to proceed with caution. An unpublished or unfinished work is likely to be more reliable the nearer it is to completion and coherence, and the closer it is in date to Montesquieu's maturity. It does not appear that any of the unpublished materials, with the exception of the "Essay on Taste," was intended by Montesquieu to be taken as seriously as his published work.

Such considerations apply with special force to the *Pensées* —scattered, abbreviated, and undated as they are. Because of the elusiveness of Montesquieu's published works, and the apparently contrasting candor of the *Pensées*, there is a tendency among scholars to rely too heavily upon them. One must never forget the "Avertissment" Montesquieu placed at the beginning of the manuscript of his *Pensées:* "These are ideas which I have not at all thought through, and which I preserve in order to think about on the proper occasion. I certainly refuse to answer for all the thoughts which are here. Most of them I have put here only because I have not had the time to reflect on them, and I will think about them when I make use of them" (*Works*, II, 974). Compare Edwin Dargan, *The Aesthetic Doctrine of Montesquieu* (New York: Burt Franklin, n.d., "originally published Baltimore, 1907"), p. 13.

21. "Essay on Taste," second section, "Of *Esprit* in General," *Works*, II, 1243.

22. "Essay on the Causes Which Can Affect the Spirits and Characters," *Works*, II, 57; cf. *Persian Letters*, no. 145 (*Works*, I, 357–58).

23. "Essay on the Causes Which Can Affect the Spirits and Characters," *Works*, II, 57–58.

24. Ibid.; "Essay on Taste," *Works*, II, 1240–43; *Pensées*,

no. 1740, in *Works*, I, 1417, and nos. 1154, 1159, 1170, in *Works*, I, 1295–96; XIX 5–8.

25. "Essay on the Causes Which Can Affect the Spirits and Characters," *Works*, II, 58, 65.

26. For Juvenal and Horace compare *Pensées*, no. 900, in *Works*, I, 1246.

27. Cf. *Pensées*, no. 916, in *Works*, I, 1249, and no. 1217, in *Works*, I, 1246.

28. On Michelangelo and Raphael compare, "Essay on Taste," *Works*, II, 1255–56, 1259, and *Voyages, Works*, I, 692. Also *Pensées*, no. 534, in *Works*, I, 1050, and no. 893, in *Works*, II, 1245, and *Voyages, Works*, I, 686–87.

There are some striking similarities between Montesquieu's remarks about literature and art in England and France and the remarks of Shaftesbury. See Shaftesbury, *Characteristics of Men, Manners, Opinions, and Times*, 2 vols. (Indianapolis: Bobbs-Merrill, 1964), I, 141–42; also 178–81. It is unlikely that this similarity is purely coincidental. In fact, it is possible that Montesquieu was thinking of Shaftesbury, in disagreement as well as agreement, in a number of places in *The Spirit of the Laws*. Apart from our general impression and the well-known fact of Shaftesbury's great influence in eighteenth-century France, we have from Shackleton evidence of a special interest in Shaftesbury among Montesquieu's intimate circle (Shackleton, pp. 58ff.). Even more important, we find that Montesquieu in the *Pensées* refers to Shaftesbury as one of the "four great poets" (no. 2095, *Works*, I, 1546).

29. Edmund Burke, *Reflections on the Revolution in France* in *Works*, 8 vols. (London: Henry G. Bohn, 1855), II, 362–64. As to the connection between the "spirit of religion" and the "spirit of a gentleman," cf. II, 351–52, and V, 214 (*Letters on a Regicide Peace*).

Notes to Chapter Six

1. See Machiavelli, *The Prince*, chap. xxv, especially in the light of chaps. xv ff. and chap. vi, the third paragraph; consider especially the references to "matter" and "form" in chaps. vi and xxvi. Compare Plato *Republic* 499^b, 592^a, 619^{c-d}, 620^c and Aristotle *Politics* 1288^b 10–1289^a 25, 1325^b 33 ff.

2. Montesquieu's preoccupation with the influence on man of

nonhuman nature appears to be connected with what we observed to be his Spinozistic or naturalistic tendency (see chapter 3 above, n. 15). Montesquieu follows Spinoza, as opposed to Hobbes, in trying to avoid the necessity of divorcing human nature from the rest of nature (consider I 1 as a whole). This naturalism is another reason for Montesquieu's avoidance of the tendency to universalistic and hence abstract legalism that colors Hobbes's description of man.

Yet Montesquieu's understanding of nature or of the whole to which man belongs is a largely mechanistic understanding. It tends to overlook or reduce the differences among beings, to view the apparent diversity of natural characteristics as effects of universal and similar causes which are the truly fundamental things in nature. Hence Montesquieu's discussion of the human body and the animal man is based largely on deductions from the nature of matter, energy, the organic, and the inorganic considered generally. Montesquieu's reflections have an abstract and unempirical quality which is particularly evident when one contrasts them with the similar reflections of Rousseau. Rousseau does not abandon the modern reductionist orientation, but he starts more from meditation on the life and behavior of animals as they appear to the naïve observer. Rousseau studies the animal as a whole; he does not concentrate on more abstract and general phenomena like the effects of heat and cold on organic tissue.

3. Cf. "Essay on the Causes Which Can Affect the Spirits and Characters," *Works*, II, 42, 47–48.

4. Ibid., 49.

5. Cf. David Lowenthal, "The Design of Montesquieu's Considerations," *Interpretation* II (1970), 156–58.

6. Cf. "Essay on the Causes Which Can Affect the Spirits and Characters," *Works*, II, 44–45; cf. XIV 10. See Destutt de Tracy, p. 194; Aron, p. 34.

7. Compare, for example, XVII 2–3 with George F. Kennan, *Memoirs, 1925–1950* (Boston: Little, Brown and Co., 1967), pp. 480–81.

8. R. G. Collingwood, *The Idea of History* (Oxford University Press, 1956), pp. 78–79. Cf. Henry J. Merry's critique of Collingwood in *Montesquieu's System of Natural Government* (West Lafayette, Indiana: Purdue University Studies, 1970), p. 29.

Notes

9. It is worth noting as a confirmation of our interpretation of Montesquieu's view of virtuous republicanism that his remarks about the inappropriateness of slavery in such a regime are rich in ambiguity. He says that slavery is "against the spirit of the constitution," but he indicates at the same time that it is less out of place in republics than in monarchies (XV 1), and he admits that in order to replace slave labor it is necessary to "join to the augmentation of labor the augmentation of gain"—that is, one must make citizens think of personal gain rather than of public duty. In addition, one must encourage technology, "the commodity of machines which art invents or applies" (XV 8).

10. Destutt de Tracy remarks (p. 197): "So unconnected are the nature of the soil, the long hair of Clodian, and the debauchery of Childeric with each other, that it is difficult to discover the chain of thought which could have conducted our author from one of these topics to the other: and it is yet more difficult to say precisely what is the subject of this book." Cf. Levin, p. 1.

11. For further reflections on the connection between the emergence of the modern science of nature and the emergence of the modern science of history, see Jacob Klein, "Phenomenology and the History of Science," in *Philosophical Essays in Memory of Edmund Husserl* (Cambridge: Harvard University Press, 1940), pp. 149–50.

12. Montesquieu relies primarily on Tacitus's *Germania* and other histories and travellers' reports for observation. In addition, he bases his conclusions on his researches into the records of the laws of the early Franks and the extrapolation from those laws to the conditions which must have existed at the time of their institution.

13. Montesquieu does allude to the existence of slaves almost from the beginning (XVIII 12, 22). His mention of slaves among the earliest men is perhaps a veiled allusion to the unhappy situation of women (note that in chapter 12 he speaks of quarrels over slaves but not over women, perhaps indicating that all women were slaves). Then too, one might suppose that the losers in war were probably sometimes enslaved. But the simplicity of the needs and the ease of escape must have made the extent of this slavery rather insignificant (cf. esp. chap. 19: "They weren't condemned to civil slavery; they would have been a burden to a simple nation which had no lands to cultivate and no need of domestic service").

14. Cf. Thucydides i 2.

15. Cf. "Essay on the Causes Which Can Affect the Spirits and Characters," *Works*, II, 61: "Nevertheless, it is necessary to admit that the timid peoples, who flee death in order to enjoy real goods like life, tranquility, pleasure, are born with a better constitution somehow than the insensitive people of the North, who sacrifice their life to a vain glory, that is to say who prefer living after themselves to living with themselves."

16. Ibid., 60.

17. See above, chap. 3, pp. 44–45, and nn. 22 and 23 below.

18. See especially Raymond Aron, *Les étapes de la pensée sociologique* (Paris: Gallimard, 1967), pp. 18–19, 27, 30–31, 33, 66, 86, 362, 367–68. Cf. Raymond Aron, *German Sociology*, trans. Mary and Thomas Bottomore (Glencoe, Ill.: The Free Press, 1957), pp. 1–4, 116–17, with Max Weber, *The Theory of Social and Economic Organization*, trans. Talcott Parsons (Glencoe, Ill.: The Free Press, 1964), pp. 88ff., and Durkheim, pp. 55ff. See also Seymour Martin Lipset, "Political Sociology," in *Sociology Today*, ed. Robert Merton, Leonard Broom, and Leonard Cotrell, Harper Torchbooks, 2 vols. (New York: Harper and Row, 1965), I, 81–83, and Claude Lévi-Strauss, *The Scope of Anthropology*, trans. Sherry and Robert Paul (London: Jonathan Cape, 1967).

19. See Taine, pp. 179–81.

20. Although it should be noted that the phrase "moral causes" is used very rarely by Montesquieu. If we are not mistaken, it occurs only twice in *The Spirit of the Laws* (VIII 21 and XIV 5; cf. *Considerations*, *Works*, I, 173; also "Essay on the Causes Which Can Affect the Spirits and Characters," *Works*, II, 53, 58, and *Defense of the Spirit of the Laws*, *Works*, II, 1137).

21. Compare X 13 with *Considerations*, chap. 15, *Works*, II, 147–48, as well as "On Policy," *Works*, I, 114.

22. Cf. Berlin, p. 276; Dedieu, p. 196; Aron, *Les grands doctrines*, pp. 50–51; Franz Neumann, "Introduction," p. xxxvi.

23. Cf. Aron, *German Sociology*, pp. 25, 37ff.

24. See n. 23 above. Consider the importance for sociology of the idea of "civilization": Aron, *German Sociology*, pp. 43–66. And compare the kindred connection between the sociological orientation and the concept of historical progress: Aron, *Les étapes*, p. 66; Durkheim, pp. 105–7. Consider the discussion of historical

methodology by Durkheim's teacher, Fustel de Coulanges: *The Ancient City*, trans. Willard Small (Anchor Books; Garden City, New Jersey: Doubleday and Co., n.d.), pp. 11–14.

25. Edmund Burke, II, 351ff., 362ff.; V, 214ff. See chap. 5, n. 29 above.

Notes to Chapter Seven

1. Book XXVIII is a part of what was called in the original printed edition an addition or appendix to *The Spirit of the Laws* proper (see the title page of the Pléiade edition). Book XX is therefore the only book in the main body of the work which has an epigraph.

2. In the first edition Book XX marked the beginning of the second volume, and the epigraph was placed on the title page of the whole volume, but in the last edition actually supervised and revised by Montesquieu, it stands as an epigraph to Book XX. Cf. *Works*, II, 1514 with the critical edition of Jean Brethe de la Gressaye, I, xlvii–li, III, 342–43.

3. See Edouard Laboulaye, ed., *Oeuvres complètes de Montesquieu*, 7 vols. (Paris: Garnier Frères, 1875–79), IV, 357–60; as well as André Masson, ed., *Oeuvres complètes de Montesquieu*, 3 vols. (Paris: Nagel, 1950–55).

4. Cf. Edmund Burke, letter to Rivarol of June 1, 1791, in *Correspondence of Edmund Burke*, ed. Thomas Copeland, 8 vols. (Chicago: University of Chicago Press, 1958–71), VI, 269–70.

5. Cf. Sorel, p. 152.

6. See "Discourse on the Motives Which Ought to Encourage Us Toward the Sciences," *Works*, I, 53ff.; *Reflections on Universal Monarchy in Europe*, *Works*, II, 19, 23.

7. The only ancient political philosopher whom Montesquieu finds helpful in understanding commerce is Xenophon (XX 18); cf. Leo Strauss, *Xenophon's Socratic Discourse* (Ithaca, New York: Cornell University Press, 1970), pp. 203–4.

8. By his reference to two different kinds of "humanity" Montesquieu shows his awareness of the fact that the understanding of humanity as primarily a virtue all men show to one another as equals represents a shift of emphasis. Traditionally, humanity was thought to be primarily a virtue one manifested toward one's inferiors. It was a result of one's sense of strength, not of one's

Notes

sense of insecurity: see, for example, Thomas Aquinas, *Summa Theologica* II ii 80, a. 1 and 2, and Machiavelli, *The Prince*, Epistle Dedicatory, chap. xv; compare Edward Huguet, *Dictionnaire de la langue française au seizième siècle*, 7 vols. (Paris: Didier, 1950), s.v. "Humain," "Humainement," "Humanité." In the passage where, according to Montesquieu, Livy speaks of "humanity," Livy in fact speaks of "the laws of mankind" (*legum humanorum*): cf. VI 15 with Livy *Ab Urbe Condita* i 28. The transformation of the notion of humanity epitomizes the transformation of morality as a whole that takes place in the thought of Montesquieu. The source of traditional morality was the generosity of self-sufficiency; the source of the new brotherhood of man is the neediness of insecurity.

9. This assessment and prediction of the contrast between English and French commerce would seem to have been accurate. Cf. Andrew Schonfield, *Modern Capitalism: the Changing Balance of Public and Private Power* (Oxford University Press, 1965), pp. 77–80.

10. Cf. the Preface, *Works*, II, 230: "In a time of ignorance one has no doubts, even when one does the greatest evils; in a time of enlightenment, one trembles even when one does the greatest good. One feels the old abuses, one sees their correction; but one also sees the abuses of that very correction."

11. Cf. XX 22. A more precise account of what Montesquieu has in mind is best postponed until our commentary on the concluding section of *The Spirit of the Laws:* see below, chapter 9.

12. Compare Burke, *Reflections on the Revolution in France, Works*, II, 352.

13. Cf. Lowenthal, "Montesquieu," pp. 486–88; "Introduction" to his edition of the *Considerations*, p. 9, bottom.

14. Shaftesbury, *Characteristics*, I, 154–57.

15. See *Beyond Good and Evil*, no. 262 and context.

16. Shaftesbury, the outstanding eighteenth-century spokesman for the tradition, states this aspect of the classical view with unrivalled clarity: "To philosophize, in a just signification, is but to carry good breeding a step higher. For the accomplishment of breeding is, to learn whatever is decent in company or beautiful in the arts; and the sum of philosophy is, to learn what is just in society and beautiful in Nature and the order of the world. 'Tis not wit

merely, but a temper which must form the well-bred man. In the same manner, 'tis not a head merely, but a heart and resolution which must complete the real philosopher. Both characters aim at what is excellent, aspire to a just taste, and carry in view the model of what is becoming and beautiful. Accordingly, the respective conduct and distinct manners of each party are regulated; the one according to the perfectest ease and good entertainment of company, the other according to the strictest interest of mankind and society; the one according to a man's rank and quality in his private station, the other according to his rank and dignity in Nature. Whether each of these offices or social parts are in themselves as convenient as becoming, is the great question" (*Characteristics*, II, 255–56).

17. Here and elsewhere I have adopted the readings of the "Essay" as it appeared when published in the *Encyclopédie*. These readings are indicated in the editor's notes to the Pléiade edition.

18. In the presentation of his reasons for admiring Stoicism, as well as in his thematic treatment of contemplation, we see in striking fashion Montesquieu's difference with Spinoza, whom he appears in a number of other respects to follow. In contrast to Montesquieu, Spinoza leaves the reader in no doubt about the ultimate superiority of the contemplative life.

19. Cf. Lowenthal, "Montesquieu," pp. 489–90.

20. Cf. Ovid *Tristia* iii 14 13.

21. See especially Plato *Laws* 804^b. Compare Pascal, *Pensées*, no. 533 (ed. Louis Lafuma), and St. Thomas More, *Utopia*, ed. and trans. Edward Surtz (New Haven: Yale University Press, 1964), p. 49.

22. Cf. Ovid *Metamorphoses* ii 553 and context with Hyginus *Fabulae*, no. 166 in *The Myths of Hyginus*, ed. and trans. Mary Grant (Lawrence, Kansas: University of Kansas Press, 1960).

23. Alain Cotta, "Le développement économique de la pensée de Montesquieu," *Revue d'histoire économique et sociale* XXXV (1957), 372. Cf. Nicos E. Devletoglou, *Montesquieu and the Wealth of Nations*, Center of Economic Research Lecture Series, no. 10 (Athens: Constantinides and Mihalas, 1963), pp. 11, 13, 16, 40–44.

24. D'Alembert, III, 473.

25. Cf. Joseph Spengler, *French Predecessors of Malthus* (Durham, North Carolina: Duke University Press, 1942), pp. 213–63; Devletoglou, pp. 56ff.

Notes

Notes to Chapter Eight

1. Cf. Lowenthal, "Montesquieu," p. 488.

2. Cf. Louis Althusser, *Montesquieu, la politique et l'histoire* (Paris: Presses universitaires de France, 1969), pp. 19–21.

3. Cf. Mathie, pp. 61ff.

4. Cf. Dedieu, pp. 304–5.

5. Cf. Leo Strauss, *Natural Right and History* (Chicago: University of Chicago Press, 1953), p. 164.

Notes to Chapter Nine

1. Montesquieu's reference to polygamy in chapter 10 reminds the reader of his very un-Christian attitude of tolerance toward this kind of marriage.

2. See chap. 4, n. 13 above.

3. *Works*, II, 1029: "It has been seen in the whole work that the laws have innumerable relationships with innumerable things. The study of jurisprudence is the study of these relationships. The laws follow these relationships, and, since the latter ceaselessly vary, the former modify themselves continually. I believe that I cannot better complete this work than by giving an example. I have chosen the Roman laws, and I have investigated what they did about successions. One will see by how many wills and pieces of luck they have been affected. What I say of them will be a species of method for those who wish to study jurisprudence."

Cf. *Works*, II, 1102: "I have taken an example, which is the origin and the generation of the Roman laws on succession; that example will serve here for the method. . . . If I have explained well the theory of the Roman laws on successions, one will be able, by the same method, to see the birth of the laws of most peoples."

4. Cf. Marc Bloch's criticism of Montesquieu in his *Feudal Society*, trans. L. A. Manyon, 2 vols. (Chicago: University of Chicago Press, 1968), I, xvii: "It may be doubted whether a highly complex type of social organization can be properly designated either by concentrating on its political aspect only, or . . . by stressing one particular form of real property."

5. Cf. Elie Carcassonne, *Montesquieu et le problème de la constitution française au XVIII⁰ siècle* (Paris: Presses universitaires, 1926), p. 87: "After having isolated by his analysis each of the relations which comprise the spirit of the laws, [Montesquieu] reconstitutes

the synthesis in a concrete example. Then that example is found to be a privileged example, which helps in understanding the origin of monarchic government in general and above all of the French government."

6. Cf. Carcassonne, p. 101.

7. For the best detailed account of this intellectual quarrel see Carcassonne, chapter i. Cf. also Dedieu, pp. 103–5; Neumann, pp. xxiv–xxvii; see also Wade's *Clandestine Organization and Diffusion of Philosophic Ideas*. Albert Mathiez's attack on Carcassonne is not only, as Neumann says, "savage," it is unintelligent: see *Annales historiques de la révolution française* IV (1927), 509–13.

8. Cf. Carcassonne, pp. 18–25, with XXX 5, 10, 25.

9. See also Carcassonne, pp. 42–45.

10. For the political-historical background, and for evidence indicating the possibility and even the persuasiveness of Montesquieu's hopes or plans, see Franklin Ford, *Robe and Sword, The Regrouping of the French Aristocracy After Louis XIV* (Cambridge: Harvard University Press, 1962). There are two flaws in Ford's otherwise careful study. On the one hand he understates the continued accessibility of the nobility of the robe to penetration from below, from the bourgeoisie. The problem manifests itself in Ford's own "Note" added to chapter seven (pp. 145–46), especially when that note is compared with pages 127ff., 149, 208, and 250. More serious is his misunderstanding of Montesquieu's thought, especially the significance and import of the theme of commerce. This leads him to miss the radical implications of Montesquieu's treatment of the nobility of the robe and the bourgeoisie.

11. See Carcassonne, pp. 222ff.

INDEX

1. Names

Alembert, Jean le Rond d', 11,
14–15, 243, 308 nn. 3, 9,
312 n. 1, 324 n. 24
Althusser, Louis, 325 n. 2
Aristophanes, 203
Aristotle, 42, 45, 47–51, 53,
56, 59–66, 69–70, 74, 76,
118–23, 161–62, 170, 182,
188–90, 210, 230, 263,
272, 278, 280–81, 310 n. 14,
312 n. 6, 313 n. 9, 315 n. 4,
316 n. 16, 318 n. 1
Aron, Raymond, 307 n. 1,
312 nn. 19, 20, 319 n. 6,
321 nn. 18, 22, 23, 24
Aube, François Richer d',
311 n. 18
Augustine, St., 264
Austen, Jane, 159

Barkhausen, Henri, 307 n. 1,
308 n. 9, 312 n. 19, 313 n. 13,
314 nn. 1, 3
Bayle, Pierre, 252–53
Benrekassa, Georges, 307 n. 1,
308 n. 2, 309 n. 9
Berlin, Isaiah, 307 n. 1,
312 n. 19, 321 n. 22
Berns, Walter, 315 n. 6
Berwick, James Fitzjames,
Duke of, 215

Bloch, Marc, 325 n. 4
Bossuet, Jacques Bénigne, 280
Boulainvilliers, Henri, comte
de, 292–93, 295–97
Brethe de la Gressaye, Jean,
316 nn. 17, 18, 322 n. 2
Broom, Leonard, 321 n. 18
Burke, Edmund, 160, 192–93,
278, 318 n. 29, 322 nn. 25, 4,
323 n. 12
Burlamaqui, Jean-Jacques,
310 n. 14

Caillois, Roger, 50
Carcassonne, Elie, 292,
325 n. 5, 326 nn. 6, 7, 8, 9, 11
Collingwood, R. G., 168,
319 n. 8
Copeland, Thomas, 322 n. 4
Corneille, 222
Cotrell, Leonard, 321 n. 18
Cotta, Alain, 242, 324 n. 23
Cropsey, Joseph, 309 n. 7,
312 n. 5, 315 n. 6

Dargan, Edwin, 317 n. 20
Dedieu, Joseph, 307 nn. 1, 2,
311 n. 18, 312 n. 19,
314 n. 3, 316 n. 17, 321 n. 22,
325 n. 4, 326 n. 7
Descartes, René, 14, 309 n. 4

Index

Destutt de Tracy, Antoine,
307 n. 2, 308 n. 9, 313 n. 14,
319 n. 6, 320 n. 10
Devletoglou, Nicos E.,
324 nn. 23, 25
Dubos, Abbé, 292–93, 295–97
Durkheim, Emil, 309 n. 9,
312 nn. 19, 20, 21, 314 nn. 2,
3, 321 nn. 18, 24

Farrand, Max, 315 n. 11
Ford, Franklin, 326 n. 10
Fustel de Coulanges, Numa
Denis, 321 n. 24

Goldwin, Robert A., 316 n. 14
Grant, Mary, 324 n. 22
Grotius, Hugo, 307 n. 1,
310 n. 14, 311 n. 18
Gurvitch, Georges, 312 n. 21

Harrington, James, 278
Hegel, Georg W. F., 5, 9,
219, 314 n. 3
Hobbes, Thomas, 4, 30, 33–39,
41–43, 50, 135, 162, 164,
167, 218–19, 259, 307 n. 1,
308 n. 1, 309 n. 10, 310 n. 15,
311 n. 16, 312 nn. 22, 4,
318 n. 2
Horace, 157, 318 n. 26
Huguet, Edward, 322 n. 8
Hume, David, 134, 315 n. 10,
316 n. 13
Husserl, Edmund, 320 n. 11
Hyginus, 324 n. 22

Ilbert, Courtney, 307 n. 2,
308 n. 9

Janet, Paul, 311 n. 18, 312 n. 3,
314 n. 3

Julian the Apostate, 254
Juvenal, 157, 202–3, 318 n. 26

Kant, Immanuel, 5, 9
Kennan, George F., 319 n. 7
Keohane, Nannerl O., 308 n. 2,
314 n. 3
Klein, Jacob, 320 n. 11

Laboulaye, Edouard, 322 n. 3
Lafuma, Louis, 324 n. 21
Lévi-Strauss, Claude, 321 n. 18
Levin, Lawrence, 307 n. 1,
314 n. 3, 320 n. 10
Lipset, Seymour Martin,
321 n. 18
Livy, 79, 96–97, 322 n. 8
Locke, John, 4, 41, 43, 135,
162, 166–67, 217, 255, 259,
309 n. 10, 315 n. 12,
316 n. 14
Loretti, Gabriel, 308 n. 9
Lowenthal, David, 88, 308 n. 3,
309 nn. 7, 8, 312 nn. 2, 5,
7, 313 nn. 10, 12, 314 n. 3,
319 n. 5, 323 n. 13, 324 n.
19, 325 n. 1
Lucretius, 243–44
Lukacs, Georg, 8, 307 n. 2

Machiavelli, Niccolò, 5, 47,
87, 136–37, 162, 164, 278,
316 n. 16, 318 n. 1, 322 n. 8
Madison, James, 315 n. 11
Marx, Karl, 5, 8
Masson, André, 322 n. 3
Masters, Roger, 311 n. 17
Mathie, William, 309 n. 7,
325 n. 3
Mathiez, Albert, 326 n. 7
Merry, Henry J., 319 n. 8
Merton, Robert, 321 n. 18

Index

Index

2. REFERENCES TO *The Spirit of the Laws*

Index

Index

Index

Index